Pushing Our Understanding of Diversity in Organizations

A Volume in Research in Social Issues in Management

Series Editors

Eden B. King
Rice University

Quinetta Roberson
Villanova University

Mikki Hebl
Rice University

Research in Social Issues in Management

Eden B. King, Quinetta Roberson, and Mikki Hebl, Editors

Pushing Our Understanding of Diversity in Organizations

edited by

Eden King
Rice University

Quinetta Roberson
Villanova University

Mikki Hebl
Rice University

INFORMATION AGE PUBLISHING, INC.
Charlotte, NC • www.infoagepub.com

Library of Congress Cataloging-in-Publication Data

CIP record for this book is available from the Library of Congress
http://www.loc.gov

ISBNs: 978-1-64113-942-7 (Paperback)

978-1-64113-943-4 (Hardcover)

978-1-64113-944-1 (ebook)

Printed in the United States of America

CONTENTS

PREFACE

Mikki Hebl, Eden King, and Quinetta Roberson

It is with delight that the three of us take on the editorship of *Research in Social Issues in Management* (RSIM). Our collaboration is what each of us would consider a dream one, and we have exciting plans for the future of RSIM.

However, we cannot begin our journey properly without first acknowledging the tremendous work of our RSIM predecessors—Stephen Gilliland (Eller College of Management at University of Arizona), Dirk Steiner (Univeristé Nice Sophia Antipolis in Nice, France), and Daniel Skarlicki (Sauder School of Business at University of British Columbia).

In 1998, these scholars led a roundtable discussion on organizational justice research at the Society of Industrial and Organizational Psychology (SIOP) conference in Dallas. The exchange of ideas, interest, and excitement was so deep that Stephen, Dirk, and Daniel responded by organizing a small, international conference the following summer. Held in Nice, France, 20 scholars from seven different countries came together to present papers and discuss research on organizational justice research. Realizing that the work of researchers doing organizational justice had been limited in many ways by the restraints of academic journals and feeling that such research was critical to understanding experiences in the workplace, Stephen, Dirk, and Daniel worked with Information Age Publishing (IAP) and initiated the newly developed series, *Research in Social*

Pushing Our Understanding of Diversity in Organizations, pp. vii–xi
Copyright © 2020 by Information Age Publishing
All rights of reproduction in any form reserved.

Issues in Management. A subset of the Nice conference attendees submitted papers, and the first volume was borne.

Together, Stephen, Dirk, and Daniel published a total of eight edited volumes of RSIM, with topics mainly focusing on organizational justice or related themes of fairness, morality, social responsibility, and ethics. These volumes include:

Gilliland, S., Steiner, D., & Skarlicki D. P. (Eds.). (2015). *The social dynamics of organizational justice*. Charlotte, NC: Information Age Publishing.

Gilliland, S., Steiner, D., & Skarlicki D. P. (Eds.). (2011). *Emerging perspectives on organizational justice and ethics*. Charlotte, NC: Information Age Publishing.

Gilliland, S., Skarlicki D. P., & Steiner, D. (Eds.). (2008). *Justice, morality, and social responsibility*. Charlotte, NC: Information Age Publishing.

Gilliland, S., Steiner, D., & Skarlicki D. P. (Eds.). (2007). *Managing social and ethical issues in organizations*. Charlotte, NC: Information Age Publishing.

Gilliland, S., Steiner, D., Skarlicki, D. P., & van den Bos, K. (Eds.). (2005). *What motivates fairness in organizations?* Greenwich CT: Information Age Publishing.

Gilliland, S., Steiner, D., & Skarlicki D. P. (Eds.). (2003). *Emerging perspectives on managing organizational justice*. Greenwich CT: Information Age Publishing.

Gilliland, S., Steiner, D., & Skarlicki D. P. (Eds.). (2002). *Emerging perspectives on values in organizations*. Greenwich CT: Information Age Publishing.

Gilliland, S., Steiner, D., & Skarlicki, D. P. (Eds.). (2001). *Theoretical and cultural perspectives on organizational justice. Research in social issues in management*. Greenwich CT: Information Age Publishing.

Indeed, they succeeded in expanding the quality, quantity, and innovation of work on organizational justice. They acknowledge that some of the papers published in their volumes shaped major theories in the field and have had a very lasting impact. They initiated and fostered national and international collaborations in the area of organizational justice. And the research has been translated into actual organizational knowledge and practice.

And so, on behalf of those who have benefitted from these volumes—the original and subsequent conference attendees, the authors and the readership over the last 15 years, and those employees whose lives have been improved because of the research—we wholeheartedly thank Stephen, Dirk, and Daniel for their work.

In the fall of 2017, Stephen, Dirk, and Daniel decided it was time to pass the reigns of the RSIM series to a new group of editors. Around this time, each of us (as well as a number of other people) received invitations to consider becoming the new editors.

Not one of us would have undertaken this alone but the idea of working together and particularly on our areas of joint interest was intriguing to say the least. After having a few conversations with each other and George Johnson, the President and Publisher of Information Age Publishing Inc., which produces RSIM, we excitedly agreed.

The joint expertise of our trio lies in the research areas of workplace discrimination, diversity and inclusion, work-family issues, and justice.

We are each called by the growing negative sociopolitical climate in which our and so many other countries find themselves. We are called by organizations that both knowingly and unknowingly continue to use discriminatory practices. We are called by the often enduring hostile and exclusive contexts that some employees perpetuate, while others must navigate. We are called by the lack of true understanding about and manifestation of what it means to be fully accepted and feel a sense of inclusion and authenticity in the workplace. We are called by the employees whose voices and experiences have not yet been given journal space.

Our plan for the series, then, is to offer a forum for research that addresses the current issues around these and related topics. Excitedly, there is a strong theme of justice in our work that will transcend from the earliest conceptions of RSIM to the present. And consistent with our predecessors, we also look forward to many of their same goals and achievements, namely to expand the work, shape major theories, and foster collaboration in the area of diversity and inclusion. We also have an added goal of wanting to strongly "push" the field—to take some real risks and to advance and expand the boundaries of diversity and inclusion (D&I) research, and to do so with a bit of edginess.

And so, for this first volume, we were motivated to come out of the starting gates with a volume featuring D&I "pushers," or people who we believe are unabashedly advancing the field by raising the questions that need to be asked, by working on topics that have received far too little research attention, and by holding researchers, practitioners, managers, organizations, and readers to task for doing what needs to be done to maximize social justice and egalitarian behaviors in the workplace.

We began by making a list of those people doing D&I research who we felt were "pushers," or researchers in D&I who help drive new ideas and perspectives. Then, we invited many of them to write a chapter, encouraging these authors to focus on innovative and/or nascent ideas that extend beyond or push the boundaries of the format of scholarly journals.

We were excited that eight of our invitees agreed and this first volume is the outcome. The chapters in this compilation raise new and provocative questions about the challenges that arise with diversity in organizations and provide new insights into potential solutions and remedies. This volume begins with the ideas of Derek Avery and Sabrina Volpone, whose work helps to frame the overarching topic. They analyze publication patterns in management journals and determine that, despite their obvious relevance and importance, demographic differences are rarely considered.

Against this backdrop, a pair of chapters dive into the nuanced experiences of one of the largest low-status demographic groups: women. Negin Toosi and colleagues broadly consider how women (compared to men) manage diverse teams, organizations, and countries. Mindy Bergman and colleagues consider how natural biological processes of menstruation, perimenopause, and (in)fertility are experienced by women. These chapters push our understanding of gender diversity in distinct and new directions. The former urges scholars to look beyond micro environments to those that are much more macro in order to understand gender dynamics. The latter challenges both scholars and managers to mention the "unmentionable" and break down taboos tied to women's biological processes.

These nuances are further unpacked in chapters that deal directly with the underexplored but increasingly salient experiences of people as a function of multiple identity groups. Kamasak and colleagues confront our tendencies to focus on demographic groups as monolithic categories and push for considerations at not only the individual level, but also the possibility of locating intersections in systems, institutions, and structures. Raymond Trau and Brent Lyons present an intersectional analysis of gay, lesbian, and bisexual workers who are racioethnic minorities, focusing on identity management experiences but integrating cross-national considerations.

Bridging from these powerful perspectives on the challenges of diversity in organizations, the final three chapters move toward potential solutions. Alison Konrad moves toward new theories of diversity and inclusion that differentiate between the experiences of high and low status identity groups, refocusing discussions of diversity as simply *difference* to diversity as differences in *power*. Moreover, in so doing, she offers ideas about the roles that leaders can play in shaping relevant norms and expectations. Andrew

Lam and Eddy Ng then point out that, despite its potentially profound consequences for diversity, backlash to affirmative action programs may get in the way of their success. Finally, Shaun Pichler specifies managerial skills—in particular, supporting, motivating, and managing conflict—that may ultimately be critical determinants of diversity and inclusion in organizations.

Each of these chapters provokes the status quo and, in so doing, pushes our understanding of diversity in organizations.

CHAPTER 1

THE PERILS OF IGNORING DEMOGRAPHIC DIFFERENCES IN MICRO ORGANIZATIONAL RESEARCH

Derek R. Avery
Wake Forest University

Sabrina D. Volpone
University of Colorado at Boulder

"When we listen and celebrate what is both common and different, we become a wiser, more inclusive, and better organization."

—Pat Wadors, Head of HR at LinkedIn

As this quote illustrates, organizational leaders are increasingly realizing that incorporating the voices of people with diverse demographics is a key factor that can contribute to an organization's success. Despite the heightened appreciation for the benefits that diversity can have for organizations, a great deal remains unknown about how employee demographics (e.g., gender, racioethnicity, age) might influence key relationships within organizational settings (Cox, Nkomo, & Welch, 2001; Ely & Padavic, 2007; Heggestad & Andrew, 2012). This suggests that management scholars

Pushing Our Understanding of Diversity in Organizations, pp. 1–19
Copyright © 2020 by Information Age Publishing

might benefit from extending the ideas put forth in the opening quote to our own management scholarship; that is, we might become a wiser, more inclusive field when we listen to the perspective that diverse demographics brings in aiding our understanding of workplace relationships. To guide our field in gaining insight into our understanding of workplace relationships, we review the literature that demonstrates how demographics can influence key relationships within organizational settings and then explore how scholars can reconceptualize how we study and report employee demographics to better demonstrate how and when diverse demographics contribute to organizations' success.

It is timely and imperative that we develop new approaches to understanding how diverse demographics can contribute to an organization's success. One pressing reason for this is because demographic changes in our society are increasing the level of demographic diversity in organizations. First, women's liberation movements and changing financial realities (i.e., increasing difficulty of raising a family on a single income) are escalating female workplace participation rates in many industrialized nations (Ortiz-Ospina & Tzvetkova, 2017; Tzvetkova & Ortiz-Ospina, 2017). Second, increasing immigration, differential birth rates among groups, and the rapid proliferation of international business is giving rise to greater racial and ethnic (i.e., racioethnic) diversity (Toossi, 2016; Toossi & Joyner, 2018). Third, the aging of the baby boomers, the largest age demographic group in many industrialized nations, is promoting higher levels of age diversity than in prior years (Lacey, Toossi, Dubina, & Gensler, 2017; Toossi & Torpey, 2017). The net effect of these changes is that the workforce is now more diverse in regards to gender, racioethnicity, and age. These trends suggest it is necessary that scholars continue to research the role of demographic characteristics in organizations, as projections (e.g., Toossi, 2012) show that these changes will continue into the foreseeable future.

Moreover, another pressing reason to consider new approaches to understanding the role of demographics is to avoid the consequences that come from ignoring these characteristics in our theories. Research shows that minority employees (e.g., female, Black, Asian, Hispanic, those over 40 years old) have unique and complex employment experiences as compared to their young White male counterparts (e.g., Hernandez, Avery, Volpone, & Kaiser, 2019; Luksyte, Waite, Avery, & Roy, 2013; McKay & Avery, 2006; McKay et al., 2007). The lack of consideration of employees' demographic characteristics suggests that our research and theories are presenting narrow views of organizational experiences that only occur for employees with certain characteristics (i.e., young White males) while overlooking the lived experiences of those with "other" demographic characteristics. This is a crucial oversight in our literature considering minority employees' increasing presence in the workforce. Specifically, if we continue to neglect the increasingly growing perspectives of employees with minority demographic characteristics, our research and theories will not represent the lived experiences of employees in today's diverse organizations.

To illustrate this point, we note that extant gender, racioethnicity, and age scholarship has demonstrated the unmistakable role that demographics have in altering how we interpret the relationship between variables. For example, research shows that gender influences the relationships between citizenship and politics (Kacmar, Bachrach, Harris, & Zivnuska, 2011), embeddedness and turnover (Jiang, Liu, McKay, Lee, & Mitchell, 2012), and weight and wages (Judge & Cable, 2011). Further, research has shown that racioethnicity influences linkages between diversity climate perceptions and turnover intentions (McKay et al., 2007), the proportion of dissimilar others and supportive peer relationships (Bacharach, Bamberger, & Vashdi, 2005), and organizational citizenship and perceived victimization (Aquino & Bommer, 2003). Similarly, age influences relationships between proactive personality and training attitudes (Bertolino, Truxillo, & Fraccaroli, 2011), human resource practices and work attitudes (Kooij, Jansen, Dikkers, & De Lange, 2010), and psychological contract breach and job attitudes (Bal, De Lange, Jansen, & Van Der Velde, 2008). As such, it is evident that the inclusion of gender, racioethnicity, and age has enlightened our understanding of workplace relationships.

However, to more fully explore the role that demographics may have in our field, we suggest that the responsibility for understanding the influence of demographic characteristics (e.g., gender, racioethnicity, age) should not be limited to researchers whose primary interest is diversity. Instead, demographic variables should be examined as moderators in research studies with non-diversity foci, as well. To write about employees in a way that our findings accurately represent *all* employees and not just the majority perspective (in most organizational settings this is represented by a White man) we must consider the representation of the samples those findings are based on. Just as scholars have argued that researchers should pay greater attention to the impact of the context of their work because it could be a moderator of the processes under investigation (e.g., Johns, 2006), a similar case can be made for considering gender, racioethnicity, and age. Accordingly, in this chapter we focus on what could be a rather significant missed opportunity to learn more about the impact of demographic differences in the workplace and better contextualize the findings of micro organizational research.

We explore these notions by discussing how gender, racioethnicity, and age can influence organizational processes. After demonstrating the moderating potential of these variables, we briefly review the extent to which micro organizational research has incorporated them within the past 10 years. In doing so, this research guides future research in two key ways.

First, we provide the impetus for organizational researchers in general to pay greater attention to the impact of individual employee demographics in their research. Second, we identify a simple, straightforward approach that should assist scholars in (a) making more efficient use of their data, (b) enhancing the theoretical contribution of their research, and (c) shedding greater light on the generality of their findings.

DEMOGRAPHIC VARIABLES IN
MICRO ORGANIZATIONAL RESEARCH

Next, we review key literature that shows how scholars' understanding of workplace relationships was expanded when they considered how organizational experiences might differ considerably depending on one's gender, racioethnicity, and age (Aguinis, Beaty, Boik, & Pearce, 2005; Cox et al., 2001; Ely & Padavic, 2007; Heggestad & Andrew, 2012). Although shedding light on the main effects of these identity markers is important (i.e., demographic differences in outcomes), so too is understanding their roles as moderators (i.e., demographic differences in linkages). In fact, it is clear that all three can influence relationships considered well established in our literature and sometimes in counterintuitive ways.

We focus on the demographic characteristics of gender, racioethnicity, and age in this chapter. Though we recognize that conceptually similar arguments can be made regarding other variables (e.g., organizational tenure), we believe that societal trends (e.g., growing demographic diversity) and practical concerns (e.g., financial costs of mismanaging diversity; James & Wooten, 2006; Wright, Ferris, Hiller, & Kroll, 1995) make our case more salient for these three.

Gender. To begin, we note that examining gender has produced some interesting findings for our literature. This work began more than 65 years ago as Kerr (1946) investigated the possibility of gender differences in employee attitudes concerning industrial music and found men to be more desirous of music at work than women. Since that time, a review of the work on gender in organizations concluded that "the field of organizational behavior has witnessed a proliferation of research documenting how the sexes differ in a variety of ways" (Ely & Padavic, 2007, p. 1121). Based on these documented differences, we argue that researchers should examine potential gender differences in important workplace relationships to more accurately understand key relationships within organizational settings.

To give an example of the importance of exploring gender as a moderator, we explore why it might influence key relationships within organizational settings. This is because the experiences of women—or employees that do not identify with the gender binary category of male is often different than the experiences that males employees have in the workplace. These different experiences (existing in the minority, where power, voice, and opportunity is often minimized) may produce different outcomes for employees that belong to a minority group, as compared to a majority group. Such gender differences have been shown across a number of studies. In our literature, the association between ethical leadership and organizational citizenship behaviors in subordinates is assumed to be positive based on social exchange theory (Cropanzano & Mitchell, 2005). That is, leaders who are trustworthy and fair (traits typical of ethical leaders; Brown & Treviño, 2006) encourage their employees to act in ways consistent with these traits (e.g., organizational citizenship behaviors). However, Kacmar et al. (2011) recently found that the relationship between ethical leadership and organizational citizenship behaviors can be fully explained only when it is examined through the lens of gender. Specifically, these authors examined gender and politics perceptions as moderators of the ethical leadership- organizational citizenship behaviors relationship and found that for women, the relationship between ethical leadership and citizenship behaviors was positive when political perceptions were low; when political perceptions were high, the relationship between ethical leadership and citizenship was slightly weaker. However, for men, the relationship was positive when political perceptions were high and when political perceptions were low, the positive relationship disappeared.

Additional evidence further suggests that testing for gender differences in research examining micro-level organizational linkages is necessary. For instance, recruitment literature shows that the relationship between certain job characteristics and applicant attraction differs depending on the gender of the applicant. Specifically, the current thinking is that women, on average, are more sensitive than men to the perceived fairness of selection systems as a result of their experiences with discrimination and unfair hiring practices in the past. However, if researchers probed these well-established relationships between job characteristics and recruitment outcomes, our field would have theory depicting that such gender differences are not always present or in the direction expected. In fact, Chapman and colleagues (Chapman, Uggerslev, Carroll, Piasentin, & Jones, 2005) conducted a meta-analysis showing that women placed less emphasis on fairness perceptions during recruitment than men did when evaluating job attractiveness. Researchers and practitioners drawing on theory explaining the relationships between job characteristics and recruitment outcomes probably found this result surprising because prior authors investigating recruitment failed to consider gender differences. This type of finding is by no means an isolated occurrence. Within the past few years, gender has been shown to influence a number of important linkages such as that between psychopathy and leadership (Landay, Harms, & Crede, 2019), and family poverty and leadership role attainment (Barling & Weatherhead, 2016) to name a few. In conclusion, these examples support our argument that investigating relationships among important organizational constructs is not enough – researchers also should examine potential gender differences in these relationships.

Racioethnicity. Like gender, an employee's racioethnicity also is apt to influence relationships between workplace antecedents and consequences. This is because the experiences of racioethnic minorities is often different than that White male employees and these different experiences may produce different outcomes for employees that belong to the racioethnic minority, as compared to the majority. Such racioethnic differences have been shown across a number of relationships, establishing that racioethnic minority employees have different experiences than White employees do when negotiating their salary, when being recruited as applicants, and in their opportunity for promotion (e.g., Hernandez, Avery, Volpone, & Kaiser, 2019; Luksyte, Waite, Avery, & Roy, 2013; McKay & Avery, 2006; McKay et al., 2007).

To demonstrate this point further, take, for instance, the case of behavioral integrity, or the perceived association between what one says and does. Prior evidence indicates managerial behavioral integrity affects employee organizational citizenship behavior (Simons, 2002). However, Simons, Friedman, Liu, and Parks (2007) had the foresight to hypothesize that this relationship could vary by racioethnicity. Their reasoning was that racioethnic minorities often feel they cannot trust dissimilar others in positions of power (Livers & Caver, 2002) and this would amplify the integrity-citizenship behavior relationship for racioethnic minorities. When these authors tested this hypothesis they found that, indeed, Black employees were more sensitive to their managers' behavioral integrity than their White counterparts.

We have also seen meta-analytic evidence indicating how relationships between predictors and outcomes often vary as a function of race. For instance, the effect of age on in-role and extra-role performance differs for White and minority employees with the linkage appearing less positive for the former than for the latter (Ng & Feldman, 2008). Race also appears to impact the relationship between age and job attitudes (Ng & Feldman, 2010) as well as the magnitude of performance returns for individual educational investments (Ng & Feldman, 2009). Overall, this work on racioethnicity has been noteworthy, as less than a decade after lamenting that racioethnic minorities were essentially "invisible" in organizational behavior and human resource management research (Cox & Nkomo, 1990), the same authors were encouraged with how the "base of knowledge about how racioethnic diversity impacts behavior in organizations has expanded dramatically in the past five or six years"

(Cox et al., 2001, p. 276). However, the examples provided here show that researchers also should examine potential racioethnic differences in workplace relationships to provide additional insights to management scholars.

Age. Finally, age is another demographic variable that can demonstrate differential affects when examined in relation to organizationally-relevant associations. It is well documented that employees if different age cohorts are impacted by different life events (e.g., wars, economic depressions, 9/11, assassinations of prominent leaders). These life events impact work habits and values that change from cohort to cohort. When workforces are comprised of multiple age cohorts theses different subgroups of employees bring different values and experiences to the workplace that impact how they experience the workplace. These different experiences would logically suggest that employees of different ages may have different outcomes in important workplace relationships based on their differing values and experiences. For example, when considering the relationships between political perceptions and work outcomes, demographics have not been examined as variables that may affect these relationships. Nevertheless, a set of researchers (Treadway, Ferris, Hochwarter, Perrewe, Witt, & Goodman, 2005) suggested that age may moderate these relationships and conducted a study to test the notion. These authors hypothesized that the relationship between political perceptions and job performance would be negative for older, but not younger, employees because older individuals have fewer personal resources to respond to political stress as compared to younger employees (Hobfoll & Wells, 1998). Their findings supported this, in that increased politics perceptions had no significant effect on younger employees but the relationship between politics perceptions and job performance for older employees was negative. More recent inquiry has shown that relationships between antecedents of life satisfaction such as growth and support vary depending on the age of the individual in question (Colbert, Bono, & Purvanova, 2016).

Despite this clear potential to influence seemingly straightforward relationships between organizational constructs, there are reasons to anticipate that the moderating effects of demographics are underexplored in current organizational research. In a 1990 article that was subsequently reprinted in 2004 as one of the journal's most influential, noted diversity scholar Taylor Cox detailed a number of reasons organizational researchers often avoid studying diversity. Among the factors that emerged from his survey of diversity researchers were that there are perceived biases against such work both during scholarly development (i.e., graduate school and as a junior faculty member) and in the manuscript review process. Their insights suggested that burgeoning scholars are often steered away from diversity oriented topics because their advisors (a) believe they are unqualified to train them in these areas, (b) question the value of such research, or (c) anticipate that the difficulties associated with building a career doing such work sufficiently outweigh any reasons for doing so. Moreover, the interviewed researchers listed a variety of obstacles in the publication process that are unique to diversity research (e.g., lack of qualified reviewers, research design challenges, and reviewer/editor bias against diversity research). To the extent that such impediments remain, we would anticipate that a low proportion of researchers incorporate gender, racioethnicity, or age in their work. This could explain, in part, why a recent review identified diversity as an area where research has lagged in top outlets over the last 45 years (Cascio & Aguinis, 2008). We also anticipate that the means by which these variables are incorporated when they do appear is likely to be minor as opposed to substantive.

Overall, this overview of the research on gender, racioethnicity, and age shows that demographics (e.g., gender, racioethnicity, age) often influence key relationships within organizational settings. As such, management scholars might benefit from exploring how scholars can reconceptualize how we study and report employee demographics to better demonstrate how and when diverse demographics contribute to organizations' success. Before we discuss ways to do this, we provide a review of micro-level organizational research to demonstrate the frequency (or lack thereof) of examining demographic characteristics in our field.

REVIEW OF DEMOGRAPHICS IN MICRO-LEVEL RESEARCH

Next, to examine the extent to which scholars are taking demographic characteristics into account when conducting micro-level organizational research, we reviewed five of the top management outlets (as defined by Podsakoff, Mackenzie, Bacharach, & Podsakoff, 2005) for the past ten years for the inclusion of papers that incorporate gender, racioethnicity, and age. Specifically, the journals included in our sample were *Academy of Management Journal* (AMJ), *Administrative Science Quarterly* (ASQ), *Journal of Applied Psychology* (JAP), *Organizational Behavior and Human Decision Processes* (OBHDP), and *Personnel Psychology* (PPsych). Though AMJ and ASQ tend to publish more research that is considered macro rather than micro, we elected to include these journals because they (a) publish some work at the employee (i.e., micro) level of analysis and (b) are clearly top-level outlets. Between 2008 and 2018, these five journals published a total of 2,991 articles that accounted for gender, racioethnicity, and age. This total eliminated work that did not focus on individual employees with original data (e.g., methodological papers, meta-analyses, editorials, erratum corrections, conceptual papers, meso- or macro-level research) and data that did not use a form of quantitative analysis.

Study Characteristics

Two considerations were examined in each study. First, we coded whether or not the study reported, controlled, or otherwise statistically incorporated the demographic characteristics of interest. Second, we examined whether or not the studies that controlled for gender or racioethnicity (the categorical variables of interest) reported a test of homogeneity of regression (i.e., interactions with focal variables in predicting the outcomes). We did so because when a categorical control variable is included in a regression-based analysis, it is assumed that the slopes of any focal variables (i.e., the main effects) are parallel across different levels of each control (Tabachnik & Fidell, 2001). In other words, controlling for gender assumes that the relationship between the independent and dependent variables is functionally equivalent for men and women. If this is not the case, the assumption of homogeneity of regression is violated and it is statistically inappropriate to include gender as a control without also accounting for the gender x independent variable interaction. Because age is a continuous, and not a categorical, variable, it is not necessary for authors to report a test of homogeneity of regression.

TRENDS IN REPORTING DEMOGRAPHICS IN MICRO-LEVEL RESEARCH

To determine the extent to which micro organizational research has incorporated gender, racioethnicity, and age within the past 10 years we looked at reporting trends. A summary of the results is provided in Table 1.1. Results showed that while the majority of studies provided the gender (73.8%) and age (72.7%) composition of their sample, the same cannot be said for racioethnicity (22.1%). In fact, authors were less than a third as likely to report racioethnicity as they were to report gender. Despite these differences in reporting rates, the usage rates (i.e., the proportion of reporters that performed some sort of statistical test with the demographic) were remarkably low across the three with 6.86% using gender, 4.72% using racioethnicity, and 5.08% using age in their statistical analyses. It is also worth noting that the very high degree of correspondence between studies that used one of these demographics with those that used another. In other words, the same small group of scholars are utilizing multiple demographics whereas the overwhelming majority of others are not using any.

Table 1.1.
Summary of Results: Publication Outlets' Inclusion of Demographic Variables from 2008–2018

	Gender	Race	Age
Described	73.82%	22.05%	72.78%
Controlled	5.06%	1.04%	3.70%
Usage	6.86%	4.72%	5.08%

We also reviewed the meta-analyses published in these top outlets over the past 10 years ($N = 172$) to determine whether these quantitative reviews were more attentive to the prospect of demographic differences than primary studies. First, we see that only a small percentage of meta-analyses (2.0%) explicitly examined sex analytically, which was roughly half the rate as in primary studies. Second, meta-analysts were significantly more likely than authors of primary studies to test for racioethnic differences (1.1% vs. 0.4%). Third, tests of age differences were half as prevalent in meta-analytic than primary studies (1.5% vs. 3.0%).

DISCUSSION

The purpose of this research was to demonstrate how demographics can influence key relationships within organizational settings while also guiding our field in gaining insight into how to reconceptualize how we study and report employee demographics. Thus far we have demonstrated that demographics can influence key relationships within organizational settings. To illustrate this point, we presented statistics to show the extent to which micro organizational researchers tend to account for or ignore gender, racioethnicity, and age in top tier level research. Our review showed that each of the three demographics we considered was routinely excluded from mention. Moreover, the majority of studies (77.9%) did not report the racioethnic composition of their samples and even those that did were unlikely to have performed any statistical analyses involving this variable as roughly one in every hundred studies examined race statistically. Scholars conducting meta-analyses were also unlikely to pay attention to demographics, but, in their defense, doing so is more difficult if primary studies do not even report this information. We now turn our attention to the implications of these research practices for our science before discussing how we can reconceptualize how we study and report employee demographics in our field.

Statistical Implications

Like other recent reviews (e.g., Bernerth & Aguinis, 2016), we found that most authors in organizational behavior do not statistically control for demographics when conducting their analyses. In some respects, this practice is actually quite appropriate. Other scholars (e.g., Breaugh, 2006; Spector & Brannick, 2011) have produced compelling arguments against the inclusion of demographic variables as controls because they see these variables as proxies for the actual source of the differences they are used to capture. For instance, it is not that authors controlling for gender are doing so because they feel the need to account for inherent biological differences between men and women. Rather, gender is most commonly used to account for differences in the experiences commonly associated with being male versus female. Statistically speaking, using demographic variables as controls amounts to employing a "coarse" measure, which can bias statistical parameter estimates (Aguinis, Pierce, & Culpepper, 2009). Thus, we neither call for future research to control for demographics nor chide prior researchers for failing to do so.

Nevertheless, scholars with a sound rationale for including these variables as controls should test for homogeneity of regression prior to doing so (Tabachnik & Fidell, 2001). When including categorical control variables in analysis of covariance or regression, it is assumed that the slopes of the focal variables in predicting the outcome variables are parallel for each category. For example, if a researcher is interested in the relationship between organizational justice and workplace deviance and wants to control for gender because women (a) tend to perceive lower justice (Cohen-Charash & Spector, 2001) and (b) are less apt to engage in counterproductive work behavior (Berry, Ones, & Sackett, 2007), they should first test to see if the justice-deviance relationship is consistent for men and women. If so, then it is statistically appropriate to use gender as a control variable. If not, the interaction between gender and justice should be reported and the authors should not merely control for gender in their analyses.

We understand that there are instances where authors would like to test for demographic effects but the sample sizes for some sub-groups (e.g., the number of racioethnic minority individuals) within the sample is not sufficient to run such tests. While we encourage authors to take extra efforts in recruiting participants so that the demographic characteristics of their sample match that of the workforce in the country(ies) they are sampling from, in the case that sample sizes for subgroups are too small, we suggest reporting the racioethnic (and other) demographic characteristics to aid readers in interpreting the results given the characteristics reported. Without reporting the racioethnicity or other demographic characteristics, readers may assume generalizability to the workforce in the country that the research was conducted; it is incumbent on authors to report demographic characteristics, even if they indicate a small sample size, to prevent the assumption that the findings are generalizable to diverse employees and workforces.

Theoretical Implications

Although the failure to consider demographic differences as controls is not necessarily statistically worrisome, it is considerably troubling theoretically. Prior evidence has shown that gender, racioethnicity, and age affect people's workplace experiences considerably (e.g., Aguinis et al., 2005; Cox et al., 2001; Ely & Padavic, 2007; Heggestad & Andrew, 2012). This calls into question what we term the universality assumption, or the belief that a process under investigation functions the same for members of all demographic groups. By pushing past the universality assumption, we might become a wiser, more inclusive field when we listen to the perspective that diverse demographics brings in aiding our understanding of workplace relationships.

Editors and reviewers typically require authors to provide contextual background information about the samples used to test their research hypotheses. In fact, the *Journal of Organizational Behavior* has added a section called the "contextual sidebar" wherein authors are expected to explain any anomalies about their sample that might influence the external validity of their conclusions. This information is used to help readers determine the limits of the generality of the study's findings. For instance, if a study relies on an all-Canadian sample, readers may question the extent to which the findings may be expected to apply to employees outside of Canada. Similarly, if a study uses an all-male or all-White sample, we should question how well its findings generalize to women and racioethnic minority populations. Reporting this type of information allowed recent scholars to criticize the overreliance on North American samples to draw inferences about organizational behavior (Shen et al., 2011).

Though many authors in the studies we reviewed took the initiative to contextualize their findings, they also missed out on an opportunity to maximize the theoretical contribution of their work. The majority of micro studies we reviewed provided descriptive information about the gender and age makeup of their participants and a sizable portion also included some information on racioethnicity. This means that almost all of these studies had the *opportunity* to examine whether or not the relationships central to their paper were consistent across these demographic boundaries. Instead of actually testing this premise, however, it seems that authors (and by extension, reviewers and editors) are content to either assume universality or state the limits of their data as opposed to actually testing for prospective differences using the readily available information. Moreover, failing to report sample descriptive information means that meta-analysts, who are significantly more likely to consider the prospect of demographic differences, cannot test for such differences. Given the diversification of the workplace and a wealth of evidence undermining the universality assumption, this represents a considerable opportunity cost of maintaining the status quo.

We should note that organizational scientists are not unique in this regard. In fact, in a very comprehensive criticism of behavioral science in general, Henrich, Heine, and Norenzayan (2010) highlighted scholars' tendency for primarily studying people from Western, educated, industrialized, rich, and democratic societies, from which they created the acronym WEIRD. Reviewing data from a variety of domains, they raised considerable questions about the extensive generalizing of findings from WEIRD data to other types of populations. Similarly, Shen et al. (2011) urged organizational researchers to broaden the base of our samples to include traditionally underrepresented groups and encouraged greater use of cross-cultural approaches. We second those recommendations and extend them by making a general plea for greater efficiency in general. In most instances, authors have the data on the demographic makeup of their participants, they simply need to use it. Doing so will help to identify instances wherein widespread generalization of conclusions is warranted and those where it is not.

Reconceptualizing How We Study and Report Demographic Information

Instead of simply ignoring demographic variables such as gender, racio-ethnicity, and age, we advocate that researchers empirically test for and report the presence or absence of differences in the relationships they examine. That is not to say demographic differences should become the primary or even secondary focus of their work. Rather, such a test is simple to perform and can be reported very succinctly, thereby informing readers about this key aspect of the study's generality without distracting from the central premise of the work. To facilitate such practices, in Table 1.2 we provide recommendations for journal reporting standards that authors may consider incorporating into their work. A couple of excellent examples of this approach are presented here. First, Chapman et al. (2005) who, after meta-analytically investigating a number of relationships in the job search process, tested the invariance of these linkages across racioethnicity and gender and reported their findings in a single paragraph in the results

Table 1.2.
Recommendations for Journal Reporting Standards

Considerations for Authors	Considerations for Journals
• Empirically test for, and report, the presence or absence of differences in the relationships examined in the study(ies).	• Consider practices that encourage the reporting of demographic effects, such as adding new sections (e.g., the contextual sidebar at *Journal of Organizational Behavior*)
• If a sound rationale exists for including a demographic variable(s) as a control variable, test for—and report the results of-homogeneity of regression before deciding to use it as a control in the analyses.	• Encourage authors to include results and discussion that help readers determine the limits or strengths of the generality of the findings.
• If the results of a homogeneity of regression analysis suggest that it is statistically appropriate to use a demographic variable(s) as a control, the results of the interaction of the demographic variable in the study model should be reported rather than merely controlling for the demographic variable in the analyses.	• Consider asking questions during the manuscript submission process that prompt authors to report the role of demographics in testing the relationships central to their study(ies).
• If conducting a meta-analysis, encourage authors to provide demographics from their data, even if not reported in the original study.	• Add prompts or questions to the reviewer guidelines that encourage journal reviewers to look specifically at the representation or generalizability of the sample demographically when reading the manuscript.
• Use footnotes, supplemental analysis, or a single paragraph in the results section, to report the results of demographic effects with minimal distraction to the reader.	• State on the journal's website that authors are encouraged to report the kinds of supplemental analyses suggested (e.g., homogeneity of regression) and why the interpretation of findings through the lens of demographic generalizability will improve scholarship.
• Where appropriate, consider testing and reporting the effect that the interaction of demographic variables have to support the growing literature on multiple identities and intersectionality.	• Discuss the journal's and editor's value of demographic generalizability at journal board meetings.
• If the sample size of a group (e.g., females, people of color, etc.) is too small in the sample, report that information instead of a homogeneity of regression analysis so that readers can be aware of the sample characteristics when interpreting findings.	• Encourage authors to use samples that represent the demographic characteristics of the workforce in the country(ies) they are conducting research in.

section. In this particular instance, the authors opted to develop arguments for differences into the theoretical model they tested, but the results did not vary much by gender (or at all by racioethnicity). Nevertheless, results of such a test of demographic differences are equally informative in the absence of a priori logic and can be incorporated regularly in a purely exploratory fashion. Second, Scott and Barnes (2011, p. 129) opted to include the following footnote in their work:

> On an exploratory basis, we examined the potential moderating influence of age and ethnicity. Results of these analyses revealed that neither age nor ethnicity moderated any of the hypothesized relationships, with one exception: the within-individual relationship between state negative affect and withdrawal was stronger for Caucasians ($b_{63} = .27, p < .05$).

This provided minimal distraction to the reader, but clearly illustrates that the phenomenon of interest in their case appears invariant across ethnicity and age (at least within their data). In sum, we believe the increasing presence of diversity calls for it to play a more integral role in *all* theorizing and theory testing, not just that which explicitly pertains to the effects of diversity in the workplace.

REFERENCES

Aguinis, H., Beaty, J. C., Boik, R. J., & Pierce, C. A. (2005). Effect size and power in assessing moderating effects of categorical variables using multiple regression: A 30-year review. *Journal of Applied Psychology, 90*, 94–107. doi:10.1037/0021-9010.90.1.94

Aguinis, H., Pierce, C. A., & Culpepper, S. A. (2009). Scale coarseness as a methodological artifact: Correcting correlation coefficients attenuated from using coarse scales. *Organizational Research Methods, 12*, 623–652. doi:10.1177/1094428108318065

Aquino, K., & Bommer, W. H. (2003). Preferential mistreatment: How victim status moderates the relationship between organizational citizenship behavior and workplace victimization. *Organization Science, 14*, 374–385. doi:10.1287/orsc.14.4.374.17489

Bacharach, S. B., Bamberger, P. A., & Vashdi, D. (2005). Diversity and homophily at work: Supportive relations among White and African-American peers. *Academy of Management Journal, 48*, 619–644. doi:10.5465/AMJ.2005.17843942

Bal, P. M., De Lange, A. H., Jansen, P. G. W., & van der Velde, M. E. G. (2008). Psychological contract breach and job attitudes: A meta-analysis of age as a moderator. *Journal of Vocational Behavior, 72*, 143–158. doi:10.1016/j.jvb.2007.10.005

Barling, J., & Weatherhead, J. G. (2016). Persistent exposure to poverty during childhood limits later leader emergence. *Journal of Applied Psychology, 101,* 1305–1318. doi:10.1037/apl0000129

Bernerth, J. B., & Aguinis, H. (2016). A critical review and best-practice recommendations for control variable usage. *Personnel Psychology, 69,* 229–283. doi:10.1111/peps.12103

Berry, C. M., Ones, D. S., & Sackett, P. R. (2007). Interpersonal deviance, organizational deviance, and their common correlates: A review and meta-analysis. *Journal of Applied Psychology, 92,* 409–423. doi:10.1037/0021-9010.92.2.410

Bertolino, M., Truxillo, D. M., & Fraccaroli, F. (2011). Age as moderator of the relationship of proactive personality with training motivation, perceived career development from training, and training behavioral intentions. *Journal of Organizational Behavior, 32,* 248–263. doi:10.1002/job.670

Breaugh, J. A. (2006). Rethinking the control of nuisance variables in theory testing. *Journal of Business and Psychology, 20,* 429–443. doi:10.1007/s10869-005-9009-y

Brown, M. E., & Treviño, L. K., 2006. Ethical leadership: A review and future directions. *Leadership Quarterly, 17,* 595–616. doi:10.1016/j.leaqua.2006.10.004

Cascio, W. F., & Aguinis, H. (2008). Research in industrial and organizational psychology from 1963 to 2007: Changes, choices, and trends. *Journal of Applied Psychology, 93,* 1062–1081. doi:10.1037/0021-9010.93.5.1062

Chapman, D. S., Uggerslev, K. L., Carroll, S. A., Piasentin, K. A., & Jones, D. A. (2005). Applicant attraction to organizations and job choice: A meta-analytic review of the correlates of recruiting outcomes. *Journal of Applied Psychology, 90,* 928–944. doi:10.1037/0021-9010.90.5.928

Cohen-Charash, Y., & Spector, P. E. (2001). The role of justice in organizations: A meta-analysis. *Organizational Behavior and Human Decision Processes, 86,* 278–321. doi:10.1006/obhd.2001.2958

Colbert, A. E., Bono, J. E., & Purvanova, R. K. (2016). Flourishing via workplace relationships: Moving beyond instrumental support. *Academy of Management Journal, 59,* 1199–1223. doi:10.5465/amj.2014.0506

Cox, T. (1990). Problems with research by organizational scholars on issues of race and ethnicity. *Journal of Applied Behavioral Science, 26,* 5–23. doi:10.1177/002188639002600103

Cox, T., & Nkomo, S. M. (1990). Invisible men and women: A status report on race as a variable in organization behavior research. *Journal of Organizational Behavior, 11,* 419–431. doi:10.1002/job.4030110604

Cox, T. H., Jr., Nkomo, S. M., & Welch, J. (2001). Research on race and ethnicity: An update and analysis. In R. Golembiewski (Ed.), *Handbook of organizational behavior* (2nd ed., pp. 255–286). New York, NY: Marcel Dekker.

Cropanzano, R., & Mitchell, M. (2005). Social exchange theory: An interdisciplinary review. *Journal of Management, 31,* 874–900. doi:10.1177/0149206305279602

Ely, R. & Padavic, I. (2007). A feminist analysis of organizational research on sex differences. *Academy of Management Review, 32,* 1121–1143. doi:10.5465/AMR.2007.26585842

Heggestad, E. D., & Andrew, A. M. (2012). Aging, personality, and work attitudes. In J. W. Hedge & W. C. Borman (Eds.), *Oxford handbook of work and aging*, (pp. 256–279). Oxford, UK: Oxford University Press.

Henrich, J., Heine, S. J., & Norenzayan, A. (2010). The weirdest people in the world? *Behavioral and Brain Sciences*, *33*, 61–135. doi:10.1017/S0140525X0999152X

Hernandez, M., Avery, D. R., Volpone, S. D., & Kaiser, C. (2019). Bargaining while Black: The role of race in salary negotiations. *Journal of Applied Psychology*, *104*, 581–592. doi:10.1037/apl0000363

Hobfoll, S. E., & Wells, J. D. (1998). Conservation of resources, stress, and aging: Why do some slide and some spring? In *Handbook of Aging and Mental Health* (pp. 121–134). Springer.

James, E. H., & Wooten, L. P. (2006). Diversity crises: How firms manage discrimination lawsuits. *Academy of Management Journal*, *49*, 1103–1118. doi:10.5465/AMJ.2006.23478091

Jiang, K., Liu, D., McKay, P. F., Lee, T. W., & Mitchell, T. R. (2012). When and how is job embeddedness predictive of turnover? A meta-analytic investigation. *Journal of Applied Psychology*, *97*, 1077–1096. doi:10.1037/a0028610

Johns, G. (2006). The essential impact of context on organizational behavior. *Academy of Management Review*, *31*, 386–408. doi:10.5465/AMR.2006.20208687

Judge, T. A., & Cable, D. M. (2011). When it comes to pay, do the thin win? The effect of weight on pay for men and women. *Journal of Applied Psychology*, *96*, 95–112. doi:10.1037/a0020860

Kacmar, K., Bachrach, D. G., Harris, K. J., & Zivnuska, S. (2011). Fostering good citizenship through ethical leadership: Exploring the moderating role of gender and organizational politics. *Journal of Applied Psychology*, *96*, 633–642. doi:10.1037/a0021872

Kerr, W. A. (1946). Worker attitudes toward scheduling of industrial music. *Journal of Applied Psychology*, *30*, 575–578. doi:10.1037/h0057718

Kooij, D., Jansen, P. G. W., Dikkers, J. S. E., & De Lange, A. H. (2010). The influence of age on the associations between HR practices and both affective commitment and job satisfaction: A meta-analysis. *Journal of Organizational Behavior*, *31*, 1111–1136. doi:10.1002/job.666

Landay, K., Harms, P. D., & Credé, M. (2019). Shall we serve the dark lords? A meta-analytic review of psychopathy and leadership. *Journal of Applied Psychology*, *104*, 183–196. doi:10.1037/apl0000357

Livers, A. B., & Caver, K. A. (2003). *Leading in Black and White: Working across the racial divide in corporate America*. San Francisco, CA: Jossey-Bass.

Luksyte, A., Waite, E., Avery, D. R., & Roy, R. (2013). Held to a different standard: Racioethnic and gender differences in the impact of lateness on promotion opportunity. *Journal of Occupational and Organizational Psychology*, *86*, 142–165. doi:10.1111/joop.12010

McKay, P. F., & Avery, D. R. (2006). What has race got to do with it? Unraveling the role of racioethnicity in job seekers' reactions to site visits. *Personnel Psychology*, *59*, 395–429. doi:10.1111/j.1744-6570.2006.00041.x

McKay, P., Avery, D., Tonidandel, S., Morris, M., Hernandez, M., & Hebl, M. (2007). Racial differences in employee retention: Are diversity climate perceptions the key? *Personnel Psychology*, *60*, 35–62. doi:10.1111/j.1744-6570.2007.00064.x

Ng, T. W. H., & Feldman, D. C. (2008). The relationship of age to ten dimensions of job performance. *Journal of Applied Psychology, 93*, 392–23. doi:10.1037/0021-9010.93.2.392

Ng, T. W., & Feldman, D. C. (2009). How broadly does education contribute to job performance? *Personnel Psychology, 62*, 89–134. doi:10.1111/j.1744-6570.2008.01130.x

Ng, T. W., & Feldman, D. C. (2010). The relationships of age with job attitudes: A meta-analysis. *Personnel Psychology, 63*, 677–718. doi:10.1111/j.1744-6570.2010.01184.x

Ortiz-Ospina, E. & Tzvetkova, S. (2017). Working women: Key facts and trends in female labor force participation. Retrieved from https://ourworldindata.org/female-labor-force-participation-key-facts

Podsakoff, P. M., Mackenzie, S. B., Bachrach, D. G., & Podsakoff, N. P. (2005). The influence of management journals in the 1980s and 1990s. *Strategic Management Journal, 26*, 473–488. doi:10.1002/smj.454

Scott, B. A., & Barnes, C. M. (2011). A multilevel field investigation of emotional labor, affect, work withdrawal, and gender. *Academy of Management Journal, 54*, 116–136. doi:10.5465/amj.2011.59215086

Shen, W., Kiger, T. B., Davies, S. E., Rasch, R. L., Simon, K. M., & Ones, D. S. (2011). Samples in applied psychology: Over a decade of research in review. *Journal of Applied Psychology, 96*, 1055–1064. doi:10.1037/a0023322

Simons, T. (2002). Behavioral integrity: The perceived alignment between managers' words and deeds as a research focus. *Organization Science, 13*, 18–35.

Simons, T., Friedman, R., Liu, L. A., & Parks, J. M. (2007). Racial differences in sensitivity to behavioral integrity: attitudinal consequences, in-group effects, and "trickle down" among Black and non-Black employees. *Journal of Applied Psychology, 92*, 650–665. doi:10.1037/0021-9010.92.3.650

Spector, P. A., & Brannick, M. T. (2011). Methodological urban legends: The misuse of statistical control variables. *Organizational Research Methods, 14*, 287–305. doi:10.1177/1094428110369842

Tabachnik, B. G., & Fidell, L. S. (2001). *Using multivariate statistics* (4th ed.). Needham Heights, MA: Allyn & Bacon.

Toossi, M. (2012). Projections of the labor force to 2050: A visual essay. *Monthly Labor Review, 135*(10), 3–16.

Toossi, M. (2016). A look at the future of the U.S. labor force to 2060. *Spotlight on Statistics*, U.S. Bureau of Labor Statistics. Retrieved from https://www.bls.gov/spotlight/2016/a-look-at-the-future-of-the-us-labor-force-to-2060/pdf/a-look-at-the-future-of-the-us-labor-force-to-2060.pdf

Toossi, M. & Joyner, L. (2018). Blacks in the labor force. *Spotlight on Statistics*, U.S. Bureau of Labor Statistics. Retrieved from https://www.bls.gov/spotlight/2018/blacks-in-the-labor-force/pdf/blacks-in-the-labor-force.pdf

Toossi, M., & Torpey, E. (2017). Older workers: Labor force trends and career options. *Career Outlook*, U.S. Bureau of Labor Statistics. Retrieved from https://www.bls.gov/careeroutlook/2017/article/older-workers.htm

Treadway, D. C., Ferris, G. R., Hochwarter, W., Perrewé, P. L., Witt, L. A., & Goodman. J. M. (2005). The role of age in the perceptions of politics-job performance relationship: A three study constructive replication. *Journal of Applied Psychology, 90*, 872–881. doi:10.1037/0021-9010.90.5.872

Tzvetkova, S., & Ortiz-Ospina, E. (2017). Working women: What determines female labor force participation? Retrieved from https://ourworldindata.org/women-in-the-labor-force-determinants

Wright, P., Ferris, S. P., Hiller, J. S., & Kroll, M. (1995). Competitiveness through management of diversity: Effects on stock price valuation. *Academy of Management Journal, 38*, 272–287. doi:10.2307/25673

CHAPTER 2

ARE WOMEN BETTER SUITED THAN MEN TO LEAD IN DIVERSE SETTINGS?

A Look at Nations, Organizations, and Teams

Negin R. Toosi
California State University

Susan E. Perkins
University of Illinois

Jaee Cho
Hong Kong University of Science and Technology

Katherine W. Phillips
Columbia University

INTRODUCTION

Who do you visualize when you think of an ideal leader? And how does the level of racial/ ethnic diversity in the context affect your answer to that question? Although women are still underrepresented at the highest levels of leadership, there has been a noticeable increase in the number of female leaders over the last few decades across nations, organizations, and top leadership teams globally (Adler, 2001; Bullough, Kroeck, Newburry, Kundu, & Lowe 2012; Perkins, Phillips, & Pearce, 2013; Pew Research Center, 2019). The number of female heads of state has tripled in the last 30 years (see Figure 2.1); the current cohort of 22 female presidents and prime ministers represents approximately 10% of all world leaders. In organizations, women now make up about 5% of CEOs and over 20% of top management team members (e.g., corporate boards) of Fortune 500 companies (Pew Research Center, 2019). In the U.S., this is a small, yet powerful cohort of 27 female CEOs. Outside of the U.S., women currently represent 15% of the top leadership teams in European countries and 4% across Asia (Global Gender Balance Scorecard, 2018), and in some countries, gender quotas for board membership promise to increase the representation of women even further (Terjesen, Aguilera, & Lorenz, 2015; Wang & Kelan, 2013). This represents a multifold increase of women in leadership positions compared to the end of the last century, and yet these numbers are still nowhere near parity.

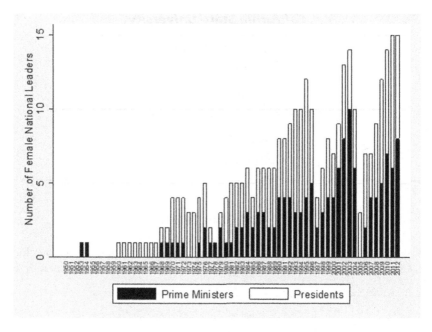

Figure 2.1. Female National Leader Trends (1950–2012).

However, what is promising about the presence of these women is the positive association between the inclusion of women in the decision making and the performance outcomes of countries, organizations, and teams. For example, in the groups/teams literature, Woolley, Chabris, Pentland, Hashmi, and Malone (2010) show that the collective intelligence of the team, which improves performance across multiple tasks, is correlated with a higher proportion of women on the team. Relatedly, at the organizational level, Dezsö and Ross (2012) found that female leaders are associated with improved managerial performance which in turn boosts overall firm performance, particularly in innovation-intensive industries. Further to this point, a recent McKinsey study on top management teams across the United Kingdom, North America, and Latin America found that firms that have gender diversity in the leadership team outperform their industry peers by 15% (Hunt, Layton, & Prince, 2015). These studies reveal that for teams and organizations, female contributions to decision making, particularly when the decisions are complex in nature, matter greatly.

This pattern of positive outcomes at the team and organizational levels can also be seen at the country level. In a recent empirical examination of more than 180 countries Perkins, Phillips, and Pearce (2013) found that when more racially/ethnically diverse countries have female heads of state (e.g., presidents and prime ministers) there is greater economic growth in the country, relative to when the country is led by a male. This global evidence connecting female leadership positively to performance outcomes in diverse, but not more homogeneous settings (note there were no significant differences in country-level performance between male and female leaders in less diverse countries) motivated us to explore this connection further in this chapter. We believe that the complexity brought on by racial/ethnic diversity in those countries make it important to have women involved in the leadership—just like more complex teams and organizations benefit from women's presence.

The need to conceptually unpack the connection between the types of leaders that best serve diverse[1] groups, organizations, and countries is increasingly important given that our social settings are becoming increasingly diverse in terms of race and ethnicity. Increased travel and migration on a global scale (UNESCO Institute for Statistics, 2009), demographic shifts due to birth rates at the country-level (U.S. Census Bureau, 2008, 2012), and continued emphasis on racial and ethnic diversity in the workplace (Dodd-Frank Act of 2010) all combined underscore the importance of understanding and navigating the complexities of diversity at each level.

Although substantial research has examined the effects of diversity on social and performance outcomes in small team settings (Mannix & Neale, 2005; Van Knippenberg & Schippers, 2007; Williams & O'Reilly, 1998) and on economic outcomes in countries (Alesina, Devleeschauwer, Easterly,

Kurlat, & Wacziarg, 2003; Alesina & La Ferrara, 2005), very little work has explicitly examined the relationship between diversity and gender in leadership. In this chapter, we intend to explore two primary questions: First: How might racial/ethnic diversity influence women's selection and emergence into leadership positions? and second: How might female leaders affect performance and outcomes for members in diverse teams, organizations, and nations differently than others leading in less diverse settings? In exploring these two questions, a secondary goal of this chapter is to identify some of the potential conditions and mechanisms that would explain the potentially mutually reinforcing nature of racial/ ethnic diversity and female leadership, and its implications for performance of teams, organizations, and nations.

In the first part of this chapter, we explore the first question by reviewing research across multiple fields that focus particularly on four such potential conditions: (1) perceived complexity,(2) sense of threat and need for change, (3) the desire for cooperation rather than competition, and 4) heterogeneity of beliefs about gender roles. We aim to make connections between these interlocking and complementary themes to further explore the conditions created by diversity and those that are conducive to increasing the representation of women in leadership roles.

In the second half of the chapter, we explore the second question about how and why women's leadership might affect outcomes in diverse settings. Once in power, female leaders may have a unique effect on racially diverse groups through their (1) symbolic presence, (2) leadership styles, and (3) policy choices and attitudes. In exploring these issues, we pull from research in social psychology, management, economics, and political science examining phenomena ranging from the group to the organization to the national level, and seek unifying themes to develop a broader vision for the impact of female leadership in diverse settings. We conclude this chapter by offering many possible future research directions that could provide evidence for the influence of female leadership in diverse settings.

2.0 DIVERSITY AND THE SELECTION OF LEADERS

The broader appeal of racial/ethnic diversity is the potential for its positive performance effects on creativity, innovation, decision making, and information processing for individuals, teams, and organizations. However, research has also shown that diversity can have detrimental effects such as intragroup conflict, exclusion of underrepresented minorities, and inequalities in resource allocations that when at their extremes can be deleterious to the positive diversity outcomes (e.g., Alesina & La Ferrara, 2005; Mannix & Neale, 2005; Williams & O'Reilly, 1998). Researchers and practitioners alike have focused on ways to mitigate the negative effects and capture the benefits of diversity, given its increasing prevalence in many aspects of life. Some micro-organizational scholars have focused on resolving these frictions of diversity through improving interpersonal interactions (Dumas, Phillips, & Rothbard, 2013; Phillips, Rothbard, & Dumas, 2009). Another, more macro, view on managing diversity suggests that leaders matter in determining policies and representing the needs of underrepresented and disenfranchised groups (Chattopadhyay & Duflo, 2004; Ely, 1994; Nishii & Mayer, 2009).

Here we make the connection and further distinguish that these negative conditions associated with racial/ ethnic diversity overlap with several of the conditions that have been demonstrated to lead to an increased preference for the selection and emergence of female leaders. For instance, diversity is associated with an increase in perceived social complexity and risk of conflict (Jehn, Northcraft, & Neale, 1999) and interactions with diverse others can evoke a sense of anxiety or threat (Toosi, Babbitt, Ambady, & Sommers, 2012; Trawalter, Richeson, & Shelton, 2009); both of these diversity concerns have been shown to affect preferences for female leaders. Diverse settings could also call forth the desire for feminine (versus masculine) leadership that would encourage cooperation rather than competition and escalation of conflict (Spisak, Homan, Grabo, & Van Vugt, 2012; Van Vugt & Spisak, 2008) and present fertile ground for voicing of non-traditional and gender-egalitarian views on leadership (Cuddy, Wolf, Glick, Crotty, Chong, & Norton, 2015; Phillips & Loyd, 2006). In the sections that follow, we examine each of these conditions in terms of how it is engendered by diverse settings and how it, it turn, affects leadership preferences.

2.1 Increased Complexity

Diversity signals increased complexity not just at the national level, but also in organizations and within teams. Diversity within a country is associated with greater potential for inter-ethnic conflict, competition for resources, and lower economic growth (Alesina et al., 2003; Alesina & La Ferrara, 2005; Collier, 2000; Easterly & Levine, 1997). Part of the challenge in building diverse societies is resolving the issue of decreased levels of participation as racial/ethnic diversity rises (Alesina & La Ferrara, 2000). Likewise, in the corporate arena, greater diversity is associated with increased complexity in the form of interpersonal and task related conflict, as well as communication difficulties (e.g., Jehn, Northcraft, & Neale, 1999; Milliken & Martins, 1996; Pelled, Eisenhardt, & Xin, 1999; see Williams & O'Reilly, 1998 for a review). At the level of the workgroup, racially diverse groups are perceived as more socially complex than homogeneous groups (e.g., Toosi, Sommers, & Ambady, 2012). Part of the reason underlying this association is that diverse settings can evoke social concerns about prejudice and self-presentation (Toosi, Babbitt, Ambady, & Sommers, 2012). For example, when asked what degree of "diplomatic and interpersonal skills" would be needed in a group with both Black and White members versus an all-White group, participants indicated the need for more social skills for the diverse group, demonstrating that racial diversity is a cue to social complexity (Toosi, Sommers, & Ambady, 2012, Study 3). At all three levels of analysis, these findings suggest that there are missed opportunities to leverage the advantages of diversity when this complexity is not adequately addressed.

Examining the situations that lead to emergence of leaders, a meta-analysis by Eagly and Karau (1991) demonstrated that although men are more likely to emerge as leaders of groups generally, women are more likely to emerge as leaders when the group tasks contained some element of social and interpersonal complexity. Because of gender roles that attribute social and affiliative roles to women, they are seen as more fitting for roles that feature complex social interactions (Eagly & Karau, 1991, 2002). Furthermore, women tend to respond to intergroup situations by becoming more engaged, a "tend-and-befriend" strategy, whereas men pull back (Littleford, Wright, & Sayoc-Parial, 2005; Taylor et al., 2000).

In an experimental test, in all-White groups deliberating as mock juries, White men dominated women in terms of speaking time, and other group members rated men as more persuasive than women. However, in racially diverse groups, White women and White men spent equal amounts of time speaking and were rated as equally persuasive (and not statistically different from the Black women and men in these groups). In other words, all group members, men and women, had more equal airtime in the racially diverse groups (Toosi, Sommers, & Ambady, 2012). This suggests that racially diverse settings may create settings where all have more equal opportunities to emerge as leaders relative to homogeneous groups, especially in cases of smaller groups which meet regularly.

At the organizational level, the question of whether more racially diverse companies are more likely to hire and promote female leaders due to a greater sense of complexity has not, to our knowledge, been addressed. However, a recent analysis of Standard & Poor's 500 companies showed that when these organizations have a chief diversity officer (about half do), they most frequently entrust women with these organizational roles: Women make up 76% of the chief diversity officers in the S&P 500 (Glasman, Paikeday, Sachar, Stuart, & Young, 2018).

At the national level, the above findings are consistent with our observations of elected female national leaders with campaigns focused on managing complex racial/ethnic tensions. Liberia, for example, has approximately twice the level of racial/ethnic diversity as the United States (see Figure 2.2), with over 15 ethnic groups.[2] After years of leadership styles that isolated and disenfranchised many groups and set the foundation for 14 years of civil war, Liberia's first female president, President Ellen Johnson Sirleaf, won the Nobel Peace Prize for her efforts to mend the complex social fractures of ethnic conflicts in that highly diverse country. In a more recent example, the Ethiopian parliament unanimously selected Sahle-Work Zewde as the new president of that highly diverse[3] country. President Zewde is currently the only female head of state in Africa. In Zewde's first speech to parliament, she conveyed her goal for "a prosperous Ethiopia free of religious, ethnic and gender discrimination" ("Ethiopia Appoints," 2018). Thus, we suggest that greater racial/ethnic diversity may lead to more emergence of female leaders.

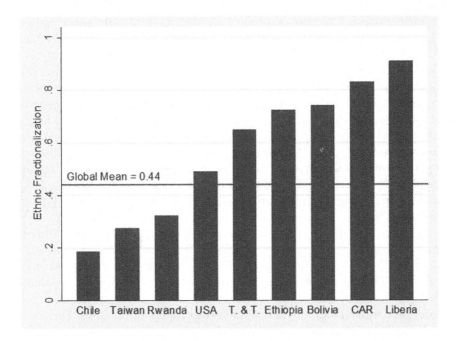

Figure 2.2.   Ethnic fractionalization by country. Ethnic fractionalization (EF) is a country-level index which measures the level of racial/ethnic diversity within a country (Alesina et al., 2003). High levels of EF correspond to a value of 1; low levels correspond to a value of 0. The global mean across 190 countries is 0.44. Countries represented include the USA and the countries with female national leaders discussed throughout this chapter. T. & T. abbreviates Trinidad and Tobago; CAR stands for Central African Republic.

2.2 Threat and Need for Change

Diversity can also be construed as a threat to the status quo. At the interpersonal level, a well-developed body of research on diversity in the form of interracial interactions has shown that diversity can evoke a stress response, particularly from members of racial majority groups (Amodio, 2009; Shelton, Richeson, & Vorauer, 2006; Toosi, Babbitt, Ambady, & Sommers, 2012; Trawalter, Richeson, & Shelton, 2009). In terms of policy preferences and diversity ideology, White Americans react to projections of the diversifying demographic shifts in the U.S. with defensiveness, concerns about discrimination against their racial in-group, and decreased support for diversity (Craig & Richeson, 2017; Danbold & Huo, 2015). Furthermore, White Americans avoid interracial interactions because of the discomfort and anxiety that it causes for them (Plant, 2004; Plant & Devine, 1998). Consistent with this feeling of threat and desire to avoid diversity, White Americans express a greater preference for colorblind approaches to race relations which de-emphasize racial and ethnic differences, rather than multicultural approaches which highlight them, because they feel excluded by the latter (Plaut, Garnett, Buffardi, & Sanchez-Burks, 2011).

To be sure, the interracial tension between ethnic groups is not a diversity problem exclusive to the United States; it is a concern globally. European countries which have been accepting large number of migrants fleeing persecution and war likewise have shown attitude shifts, depending on levels of racial prejudice and perceived economic competition (Card, Dustmann, & Preston, 2005; Gang, Rivera-Batiz, & Yun, 2002). An increased number of ethnic groups within a country is associated with greater risk of ethnic conflict (Fearon & Laitin, 2003), and when grievances are not resolved and further antagonism persists, the risk of civil war is very high (Fearon & Laitin, 2003).

This sense of threat as a result of increasing diversity, especially among racial majority group members, may disrupt typical preferences for male over female leaders. The psychological experience of threat or risk may lead to a preference for a new direction in leadership (Brown, Diekman, & Schneider, 2011; Haslam & Ryan, 2005, 2008). Because femininity is associated with change and masculinity is associated with stability (Diekman & Eagly, 2000; Diekman, Goodfriend, & Goodwin, 2004), individuals have shown increased positive attitudes towards female leaders in change-oriented situations. Brown and colleagues (2011), for example, found that when a sense of threat was induced in participants (e.g. by having them write about challenges faced by their local community, such as economic instability or crime), they were more likely to express preferences for female leaders, thereby reducing or reversing the typical preference for male leaders.

Furthermore, archival evidence and experiments demonstrate that when organizations are in crisis women are more likely to be selected as leaders, whereas men are preferred as leaders when organizations are stable or improving (the "glass cliff" effect; Haslam & Ryan, 2005, 2008). Furst and Reeves (2008) explored similar themes in their exploration of "creative destruction" as a pathway to emergent female leadership, using profiles of several female executives. They suggested that turbulent environments are conducive to women's emergence as leaders, because they trigger a need for change, new talent, and innovation, which are associated with women's leadership styles. As an example at the national level, Bolivia's first (and to date only) female President Lidia Gueiler Tejada was selected as provisional president (1979–1980) to bring back stability to the country after the former President Wálter Guevara was overrun by a coup and the new dictator, Alberto Natusch, was rejected by a national rebellion to his power.

We suggest that, to the extent that individuals construe the presence of racial/ethnic diversity as a threat and correspondingly feel a need for change, racial/ethnic diversity may lead to an increased preference for female leaders. However, this pathway may be limited by the extent to which the response to racial/ethnic diversity is derived from a social dominance approach to group relations, signifying a preference for inequality among social groups in terms of race as well as gender (Sanchez, Chaney, Manuel, Wilton, & Remedios, 2017; Sidanius & Pratto, 1999). In such cases, the sense of threat evoked by increasing racial diversity would not lead to greater support for female leaders, as this would represent a further threat to the status hierarchy.

2.3 Cooperation Rather Than Competition

Diverse settings may present a need for a leader who can nurture positive intragroup relations. Diverse groups are often perceived as having more conflict than homogeneous groups (Jehn et al., 1999; Pelled et al., 1999) even if the groups' members are saying and doing the exact same things as equivalent homogeneous groups (Lount, Sheldon, Rink, & Phillips, 2012). Diversity signals difficulties in communication and less cohesion (Hoffman, 1985; Mehra, Kilduff, & Brass, 1998). Similarly, at the country level, diversity creates competition for resource allocation because of "within group" versus "between group" preferences across ethnicities (Alesina & La Ferrara, 2005). In settings where intergroup or identity-based conflicts are possible, such as small racially diverse task groups, companies seeking to increase diversity and inclusion among their employees, or most countries (excluding those who are intending to break apart due to internal civil divisions), strategies for avoiding and/or resolving these conflicts in a peaceful way are needed. Institutions or leaders that change the "rules of the game" towards more inclusion are thought to be a viable solution in mitigating these challenges of diversity (Alesina & La Ferrara, 2005).

Research demonstrates that in situations where it is necessary to build positive, harmonious, and cooperative relationships between groups, people tend to prefer female leaders. Conversely, in situations where the preference is for a dominant leader who emphasizes competition with other groups for the benefit of the in-group, male leaders are more likely to be selected (Spisak, Homan, Grabo, & Van Vugt, 2012; Van Vugt & Spisak, 2008).

To the extent that challenges associated with diversity within a country, organization, or group are considered to be worth resolving for the sake of the whole group, female leadership may be preferred. It is not always true that the parties to a conflict want to resolve these conflicts. Differences of scale may play a role here. For instance, compared to small workgroups, the complex interplay of multiple racial, ethnic, and tribal groups at the larger scale of organizations and countries may interfere with a desire for unity. Competition for scarce resources in these larger contexts can trigger intractable intergroup conflicts that can lead to desires for partition or secession.

Yet, at the organizational level, leaders have recognized that female leadership styles that put an emphasis on cooperation may be better for organizational success. For instance, as illustrated by an interview with George Halvorson, former CEO of Kaiser Permanente, "when you've got a complex project involving multiple layers, you need a leader who is collaborative and more often than not, that leader is a woman" (Groysberg & Connolly, 2013). At the national level, there are also examples such as the first and, thus far, only female Prime Minister in Rwanda, Agathe Uwilingiyimana, who was appointed by the president with the hopes that she would be key in negotiating a peace agreement between the Hutus and Tutsis to end the civil war. Unfortunately, she was assassinated as one of the first victims of the Rwandan genocide of 1994. More recently, President Catherine Samba-Panza, the first female president of the Central African Republic (CAR), was elected by the transition team of her postwar country largely to be the peacemaker. The electorate expected her to quell long-standing ethnic conflict, to foster peace and social cohesion through the gateways of tolerance and cooperation. Dubbed by her fellow countrymen as "Mother Courage," President Samba-Panza felt that her country "didn't want any more male politicians," and instead wanted a female leader "who could calm things, reconcile people" (RFI, 2014).

2.4 Heterogeneity of Beliefs About Gender Roles

Finally, a diversity of racial/ethnic backgrounds within a group, organization or country suggests that there may be heterogeneity in beliefs among the members about what makes an effective leader, as well as in beliefs about gender roles. Racial differences in attitudes towards female leadership exist. For example, in a survey of over 3,600 American respondents, more African American and Latino men than White men expressed support for a potential female candidate for president and expected that they would see a female president in their lifetime; this held true even when controlling for political party identification (Maxwell, Ford-Dowe, Jimeno, & Shields, 2013). Even the mere presence of diversity may be enough to disrupt assumptions about women's suitability for leadership (e.g. Bridges & Nelson, 1989; Tomaskovic-Devey, 1993), given that being in diverse groups can reduce people's tendency to assume that others will agree with them compared to homogeneous groups (Phillips & Loyd, 2006; Phillips, Northcraft, & Neale, 2006; Sommers, Warp, & Mahoney, 2008).

Furthermore, although an association between men and leadership roles seems largely consistent across different countries, over time, and even across age groups (Ayman & Korabik, 2010; Ayman-Nolley & Ayman, 2005; Heilman, 2001; Lam, 1992; Powell, Butterfield, & Parent, 2002; Schein, 2001; Schein, Müller, Lituchy, & Liu, 1996), the aggregate statistics may conceal differences in the association of specific traits with leadership and gender roles. People from various countries identify different traits in their prototypical leaders (Dickson, Den Hartog, & Mitchelson, 2003; Gerstner & Day, 1994; Rule et al., 2010). Research by Cuddy and colleagues (2015) illustrates how these different leadership profiles may relate to gender roles: In countries where assertiveness is valued (e.g., the United States) men are attributed greater assertiveness, whereas women are considered to be more communal. On the other hand, in countries where social values emphasize a communal orientation (e.g., Korea), men are considered to be more communal, and women are seen as more assertive. In both cases, men are higher-status, and the proportion of men in leadership positions is similar, but the specific social roles assigned to men versus women are different, based on whichever traits are more valued. Because diversity brings together people who may hold differing beliefs about the specific leadership traits associated with gender roles, women demonstrating some of the relevant traits may be considered as possible leaders by people from other groups, potentially creating opportunities for them to rise to positions of leadership. Consistent with this possibility, an analysis of factors leading to women's promotions to CEO in Fortune 500 companies over a 20-year period highlighted the role of decision-maker diversity in increasing the likelihood of selecting women for those leadership positions (Cook & Glass, 2014).

3.0 OUTCOMES AND PERFORMANCE

Once women attain these positions of leadership in diverse organizations, how might their performance as leaders differ from those of males? In the only published study, we are aware of that examines racial/ethnic diversity and its relationship to women's leadership, Perkins, Phillips, and Pearce (2013) analyzed the country-level effects of ethnic diversity on the economic performance of a nation, measured by gross domestic product (GDP). They found that in general, increased ethnic diversity tended to be associated with lower GDP growth, concurring with previous findings on the effects of diversity on economic growth (Alesina et al., 2003); however, the results were reversed when moderated by the gender of the leader. Highly diverse countries with female leaders actually had higher growth rates than their male counterparts in these settings. For example, countries with the highest possible ethnic fractionalization (EF = 1) that were led by a female had a 6.6% GDP growth rate in the subsequent year compared to a 0.45% growth rate for male leaders in these same settings. We explore below some potential pathways for why this boost in performance in diverse settings occurs with the presence of female leadership, ranging from the symbolic impact of female leaders to gender differences in leadership styles and policy decisions and behavior while in office.

3.1 Symbolic Impact of Female Leaders

The first pathway that we consider is the symbolic effect of having a woman in charge (that is, not taking into account potential differences in leadership styles or policy decisions). How might the mere presence of a woman—a member of what is typically the lower-status gender group—in a high-status position affect performance outcomes? First, female role models affect the attitudes of younger generations (Beaman, Duflo, Pande, & Topalova, 2012; Smith & Erb, 1986). For example, in a study of thousands of adolescents and their parents across almost 500 villages in India, Beaman and colleagues (2012) found that in villages randomly assigned to have female leaders, gender gaps in aspirations were narrowed and the gender gap in educational attainment was eliminated, compared to villages with no assigned female leader (Beaman et al., 2012). Second, the presence of women in leadership positions also impacts the engagement and motivation of other women lower in the ranks (Dezsö & Ross, 2012; Ely, 1994; Lee, Smith, & Cioci, 1993). For example, in organizations with higher numbers of women in senior management positions, other women were more likely to consider gender as a positive basis for identification with and support from their female colleagues rather than as a source of competition (Ely, 1994). Third, organizations with women in top leadership positions may be seen as signaling an environment conducive to the advancement of other women (Bilimoria, 2006; Daily & Dalton, 2003), and may be more attractive to women who want to advance in their careers.

We suggest that having a female leader may lead to positive outcomes not only for other females, but also for racial minority group members, due to the symbolic effect of having a member of a low-status group in a high-status role (e.g. Marx & Goff, 2005; Nguyen, 2008; Plant et al., 2009). An illustration of this occurs in a survey of U.S citizens by the Pew Research Center (2009), which found that Black Americans were more likely than White Americans (36% vs. 26%) to state that female leaders would do a better job of representing their interests than male leaders. Some recent research on the "stigma by prejudice transfer" effect also bears on this question. White American women reading about a racist White man expected him to also be sexist, and Black and Latino American men likewise perceived a sexist White man as racist as well (Sanchez, Chaney, Manuel, Wilton, & Remedios, 2017). If sexist attitudes can lead to expectations of racial prejudice, then indicators of gender egalitarianism may do the opposite, suggesting that racial minorities may experience less social identity threat under the leadership of a woman (or gender-egalitarian man). One effect of female leadership may be to reduce the perceived barriers for low-status individuals, thus leading to greater engagement and empowerment. This status equalization may lead to better performance outcomes for the whole group (Woolley et al., 2010). Therefore, we suggest that the effect of seeing one member of a low-status group as a role model may spill over to evoke positive performance outcomes for other low-status individuals and the group as a whole. This symbolic effect may be a stronger factor in leadership at the larger scale such as nations and large organizations, rather than in smaller groups where the leader's interactions with group members may play a more prominent role in determining effectiveness.

3.2 Leadership Style

Moving beyond the symbolic effects of having a female leader, several meta-analyses have shown that women and men tend to differ in their leadership styles (Eagly, Johannesen-Schmidt, & van Engen, 2003; Eagly & Johnson, 1990; van Engen & Willemsen, 2004). Women tend to display more empowering leadership styles than men, which may especially benefit members of racial minorities in diverse settings. Female leaders, compared to male leaders, also engage in transformational leadership more (Eagly et al., 2003). Transformational leadership is an approach that involves inspiring, mentoring, gaining the confidence of, and (especially) empowering group members (Bass, 1985, 1999; Burns 1978; Krishnan, 2012). In addition, women display more democratic/participatory styles than men, who are more likely to tend towards autocratic styles and social dominance orientation (Eagly & Johnson, 1990; Pratto, Sidanius, Stallworth, & Malle, 1994; van Engen & Willemsen, 2004). In a series of structured interviews, Cheung and Halpern (2010) found that female leaders rarely mentioned their own power, but rather emphasized collaboration, building consensus, and empowering others.

Organizational researchers have also established the idea that female leaders enrich others' engagement. For instance, Dezsö and Ross (2011) studied the effects of having women in top management teams and found improved performance outcomes, especially for firms with an innovation-focused strategy, a strategy which requires encouraging the expression of unique perspectives and ideas. They argued that female representation in leadership positions brought to the firm the benefits of informational and social diversity noted by previous research (Van Knippenberg, De Dreu & Homan, 2004; Phillips & Loyd, 2006). Furthermore, the percentage of female managers in a workplace can shape the entire organization's practices: Melero (2011) found that workplaces with a higher proportion of women in their management teams paid more attention to employee development, as well as promoting more communication, listening to employee feedback, and encouraging employee participation in decision making.

At the national level, we have also observed that some female leaders' governing style specifically emphasized status equalization between groups rather than dominance of one ethnic group over the others. For example, soon after coming to power, Taiwan's first female president, Tsai Ing-wen, apologized to Taiwan's 16 indigenous tribes including the Amis, Atayal, and Paiwan, the largest three minority groups. Her apology to those groups violated by over four centuries of unjust policies was the first such apology and powerfully redirected the national conversation to focus on including and respecting underrepresented groups (Domonoske, 2016).

Researchers have found the transformational approach to leadership that emphasizes empowerment of group members to be more effective than other forms of leadership (Foels, Driskell, Mullen, & Salas, 2000; Lowe, Kroeck, & Sivasubramaniam, 1996). Leadership styles that emphasize empowerment of group members may underlie findings at the organizational and group levels that connect women in power with improved performance (Adler, 2001; Catalyst, 2004; Dezsö & Ross, 2012; Krishnan & Park, 2005; Smith, Smith, & Verner, 2006; Woolley et al., 2010). More directly, in diverse groups, transformational leadership styles result in positive effects of diversity on performance, through improving information sharing and elaboration (Kearney & Gebert, 2009).

Possible reasons why an empowering approach to leadership may be more prevalent among women are explored quite thoroughly elsewhere (Eagly & Chin, 2010; Eagly et al., 2003), but the findings of two articles—Brescoll (2012) and Tost, Gino, and Larrick (2012)—together may serve to illustrate this effect and how it may affect low-status group members. Brescoll (2012) demonstrated, through both experimental data and archival analysis of U.S. Senators' talking behavior on the Senate floor, that power was linked with increased volubility in men, but not women. However, volubility may itself have negative consequences. Tost, Gino, and Larrick (2012) found that verbal dominance on the part of a formal leader in a group setting actually sent the message to other, lower-status group members that their perspectives were not valued. Excessive volubility thus signaled a lack of openness to input, reduced communication within the group, and hurt performance. If female leaders do not dominate the floor but rather provide space for the input of others, this could result in a more positive experience for lower-status group members, making them feel more empowered to contribute, and leading to improved performance overall.

This may be particularly critical in the case of group members who are lower-status not only by virtue of not being in formal leadership positions but also because of their racial/ethnic minority identity. A style of leadership that empowers and creates a space for racial minorities to participate and contribute may be more effective; and this seems to be the style of leadership more commonly demonstrated by women. Transformational leadership, at all levels, unlocks the performance benefits associated with a diversity paradigm that recognizes and utilizes the strength of its diverse elements for the benefit of the whole (Ely & Thomas, 2001; Kearney & Gebert, 2009; Thomas & Ely, 1996).

3.3 Policy Choices and Attitudes

The final possible pathway we offer to explain why female leaders may improve outcomes in diverse settings is that, in addition to their symbolic effect, different leadership styles, and sociopolitical attitudes, women may make different policy choices. Chattopadhyay and Duflo (2004) studied public goods provisions in Indian villages where the position of head of the village council was randomly designated to be reserved for women (part of a policy in India since the mid-1990s). They found that the leader's gender influenced policy decisions: The decisions made by female leaders reflected more closely the issues that were relevant to villagers, such as access to clean drinking water and improved roads. Further research in the same setting also demonstrated that in villages with female leaders, there was a greater quantity of public goods (without a reduction in quality), and villagers were less likely to pay bribes (Duflo & Topalova, 2004). Other research is also suggestive that women in leadership roles are associated with less governmental corruption (Dollar, Fisman, & Gatti, 2001), more worker compensation and child support enforcement policies (Besley & Case, 2000), and greater corporate social responsibility (Bear, Rahman, & Post, 2010).

Although no research that we are aware of has examined the effects of women in leadership on policies directly related to diversity, women in general do express more support for diversity programs than men (Chen & Hooijberg, 2000). Furthermore, women tend to have more egalitarian attitudes than men: Women report lower scores than men on measures of social dominance orientation, or a preference for group-based hierarchy (e.g. "To get ahead in life, it is sometimes necessary to step on other groups": Sidanius & Pratto, 1999; Sidanius, Pratto, & Bobo, 1994); this gender difference in social dominance orientation seems to be mediated by higher cognitive complexity among women (Foels & Reid, 2010). Women also score higher on motivation to control prejudice (e.g. "I am personally motivated by my beliefs to be nonprejudiced toward Black people": Hausmann & Ryan, 2004) and social compassion issues (e.g. "The government should not be responsible for helping blacks or other minorities improve their living standard," reversed: Eagly, Diekman, Johannesen-Schmidt, & Koenig, 2004).

These attitudes may arise from gender roles that position women as more friendly, nurturing, and supportive of egalitarianism (Berger, Rosenholtz, & Zelditch, 1980; Eagly, 1987; Johnson & Marini, 1998; Rudman & Glick, 2008). It may also be that women, having experience with being low-status in one identity dimension (gender) may be better able to recognize and address the challenges faced by low-status individuals in another dimension (race/ethnicity)—a sort of cross-identity competence (e.g., McIntosh, 1992).

With women in leadership positions in small group settings, this may take the form of less bias and disrespect shown to racial minority members of the group, thus encouraging them to participate. At organizational and national levels, these attitudes may influence outcomes for group members through public statements and policy that translates these more egalitarian attitudes into actual differences in outcomes. Some examples of female national leaders' policy agendas suggest this is the case. Many of the female national leaders that we studied put new policies in place to ensure a future pipeline of female leaders with the hopes that the next generation of women will live in a world less constrained. Michele Bachelet, the first female president of Chile and the only two-term serving (2006–2010, 2014–2018) president in Chile's history, reset the agenda for gender inclusion in her first term by appointing a cabinet representing gender parity (10 female and 10 male ministers). This set the tone for her subsequent policy shifts aimed to alleviate gender inequalities in the workplace and tripled the number of free childcare centers for disenfranchised families being economically left behind. Her policy moves to advance gender inclusion in the public and private sector led to her appointment to lead the newly created United Nations Entity for Gender Equality and the Empowerment of Women in 2010. Similarly, Kosovo's first female president, President Atifete Jahjaga, through the Pristina Principles, created mandates for female political representation in her country in 2012. Others have taken the lead on institutional changes that would force inclusion and balancing between the diverse ethnic and racial groups. Trinidad and Tobago's first female Prime Minister, Kamla Persad-Bissessar, in the second year of her term developed a new government ministry in her cabinet named the Ministry of National Diversity and Social Integration. The vision of this new institution is "to create a socially inclusive and cohesive society" and "is charged with the responsibility of promoting diversity and inclusion through ... policy measures and institutional reforms." Prime Minister Persad-Bissessar created a mechanism to channel the voices and needs of the different ethnic and religious groups in the country through representation in the national policy formation agenda to insure equality and social integration of all parts of society.

Leaders' attitudes towards race and diversity affect how much minority group members feel accepted and the amount of relationship conflict within the group (Meeussen, Otten, & Phalet, 2014); these provide a boost to performance in diverse groups as well (Homan, Van Knippenberg, Van Kleef, & De Dreu, 2007; Van Knippenberg, Haslam, & Platow, 2007). Therefore, we propose that more women in leadership positions may result in policies more likely to decrease racial inequality and bring forth the benefits of diverse perspectives and groups. Future research should examine this directly.

3.4 The Central Role of Empowerment and Egalitarian Values

In summary, a number of different aspects of female leadership may contribute to better performance in diverse groups. Either alone or together, the mere symbolic impact of a female leader, the leadership styles that tend to characterize women, and finally the policy choices and attitudes of women, might enhance the performance of diverse groups under female in comparison to male leadership. The common thread through many of these possible pathways is empowerment to reflect egalitarian values. In many cases, we would expect that the most impact would be on empowering members of low-status, racial minority, or disadvantaged groups. Their increased engagement and contribution, as a result, would boost the outcomes for the group as a whole. This may be what is happening on a national level (Perkins et al., 2013), and further research will, we hope, ascertain the role it plays in improved performance in corporations with more females in top management teams (e.g., Dezsö & Ross, 2012; Krishnan & Park, 2005) and in other settings as well.

4.0 DISCUSSION

In this chapter we sought to bring together two areas of research: the first about gender and leadership, and the second about the influence of racial/ethnic diversity on group, organizational and country-level outcomes. By examining them together, we were able to identify several overlapping themes. First, many of the conditions created by diverse settings are the same ones that have been found to increase the representation of women in leadership roles, namely, an increased sense of complexity, threat and need for change, desire for cooperation rather than competition, and heterogeneity of perspectives. Second, several of the unique aspects of women in leadership positions, such as the symbolic presence of a low-status person in a high-status position, leadership styles more common among women, and policy choices and attitudes, may be particularly advantageous to boosting performance in diverse settings. Taken together, this presents an encouraging cycle of increasing racial/ethnic diversity leading to more equitable gender representation in leadership positions leading to greater ability to benefit from diversity. We explore the theoretical questions raised by this chapter as well as the practical implications below.

4.1 Directions for Future Research

We have suggested several lines of subsequent inquiry throughout the text, such as comparing the ways that racial minorities and majorities perceive diversity and its impact on their preference for female or male leaders, or assessing the spillover symbolic effect of a leader of one low-status group on members of other low-status groups. In addition to these, future research should also explore questions of intersectionality.

Due to space constraints, we did not delve into how both gender and racial identities of leaders might impact outcomes, although some of our suggestions may have been more applicable to racial majority or minority leaders. The literature on intersectionality, which originated in legal scholarship (Crenshaw, 1991) and has expanded to address face perception (Johnson, Freeman, & Pauker, 2012), group dynamics (Toosi, Sommers, & Ambady, 2012), evaluations of social groups (Purdie-Vaughns & Eibach, 2008; Sesko & Biernat, 2010), negotiation behavior (Toosi, Mor, Semnani-Azad, Phillips, & Amanatullah, 2018), and more (for reviews see Babbitt, 2013; Cole, 2009), is also highly relevant to understanding leadership. For example, recent research shows that both Black women and Asian men, due to the combinations of racial and gender stereotypes associated with them, may be perceived as particularly suited for androgynous managerial roles (Galinsky, Hall, & Cuddy, 2013). Future research might continue to examine the influence of leader's race, gender, and other social categories on the link between diversity and leadership.

Another important aspect to consider is the role played by modern quota systems designed to incentivize gender parity in leadership decision-making. Several countries have instituted both hard and soft reforms on women's political participation, which usually creates more opportunities for women to attain leadership roles. For example, Rwanda created a new constitution in 2003 declaring that at least 30% of seats in all decision-making governing bodies (e.g., upper house, lower house and sub-national levels) must be held by women; by 2016, Rwanda had the world's highest number of women in parliament (64%; World Bank, 2016; see Figure 2.3). Other countries, at the organizational level, have also mandated participation of women on governing boards (e.g., 40% of seats in Norway; 30% of seats in Germany; new minimums most recently ratified in California). A recent study including 90 countries provided evidence that these country-level regulations are increasing female leadership on corporate boards (Catalyst, 2018). Countries with specific targets in place, quotas, and/or penalties for not having female board representation on average had 34% female board members compared to 18% in countries without any regulations. Not only do such strategies improve the number of female leadership representation towards parity but also save lost time. Do female leaders who come to power due in part to quotas have the same effects with regards to racial diversity as those who are elected by popular vote, in terms of symbolic influence, popularization of egalitarian attitudes, and empowering approaches to leadership and policy? Future research should investigate this question.

Moving from the focus on business and political settings, these questions could also be examined in the domain of higher education, which we did not cover in this chapter. About 30% of American colleges and universities

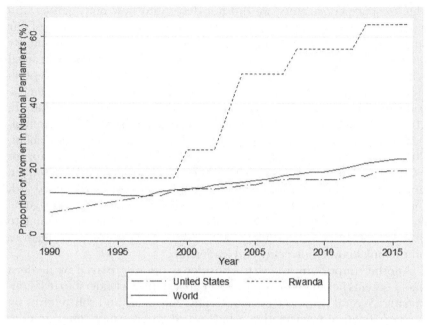

Source: World Bank, World Development Indicators, Inter-Parliamentary Union (IPU) data, 2018.

Figure 2.3. Percentage of seats in national parliaments held by women.

have female presidents (American Council on Education, 2017). Future research may examine whether having a female president in a more diverse college may lead to better academic outcomes and better overall retention and graduation rates compared to having a male president.

Furthermore, although we discussed aspects of selection and emergence of leaders, and their performance and group outcomes, we did not directly touch upon the question of evaluation of male versus female leaders as it might relate to diverse or homogeneous settings (Eagly, 2007; Eagly & Carli, 2003; Eagly, Makhijani, & Klonsky, 1992; Hekman, Johnson, Foo, & Yang, 2017). Research has shown differences in evaluations of, and backlash against, racial minority female leaders compared to racial majority female leaders or racial minority male leaders (Livingston, Rosette, & Washington, 2012; Rosette & Livingston, 2012). Investigating whether diverse groups will actually evaluate female leaders compared to male leaders in a less biased way than homogeneous groups could be a fruitful direction for future research. Relatedly, are women in leadership roles less concerned about and/or less likely to experience backlash from diverse groups compared to homogeneous groups? Another direction for future research is to empirically explore whether the presence of female leaders would generate more tolerance for individual differences in diverse settings (e.g., countries or organizations with high levels of ethnic and racial tension).

4.2 Public Policy Implications

The challenges currently associated with management of diversity and the concurrent underrepresentation of women in leadership positions suggests that there is an important role for this theoretical work. Throughout this paper, we considered these issues at three levels of analysis where possible, and in doing so, chose to focus on the unifying themes across the research, rather than to delineate their distinctions. Our decision to traverse different disciplines and levels of analysis was born out of the vast possibilities and practical implications we see for this research. These ideas may have implications for how leadership roles are assigned in organizations, how leaders are elected in countries, the use of quotas to increase the number of women in leadership positions, how small groups perform under pressure, and whether female or male teachers are better for more racially diverse classrooms, to provide just a few examples.

One specific arena that could be affected is leadership development. In training and preparing new generations of leaders for increasingly diverse organizations, it may be particularly beneficial to seek out and encourage women, on the one hand, and to encourage transformational styles of leadership and egalitarian attitudes amongst all future leaders, male or female, on the other hand. In striving to attain equal representation of women in leadership positions, it may also be valuable to emphasize the complexity that an increasingly diverse world presents, and the resulting need for new directions in leadership that emphasize cooperation rather than competition.

4.3 Limitations

One limitation of this chapter is that it provides little evidence of causality between female leadership positions and heterogeneity in performance outcomes in comparison to male leaders. The significant associations found are suggestive that the directionality of female leaders could objectively be a combination of attainment and selection factors as well as performance factors associated with leadership once in office or the position. We make no claims or assumptions that empirically would distinguish the two. Future studies can design experiments to disentangle the directionality and provide support towards causality.

One aspect to keep in mind when considering the role of female leaders in affecting outcomes for diverse groups is how one measures success. Economic output is one measure of success but not by any means the only one. At the small group level, if a team takes more time to produce a higher quality product, is that calculated as a loss in efficiency or a gain in quality? If an organization breaks off relationships with certain suppliers, temporarily decreasing production, in order to become more environmentally sustainable, how is that portrayed? If a country increases its GDP but also its levels of income inequality and child mortality, is that characterized as progress or decline? The underlying assumptions about what is a gain and what is a loss must be articulated and carefully assessed, keeping in mind that these values also may be gendered in their connotations.

In addition, we are also aware that the different levels of analysis referenced throughout the paper—groups, organizations, countries—bring different challenges and relevant moderators and mediators. The theoretical claims made here must be tested to uncover boundary conditions that increase the emergence of female leadership across differing levels. Likewise, the mechanisms connecting female leaders with improved outcomes should be explored in future studies with a careful attention to the differences between group, organization, and country levels. Given the overall discrimination, prejudice, low status, and pressures to fill very constrained gender roles that women often face (Appold, Siengthai, & Kasarda, 1998; Baxter & Wright, 2000; Elliott & Smith, 2004; Foschi, 2000), we state our claims with caution. We also note that even if women do emerge into leadership positions and accomplish improved performance and outcomes, they might not receive the credit that is due to them and may fall easily from grace.

4.4 Summary and Conclusions

While little empirical research has explored the environmental conditions in which women are more likely to succeed and outperform their male counterparts, this chapter provides an opportunity to make connections across literatures and levels of analysis. This chapter lays out plausible points of connection between leadership attributes more commonly associated with women and how they fit uniquely with the needs of more diverse and complex environments. We hope this chapter spurs an ongoing research program that will elucidate some vitally important theoretical and practical aspects of racial diversity and women in leadership.

NOTES

1. Diversity is referred to and defined throughout the chapter as racial and ethnic composition within a group, organization, or country.
2. Ethnic groups in Liberia include Kpelle 20.3%, Bassa 13.4%, Grebo 10%, Gio 8%, Mano 7.9%, Kru 6%, Lorma 5.1%, Kissi 4.8%, Gola 4.4%, Krahn 4%, Vai 4%, Mandingo 3.2%, Gbandi 3%, Mende 1.3%, Sapo 1.3%, and other Liberian 1.7% (Central Intelligence Agency, 2016)
3. Ethnic groups in Ethiopia include Oromo 34.4%, Amhara (Amara) 27%, Somali (Somalie) 6.2%, Tigray (Tigrinya) 6.1%, Sidama 4%, Gurage 2.5%, Welaita 2.3%, Hadiya 1.7%, Afar (Affar) 1.7%, Gamo 1.5%, Gedeo 1.3%, Silte 1.3%, Kefficho 1.2%, and other Ethiopian 8.8% (Central Intelligence Agency, 2016)

REFERENCES

Adler, N. (1996). Global women political leaders: an invisible history, an increasingly important future. *The Leadership Quarterly, 7*, 133–161.
Adler, R. D. (2001). Women in the executive suite correlate to high profits. *Harvard Business Review, 79*, 131–137.
Alesina, A., Devleeschauwer, A., Easterly, W., Kurlat, S., & Wacziarg, R. (2003). "Fractionalization." *Journal of Economic Growth, 8*(2), 155–194.
Alesina, A., & La Ferrara, E. (2005). Ethnic diversity and economic performance. *Journal of Economic Literature, 43*, 762–800.
Alesina, A., & La Ferrara, E. (2000) Participation in heterogeneous communities. *Quarterly Journal of Economics, 115*(3), 847–904.
American Council on Education. (2017). *Ready to lead: Women in the presidency.* Retrieved from https://www.acenet.edu/news-room/Pages/Ready-to-Lead-Women-in-the-Presidency.aspx
Amodio, D. M. (2009). Intergroup anxiety effects on the control of racial stereotypes: A psychoneuroendocrine analysis. *Journal of Experimental Social Psychology, 45*, 60–67.
Appold, S. J., Siengthai, S., & Kasarda, J. D. (1998). The employment of women managers and professionals in an emerging economy: Gender inequality as an organizational practice. *Administrative Science Quarterly, 43*, 538–565.
Ayman, R., & Korabik, K. (2010). Leadership: Why gender and culture matter. *American Psychologist, 65*, 157–170.
Ayman-Nolley, S., & Ayman, R. (2005). Children's implicit theory of leadership. In B. Schyns & J. R. Meindl (Eds.), *Implicit leadership theories: Essays and explorations* (pp. 189–233). Greenwich, CT: Information Age.
Babbitt, L. G. (2013). An intersectional approach to Black/White interracial interactions: The roles of gender and sexual orientation. *Sex Roles, 68*, 791–802.
Bass, B. M. (1985). *Leadership and performance beyond expectations.* New York, NY: Free Press.

Bass, B. M. (1999). Two decades of research and development in transformational leadership. *European Journal of Work and Organizational Psychology, 8,* 9–32.

Baxter, J., & Wright, E. O. (2000). The glass ceiling hypothesis: A comparative study of the United States, Sweden, and Australia. *Gender & Society, 14,* 275–294.

Beaman, L., Duflo, E., Pande, R., & Topalova, P. (2012). Female leadership raises aspirations and educational attainment for girls: A policy experiment in India. *Science, 335,* 582–586.

Bear, S., Rahman, N., & Post. C. (2010). The impact of board diversity and gender composition on corporate social responsibility and firm reputation. *Journal of Business Ethics, 97,* 207–221.

Berger, J., Rosenholtz, S. J., & Zelditch, M. (1980). Status organizing processes. *Annual Review of Sociology,* 479–508.

Besley, T., & Case, A. (2000). Unnatural experiments? Estimating the incidence of endogenous policies. *The Economic Journal, 110,* 672–694.

Bilimoria, D. (2006). The relationship between women corporate directors and women corporate officers. *Journal of Managerial Issues, 18,* 47–61.

Brescoll, V. L. (2012). Who takes the floor and why: Gender, power, and volubility in organizations. *Administrative Science Quarterly, 56,* 622–641.

Bridges, W. P., & Nelson, R. L. (1989). Markets in hierarchies: Organizational and market influences on gender inequality in a state pay system. *American Journal of Sociology, 95,* 616–658.

Brown, E. R., Diekman, A. B., & Schneider, M. C. (2011). A change will do us good: Threats diminish typical preferences for male leaders. *Personality and Social Psychology Bulletin, 37,* 930–941.

Bullough, A., K. G. Kroeck, W. Newburry, S. K. Kundu, K. B. Lowe. 2012. Women's political leadership participation around the world: An institutional analysis. *The Leadership Quarterly, 23*(3) 398–411.

Burns, J. M. (1978). *Leadership.* New York, NY: Harper & Row.

Card, D., Dustmann, C., & Preston, I. (2005). Understanding attitudes to immigration: The migration and minority module of the first European Social Survey. *Center for Research and Analysis of Migration Discussion Paper Series No. 3.* Retrieved from http://discovery.ucl.ac.uk/14315/1/14315.pdf

Catalyst. (2004). *The bottom line: connecting corporate performance and gender diversity.* Retrieved from www.catalystwomen.org

Catalyst. (2018). *Quick take: Women on corporate boards.* Retrieved from https://www.catalyst.org/research/women-on-corporate-boards/

Chattopadhyay, R., & Duflo, E. (2004). Women as policy makers: Evidence from a randomized policy experiment in India. *Econometrica, 72,* 1409–1443.

Chen, C. C., & Hooijberg, R. (2000). Ambiguity intolerance and support for valuing-diversity interventions. *Journal of Applied Social Psychology, 30,* 2392–2408.

Cheung, F. M., & Halpern, D. F. (2010). Women at the top: powerful leaders define success as work+ family in a culture of gender. *American Psychologist, 65,* 182–193.

Central Intelligence Agency. (2016) *The World Factbook 2016–17.* Washington, DC: Central Intelligence Agency. Retrieved from https://www.cia.gov/library/publications/the-world-factbook/index.html

Cole, E. R. (2009). Intersectionality and research in psychology. *American Psychologist*, *64*, 170.

Collier, P. (2000). Ethnicity, politics and economic performance. *Economics & Politics*, *12*, 225–245.

Cook, A., & Glass, C. (2014). Women and top leadership positions: Towards an institutional analysis. *Gender, Work & Organization*, *21*(1), 91–103.

Craig, M. A., & Richeson, J. A. (2017), Information about the US racial demographic shift triggers concerns about anti-White discrimination among the prospective White "minority". *PLoS One 12*(9), e0185389.

Crenshaw, K. (1991). Mapping the margins: Intersectionality, identity politics, and violence against women of color. *Stanford Law Review*, 1241–1299.

Cuddy, A. J., Wolf, E. B., Glick, P., Crotty, S., Chong, J., & Norton, M. I. (2015). Men as cultural ideals: Cultural values moderate gender stereotype content. *Journal of Personality and Social Psychology*, *109*(4), 622.

Daily, C. M., & Dalton, D. R. (2003). Women in the boardroom: A business imperative. *Journal of Business Strategy*, *24*, 8–9.

Danbold, F., & Huo, Y. J. (2014). No longer "All-American"? Whites' defensive reactions to their numerical decline. *Social Psychological and Personality Science*, *6*, 210–218.

Dezsö, C. L., & Ross, D. G. (2012). Does female representation in top management improve firm performance? A panel data investigation. *Strategic Management Journal*, *33*, 1072–1089.

Dickson, M. W., Den Hartog, D. N., & Mitchelson, J. K. (2003). Research on leadership in a cross-cultural context: Making progress, and raising new questions. *The Leadership Quarterly*, *14*, 729–768.☐

Diekman, A. B., & Eagly, A. H. (2000). Stereotypes as dynamic constructs: Women and men of the past, present, and future. *Personality and Social Psychology Bulletin*, *26*, 1171–1188.

Diekman, A. B., Goodfriend, W., & Goodwin, S. (2004). Dynamic stereotypes of power: Perceived change and stability in gender hierarchies. *Sex Roles, 50*, 201–215.

Dodd-Frank Wall Street Reform and Consumer Protection Act of 2010, 12 U.S.C. §§ 5301-5641 (2012).

Dollar, D., Fisman, R., & Gatti, R. (2001). Are women really the "fairer" sex? Corruption and women in government. *Journal of Economic Behavior & Organization*, *46*, 423–429.

Domonoske, C. (2016, August 1). Taiwanese president issues country's first apology to indigenous people. *National Public Radio*. Retrieved from https://www.npr.org/sections/thetwo-way/2016/08/01/488250700/taiwanese-president-issues-countrys-first-apology-to-indigenous-people

Duflo, E., & Topalova, P. (2004). *Unappreciated service: Performance, perceptions, and women: Leaders in India*. Cambridge, MA: MIT Department of Economics. Retrieved from http://karlan.yale.edu/fieldexperiments/papers/00233.pdf

Dumas, T. L., Phillips, K. W., & Rothbard, N. P. (2013). Getting closer at the company party: Integration experiences, racial dissimilarity, and workplace relationships. *Organization Science, 24*, 1377–1401.

Eagly, A. H. (1987). *Sex differences in social behavior. A social role interpretation.* Hillsdale, NJ: Erlbaum.

Eagly, A. H. (2007). Female leadership advantage and disadvantage: Resolving the contradictions. *Psychology of Women Quarterly, 31,* 1–12.

Eagly, A. H., & Carli, L. L. (2003). The female leadership advantage: An evaluation of the evidence. *The Leadership Quarterly, 14,* 807–834.

Eagly, A. H., & Chin, J. L. (2010). Diversity and leadership in a changing world. *American Psychologist, 65,* 216–224.

Eagly, A. H., Diekman, A. B., Johannesen-Schmidt, M. C., & Koenig, A. M. (2004). Gender gaps in sociopolitical attitudes: A social psychological analysis. *Journal of Personality and Social Psychology, 87,* 796–816.

Eagly, A. H., Johannesen-Schmidt, M. C., & Van Engen, M. L. (2003). Transformational, transactional, and laissez-faire leadership styles: A meta-analysis comparing women and men. *Psychological Bulletin, 129,* 569–591.

Eagly, A. H., & Johnson, B. T. (1990). Gender and leadership style: A meta-analysis. *Psychological Bulletin, 108,* 233–256.

Eagly, A. H., & Karau, S. J. (1991). Gender and the emergence of leaders: A meta-analysis. *Journal of Personality and Social Psychology, 60,* 685–710.

Eagly, A. H., & Karau, S. J. (2002). Role congruity theory of prejudice toward female leaders. *Psychological Review, 109,* 573–598.

Eagly, A. H., Makhijani, M. G., & Klonsky, B. G. (1992). Gender and the evaluation of leaders: A meta-analysis. *Psychological Bulletin, 111,* 3–22.

Easterly, W., & Levine, R. (1997). Africa's growth tragedy: Policies and ethnic divisions. *Quarterly Journal of Economics, 112,* 1203–1250.

Elliott, J. R., & Smith, R. A. (2004). Race, gender, and workplace power. *American Sociological Review, 69,* 365–386.

Ely, R. J. (1994). The effects of organizational demographics and social identity on relationships among professional women. *Administrative Science Quarterly, 39,* 203–238.

Ely, R. J., & Thomas, D. A. (2001). Cultural diversity at work: The effects of diversity perspectives on work group processes and outcomes. *Administrative Science Quarterly, 46,* 229–273.

Ethiopia appoints career diplomat Sahle-Work Zewde as Africa's only female president. (2018, October 25). *The Telegraph.* Retrieved from https://www. telegraph.co.uk/news/2018/10/25/ethiopia-appointscareer-diplomat-sahle-work-zewde-africas-female/

Fearon, J., & Laitin, D. (2003). Ethnicity, insurgency, and Civil War. *American Political Science Review, 97*(1), 75–90.

Foels, R., Driskell, J. E., Mullen, B., & Salas, E. (2000). The effects of democratic leadership on group member satisfaction: An integration. *Small Group Research, 31,* 676–701.

Foels, R., & Reid, L. D. (2010). Gender differences in social dominance orientation: The role of cognitive complexity. *Sex Roles, 62,* 684–692.

Foschi, M. (2000). Double standards for competence: Theory and research. *Annual Review of Sociology, 26,* 21–42.

Furst, S. A., & Reeves, M. (2008). Queens of the hill: Creative destruction and the emergence of executive leadership of women. *The Leadership Quarterly, 19,* 372–384.

Galinsky, A. D., Hall, E. V., & Cuddy, A. J. (2013). Gendered races: Implications for interracial marriage, leadership selection, and athletic participation. *Psychological Science, 24,* 498–506.

Gang, I., Rivera-Batiz, F., & Yun, M. S. (2002). Economic strain, ethnic concentration and attitudes towards foreigners in the European Union. *IZA Discussion Paper No. 578.* Retrieved from https://ssrn.com/abstract=331475

Gerstner, C. R., & Day, D. V. (1994). Cross-cultural comparison of leadership prototypes. *The Leadership Quarterly, 5,* 121–134.

Glasman, R., Paikeday, T., Sachar, H., Stuart, A., & Young, C. (2018). A leader's guide: Finding and keeping your next chief diversity officer. United States: Russell Reynolds Associates. Retrieved from https://www.russellreynolds.com/insights/thought-leadership/a-leaders-guide-finding-and-keeping-your-next-chief-diversity-officer

Global Gender Balance Scorecard. (2018, February). 20-first. Retrieved from http://ww1.prweb.com/prfiles/2018/02/06/15174494/2018%2020-first%20Global%20Gender%20Balance%20Scorecard.pdf

Groysberg, B., & Connolly, K. (2013, September). Great leaders who make the mix work. *Harvard Business Review,* 68–76.

Haslam, S. A., & Ryan, M. K. (2005). The glass cliff: Evidence that women are over-represented in precarious leadership positions. *British Journal of Management, 16,* 81–90.

Haslam, S. A., & Ryan, M. K. (2008). The road to the glass cliff: Differences in the perceived suitability of men and women for leadership positions in succeeding and failing organizations, *The Leadership Quarterly, 19,* 530–546.

Hausmann, L. R. M., & Ryan, C. S. (2004). Effects of external and internal motivation to control prejudice on implicit prejudice: The mediating role of efforts to control prejudiced responses. *Basic and Applied Social Psychology, 26,* 215–225.

Heilman, M. E. (2001). Description and prescription: How gender stereotypes prevent women's ascent up the organizational ladder. *Journal of Social Issues, 57,* 657–674.

Hekman, D., Johnson, S., Foo, M., & Yang, W. (2017) Does diversity-valuing behavior result in diminished performance ratings for non-White and female leaders? *Academy of Management Journal, 60,* 771–797.

Hoffman, E. (1985). The effect of race-ratio composition on the frequency of organizational communication. *Social Psychology Quarterly, 48,* 17–26.

Homan, A. C., Van Knippenberg, D., Van Kleef, G. A., & De Dreu, C. K. (2007). Bridging faultlines by valuing diversity: diversity beliefs, information elaboration, and performance in diverse work groups. *Journal of Applied Psychology, 92,* 1189–1199.

Hunt, V., Layton, D., & Prince, S. (2015). Diversity matters. McKinsey & Company. Retrieved from https://www.mckinsey.com/~/media/mckinsey/business%20functions/organization/our%20insights/why%20diversity%20matters/diversity%20matters.ashx

Jehn, K. A., Northcraft, G. B., & Neale, M. A. (1999). Why differences make a difference: A field study of diversity, conflict and performance in workgroups. *Administrative Science Quarterly, 44*, 741–763.

Johnson, K. L., Freeman, J. B., & Pauker, K. (2012). Race is gendered: How covarying phenotypes and stereotypes bias sex categorization. *Journal of Personality and Social Psychology, 102*, 116–131.

Johnson, M. K., & Marini, M. M. (1998). Bridging the racial divide in the United States: The effect of gender. *Social Psychology Quarterly, 61*, 247–258.

Kearney, E., & Gebert, D. (2009). Managing diversity and enhancing team outcomes: The promise of transformational leadership. *Journal of Applied Psychology, 94*, 77–89.

Krishnan, H. A., & Park, D. (2005). A few good women—on top management teams. *Journal of Business Research, 58*, 1712–1720.

Krishnan, V. R. (2012). Transformational leadership and personal outcomes: Empowerment as mediator. *Leadership & Organization Development Journal, 33*, 550–563.

Lam, A. C. L. (1992). *Women and equal employment opportunities in Japan.* Oxford, England: Nissan Institute of Japanese Studies.

Lee, V. E., Smith, J. B., & Cioci, M. (1993). Teachers and principals: Gender-related perceptions of leadership and power in secondary schools. *Educational Evaluation and Policy Analysis, 15*, 153–180.

Littleford, L. N., Wright, M. O., & Sayoc-Parial, M. (2005). White students' intergroup anxiety during same-race and interracial interactions: A multimethod approach. *Basic and Applied Social Psychology, 27*, 85–94.

Livingston, R. W., Rosette, A. S., & Washington, E. F. (2012). Can an agentic black woman get ahead? The impact of race and interpersonal dominance on perceptions of female leaders. *Psychological Science, 23*(4), 354–358.

Lount R. B., Jr., Sheldon, O. J., Rink, F., & Phillips, K. W. (2012). How much relationship conflict really exists? Biased perceptions of racially diverse teams. In *Annual Interdisciplinary Network for Group Research Conference, Chicago, IL.*

Lowe, K. B., Kroeck, K. G., & Sivasubramaniam, N. (1996). Effectiveness correlates of transformational and transactional leadership: A meta-analytic review of the MLQ literature. *The Leadership Quarterly, 7*, 385–425.

Mannix, E., & Neale, M. A. (2005). What differences make a difference? The promise and reality of diverse teams in organizations. *Psychological Science in the Public Interest, 6*, 31–55.

Marx, D. M., & Goff, P. A. (2005). Clearing the air: The effect of experimenter race on target's test performance and subjective experience. *British Journal of Social Psychology, 44*, 645–657.

Maxwell, A., Ford-Dowe, P., Jimeno, R., & Shields, T. (2013) Is there a war on women? Attitudes about women in the workplace and in politics: A report from the 2012 Blair Center-Clinton School Poll. Retrieved from http://blaircenterclintonschoolpoll.uark.edu/6759.php

McIntosh, P. (1992). White privilege: Unpacking the invisible knapsack. *Multiculturalism*, 30–36.

Meeussen, L., Otten, S., & Phalet, K. (2014). Managing diversity: How leaders' multiculturalism and colorblindness affect work group functioning. *Group Processes & Intergroup Relations, 17,* 629–644.

Mehra, A., Kilduff, M., & Brass, D. J. (1998). At the margins: A distinctiveness approach to the social identity and social networks of underrepresented groups. *Academy of Management Journal, 41,* 441–452.

Melero, E. (2011) Are workplaces with many women in management run differently? *Journal of Business Research, 64,* 385–393.

Milliken, F. J., & Martins L. L. (1996). Searching for common threads: Understanding the multiple effects of diversity in organizational groups. *The Academy of Management Review, 21*(2), 402–433.

Nguyen, T. (2008). *Information, role models and perceived returns to education: Experimental evidence from Madagascar* (Job market paper). Cambridge, MA: MIT Economics Department.

Nishii, L. H., & Mayer, D. M. (2009). Do inclusive leaders help to reduce turnover in diverse groups? The moderating role of leader-member exchange in the diversity to turnover relationship. *Journal of Applied Psychology, 94,* 1412–1426.

Pelled, L. H., Eisenhardt, K. M., & Xin, K. R. (1999). Exploring the black box: An analysis of work group diversity, conflict and performance. *Administrative Science Quarterly, 44,* 1–28.

Perkins. S. E., Phillips, K. W., & Pearce, N. A. (2013). Ethnic diversity, gender, and national leaders. *Journal of International Affairs, 67,* 85–105.

Pew Research Center. (2019). *The data on women leaders.* Retrieved from http://www.pewsocialtrends.org/fact-sheet/the-data-on-women-leaders/

Pew Research Center. (2008). *Men or women: Who's the better leader? A paradox in public attitudes.* Retrieved from http://www.pewsocialtrends.org/files/2010/10/gender-leadership.pdf

Phillips, K. W., & D. L. Loyd. (2006). When surface and deep-level diversity collide: The effects on dissenting group members. *Organizational Behavior and Human Decision Processes, 99*(2), 143–160.

Phillips, K. W., Northcraft, G. B., & Neale, M. A. (2006). Surface-level diversity and decision-making in groups: When does deep-level similarity help? *Group Processes & Intergroup Relations, 9,* 467–482.

Phillips, K. W., Rothbard, N. P., & Dumas, T. L. (2009). To disclose or not to disclose? Status distance and self-disclosure in diverse environments. *Academy of Management Review, 34,* 710–732.

Plant, E. A. (2004). Responses to interracial interactions over time. *Personality and Social Psychology Bulletin, 30,* 1458–1471.

Plant, E. A., & Devine, P. G. (1998). Internal and external motivation to respond without prejudice. *Journal of Personality and Social Psychology, 75,* 811–832.

Plant, E. A., Devine, P. G., Cox, W. T., Columb, C., Miller, S. L., Goplen, J., & Peruche, B. M. (2009). The Obama effect: Decreasing implicit prejudice and stereotyping. *Journal of Experimental Social Psychology, 45,* 961–964.

Plaut, V. C., Garnett, F. G., Buffardi, L. E., & Sanchez-Burks, J. (2011). "What about me?" Perceptions of exclusion and Whites' reactions to multiculturalism. *Journal of Personality and Social Psychology, 101,* 337–353.

Powell, G. N., Butterfield, D. A., & Parent, J. D. (2002). Gender and managerial stereotypes: have the times changed? *Journal of Management, 28*, 177–193

Pratto, F., Sidanius, J., Stallworth, L. M., & Malle, B. F. (1994). Social dominance orientation: A personality variable predicting social and political attitudes. *Journal of Personality and Social Psychology, 67*, 741–763.

Purdie-Vaughns, V., & Eibach, R. P. (2008). Intersectional invisibility: The distinctive advantages and disadvantages of multiple subordinate-group identities. *Sex Roles, 59*, 377–391.

RFI. (2014, January 23). Central Africans 'fed up of male politicians' says President Samba-Panza. *RFI All Africa*. Retrieved from http://en.rfi.fr/africa/20140123-central-africans-fed-male-politicians-says-president-samba-panza.

Rosette, A. S., & Livingston, R. W. (2012). Failure is not an option for black women: Effects of organizational performance on leaders with single versus dual-subordinate identities. *Journal of Experimental Social Psychology, 48*(5), 1162–1167.

Rudman, L. A., & Glick, P. (2008). *The social psychology of gender: How power and intimacy shape gender relations*. New York, NY: Guilford Press.

Rule, N. O., Ambady, N., Adams, R. B., Jr., Ozono, H., Nakashima, S., Yoshikawa, S., & Watabe, M. (2010). Polling the face: Prediction and consensus across cultures. *Journal of Personality and Social Psychology, 98*, 1–15.

Sanchez, D. T., Chaney, K. E., Manuel, S. K., Wilton, L. S., & Remedios, J. D. (2017). Stigma by prejudice transfer: Racism threatens White women and sexism threatens men of color. *Psychological Science, 28*, 445–461.

Schein, V. E. (2001). A global look at psychological barriers to women's progress in management. *Journal of Social Issues, 57*, 675–688.

Schein, V. E., Müller, R., Lituchy, T., & Liu, J. (1996). Think manager-think male: a global phenomenon? *Journal of Organizational Behavior, 17*, 33–41.

Sesko, A. K., & Biernat, M. (2010). Prototypes of race and gender: The invisibility of black women. *Journal of Experimental Social Psychology, 46*, 356–360.

Shelton, J. N., Richeson, J. A., & Vorauer, J. D. (2006). Threatened identities and interethnic interactions. *European Review of Social Psychology, 17*, 321–358.

Sidanius, J., & Pratto, F. (1999). *Social dominance: An integrative theory of social hierarchy and oppression*. Cambridge, UK: Cambridge University Press.

Sidanius, J., Pratto, F., & Bobo, L. (1994). Social dominance orientation and the political psychology of gender: A case of invariance? *Journal of Personality and Social Psychology, 67*, 998–1011.

Smith, N., Smith, V., & Verner, M. (2006). Do women in top management affect firm performance? A panel study of 2,500 Danish firms. *International Journal of Productivity and Performance Management, 55*, 569–593.

Smith, W. S., & Erb, T. O. (1986). Effect of women science career role models on early adolescents' attitudes toward scientists and women in science. *Journal of Research in Science Teaching, 23*, 667–676.

Sommers, S. R., Warp, L. S., & Mahoney, C. C. (2008). Cognitive effects of racial diversity: White individuals' information processing in heterogeneous groups. *Journal of Experimental Social Psychology, 44*, 1129–1136.

Spisak, B. R., Homan, A. C., Grabo, A., & Van Vugt, M. (2012). Facing the situation: Testing a biocontingency model of leadership in intergroup relations using masculine and feminine faces. *The Leadership Quarterly, 23*, 273–280.

Taylor, S. E., Klein, L. C., Lewis, B. P., Gruenewald, T. L., Gurung, R. A. R., & Updegraff, J. A. (2000). Biobehavioral responses to stress in females: Tend-and-befriend, not fight-or-flight. *Psychological Review, 107*, 411–429.

Terjesen, S., Aguilera, R. V., & Lorenz, R. (2015). Legislating a woman's seat on the board: Institutional factors driving gender quotas for boards of directors. *Journal of Business Ethics, 128*(2), 233–251.

Thomas, D. A., & Ely, R. J. (1996). Making differences matter: A new paradigm for managing diversity. *Harvard Business Review, 74*, 79–90.

Tomaskovic-Devey, D. (1993). *Gender & racial inequality at work: The sources and consequences of job segregation* (No. 27). Cornell University Press.

Toosi, N. R., Babbitt, L. G., Ambady, N., & Sommers, S. R. (2012). Dyadic interracial interactions: a meta-analysis. *Psychological Bulletin, 138*, 1–27.

Toosi, N. R., Mor, S., Semnani-Azad, Z., Phillips, K. W., & Amanatullah, E. T. (2018). Who can lean in? The intersecting role of race and gender in negotiations. *Psychology of Women Quarterly*. Advance online publication.

Toosi, N. R., Sommers, S. R., & Ambady, N. (2012). Getting a word in group-wise: Effects of racial diversity on gender dynamics. *Journal of Experimental Social Psychology, 48*, 1150–1155.

Tost, L., Gino, F., & Larrick, R. (2012). When power makes others speechless: The negative impact of leader power on team performance. *Academy of Management Journal, 117*, 53–65.

Trawalter, S., Richeson, J. A., & Shelton, J. N. (2009). Predicting behavior during interracial interactions: A stress and coping approach. *Personality and Social Psychology Review, 13*, 243–268.

U.S. Census Bureau. (2008). An older and more diverse nation by midcentury. Retrieved from http://www.census.gov/newsroom/releases/archives/population/ cb08-123.html

U.S. Census Bureau, Population Division. (2012, December). Table 4. Projections of the population by sex, race, and Hispanic origin for the United States: 2015 to 2060 (NP2012-T4). Retrieved from http://www.census.gov/population/projections/data/national/2012/summarytables.html

UNESCO Institute for Statistics. (2009). *Investing in Cultural Diversity and Intercultural Dialogue*. Retrieved from http://unesdoc.unesco.org

Van Engen, M. L., & Willemsen, T. M. (2004). Sex and leadership styles: A meta-analysis of research published in the 1990s. *Psychological Reports, 94*, 3–18.

Van Knippenberg, D., De Dreu, C. K. W., Homan, A. C. (2004). Work group diversity and group performance: An integrative model and research agenda. *Journal of Applied Psychology, 89*, 1008–1022.

Van Knippenberg, D., Haslam, S. A., & Platow, M. J. (2007). Unity through diversity: Value-in-diversity beliefs, work group diversity, and group identification. *Group Dynamics: Theory, Research, and Practice, 11*, 207–222.

Van Knippenberg, D., & Schippers, M. C. (2007). Work group diversity. *Annual Review of Psychology, 58*, 515–541.

Van Vugt, M., & Spisak, B. R. (2008). Sex differences in the emergence of leadership during competitions within and between groups. *Psychological Science, 19*, 854–858.

Wang, M., & Kelan, E. (2013). The gender quota and female leadership: Effects of the Norwegian gender quota on board chairs and CEOs. *Journal of Business Ethics, 117*(3), 449–466.

Williams, K. Y., & O'Reilly, C. A. (1998). Demography and diversity in organizations: A review of 40 years of research. *Research in Organizational Behavior, 20*, 77–140.

Woolley, A. W., Chabris, C. F., Pentland, A., Hashmi, N., & Malone, T. W. (2010). Evidence for a collective intelligence factor in the performance of human groups. *Science, 330*, 686–688.

World Bank. (2016), World Development Indicators. Retrieved from https://datacatalog.worldbank.org/dataset/world-development-indicators

CHAPTER 3

REPRODUCTIVE ISSUES IN PRODUCTION SPACES

Managing Menstruation, Perimenopause, and Infertility Treatments in the Workplace

**Mindy E. Bergman, Rose L. Siuta,
Sin-Ning C. Liu, and Briana G. Capuchino**
Texas A&M University

At any moment, approximately 800 million people in the world are menstruating (Barron, 2017). Worldwide, around 1.9% of women experience primary infertility (i.e., incapability of having a first biological baby) and 10.5% experience secondary infertility (i.e., incapability of having a biological baby after having at least one other biological child; Mascarenhas, Flaxman, Boerma, Vanderpoel, & Stevens, 2012). Additionally, all menstruators will eventually stop menstruating, either through natural means (i.e., menopause) or other means (e.g., hysterectomy). While all of this is happening, many of these people go to work—and yet, as a field, we are not talking about it.

The purpose of this chapter is to begin the discussion of how reproductive issues, beyond pregnancy and parenting, are an important topic

Pushing Our Understanding of Diversity in Organizations, pp. 53–90

for industrial-organizational (IO) psychology. This is not to suggest that pregnancy and parenting and their interface with work are unimportant. To the contrary, these are important topics that have considerable impact on people's lives inside and outside the workplace, such as the motherhood penalty (Avellar & Smock, 2003; Budig & Hodges, 2010; Correll, Benard, & Paik, 2007), the fatherhood uplift (Hodges & Budig, 2010), pregnancy stigma (King & Botsford, 2009), and work-family conflict (Allen, Herst, Bruck, & Sutton, 2000; Allen & Martin, 2017). However, in the IO psychology, organizational behavior, and management literatures, little attention has been paid to reproductive health in the workplace. Anecdotal evidence indicates that there are a number of concerns for employees and how their reproductive health intersects with institutional policies and events, in the workplace (Chandler, 2017b; Habersham, 2017) and beyond (Chandler, 2017a; Held, 2018).

Additionally, we specifically highlight the experiences of trans and nonbinary persons[1],as they are often in more jeopardy than cispersons when we consider these factors. The potential for trans and nonbinary people to have complicated reproductive health is high. Additionally, situations that involve reproductive-related experiences increase the odds that stealth trans or nonbinary people will be outed[2].

ORGANIZATIONS AS GENDERED INSTITUTIONS

A key aspect of understanding why issues regarding reproduction have been overlooked in workplaces and in organizational research is the gendered nature of work and workplaces (Britton & Logan, 2008). Acker (1992) notes a divide in society between production and reproduction, with the former (i.e., work) being the space of men and the masculine and the latter (i.e., family) being the milieu of women and the feminine. Acker (1990, 2006, 2012) argued that this difference is part of the fundamental fabric of modern organizations: organizations are not gender neutral but instead are masculine institutions with rules and roles that were created to reflect masculinity and masculine roles and to support a masculine idealized worker. This ideal worker has both stereotypically masculine traits (e.g., size, strength, communication styles) and stereotyped needs in the workplace (e.g., working hours, childcare needs; Britton & Logan, 2008; Connell, 2005). Thus, policies and practices reflect the masculinized ideal. Despite the changes in work and the economy over recent years, the masculine nature of work and workplaces still persists (Williams, Muller, & Kilanski, 2012).

This notion of a masculine organization built for masculine ideal workers draws on the concept of hegemonic masculinity. Hegemonic masculinity is a part of the gendered order of society, which generally positions and legitimizes men as in higher in social power and women as lower in social power (Connell, 1985). Hegemonic masculinity provides benefits to people who accrue more symbols of the hegemonic (masculine) ideal, which in Western societies is: biological markers of maleness, cisgender, stereotypical masculine behavior and traits, Whiteness, heterosexuality, and Christianity (Connell, 2005). Thus, the hegemonic ideal does not include all men and masculinities (i.e., some masculinities are subordinated) and can privilege some women over some men in some circumstances (Connell, 2005; Connell & Messerschmidt, 2005; Crenshaw, 1989; McIntosh, 2004, 2007; Rothenberg, 2008).

Hegemonic masculinity is not a simple social categorization, but rather a system of oppressions and privileges at the societal level. It normalizes some ways of being (i.e., the hegemonic ideal) and marginalizes others. Because institutions and systems are constructed to reflect the hegemonic ideal (Acker, 1990, 2012), people who match this ideal tend to benefit more from systems. Their power then allows them to continue to construct systems and institutions that benefit them (Acker, 2012; Britton & Logan, 2008; Connell, 2005; Crenshaw, 1995). Further, because of the benefits that come from hegemonic power structures, people strive toward the ideal themselves.

Notably, hegemonic masculinity is normative even though it is not commonly embodied within a society as few people fully embody the hegemonic ideal. Yet through normalization, hegemonic masculinity is integrated into society, systems, and institutions to the point that it is unquestioned and unnoticed. As a result, problems experienced by people who diverge from the ideal are often not recognized by powerful decision makers, or when they are recognized, are seen as being of little consequence because they are not "normal" problems.

This analysis explains why reproduction has been overlooked in the workplace. Everyday reproduction-related issues—such as menstruation—are not aligned with hegemonic masculinity or the people who embody it. In fact, by overlooking the reproductive problems that are primarily shouldered by bodies that are potentially pregnant, the hegemonic masculine system of power is further reinforced, because some people's needs are not attended to and therefore those people have less opportunity to participate in the workplace.

These processes have also led to the silence about these topics in the IO psychology literature (Chrisler, 2011; Coutts & Berg, 1993; Houppert, 1999; Kissling, 1996; Merskin, 1999). Menstruation, perimenopause, and infertility are part of the reproduction, rather than production, sphere. Because of the hegemonic power structure in society (Acker, 1990, 2012; Connell, 2005; Connell & Messerschmidt, 2005) and the gendered nature of science (Keller, 1985), these problems appear to be fringe and affecting few people and therefore undeserving of journal space, rather than common and affecting many and therefore of great consequence when considering how to improve the lives of workers and the efficacy of organizations.

This chapter focuses on three different reproductive processes that primarily are experienced by people outside of the hegemonic ideal: menstruation and menstrual hygiene, perimenopause and menopause, and infertility and infertility treatments. Each of these topics are briefly reviewed, followed by some suggestions for research. Following this, we make recommendations for organizational actions and societal actions that could alleviate some of the challenges that people who menstruate experience in the workplace. We close with a brief discussion of the broader theoretical models that might contribute to understanding these issues. At the outset, we should note that our suggestions for organizational supports and for research are biased by our knowledge of and experience in the U.S. health insurance system, in which health insurance is predominantly an employment benefit rather than a central, single payer system that is a social good to support the country. Authors from other systems might have a different set of suggestions.

MENSTRUATION

The menstrual cycle is a process of hormonal changes that prepares a body for pregnancy, via the maturation and release of ova, the thickening of the endometrial lining of the uterus, and other biological changes that make a body receptive to fertilization of ova and subsequent pregnancy. In humans, the menstrual cycle is approximately one month long, although there are considerable variations across people. Menstruation ends the menstrual cycle, with the sloughing off of the endometrial lining when a pregnancy has not occurred. Without intervention (e.g., menstrual cycle suppression; Hillard, 2014), menstruation occurs approximately 400–500 times in a menstruator's lifetime; this variability depends on the onset of menstruation (i.e., menarche), the end of menstruation (i.e., menopause), the number of pregnancies a person experiences, other conditions that affect menstruation (e.g., lactational amenorrhea), and cycle length. Considering that menstruation lasts 2–7 days for most people, menstruators can spend up to 3,500 days (nearly 10 years) menstruating in their lifetimes.

Stigma and Stereotypes Surrounding Menstruation

Despite the fact that menstruation is common, there is considerable stigma associated with menstruation throughout the world because menstruation is seen as an indicator of femaleness, and generally femaleness is itself stigmatized and disempowered (Chrisler, 2011; Johnston-Robledo & Chrisler, 2013; Kissling, 1996; Peranovic & Bentley, 2017). Menstruation in general and menstruating women in particular have been viewed negatively by men (Forbes, Adams-Curtis, White, & Holmgren, 2003; Marván, Cortés-Iniestra, & González, 2005; Marván, Vazquez-Toboada, & Chrisler, 2014; Roberts, Goldenberg, Power, & Pyszczynski, 2002) and by many contemporary and historical societies, cultures, and religions (see Delaney, Lupton, & Toth, 1988). Menstruation is often depicted as "none of men's business," having little relevance to them, and in need of being kept secret from them (Peranovic & Bentley, 2017; Wong et al., 2013). Considering the gendered nature of organizations and power structures, this negativity regarding menstruation perpetuates sex-based power structures and reifies the lack of organizational consideration for menstrual needs.

Cultural and religious beliefs influence the stigmatization of menstruation. These beliefs are often based on misconceptions regarding the cleanliness of menstruation (Kaur, Kaur, & Kaur, 2018). Some of these beliefs lead to restrictions on menstruators' participation in work, sex, hygiene, religious, and/or cooking activities (Dunnavant & Roberts, 2013; Guterman, Mehta, & Gibbs, 2008; Leslie, 1991; Maghen, 1999; Steinberg, 1997). Thus, it is not just organizations that affect the menstruation-work relationship, but also broader societal norms and mores.

Stereotypes regarding menstruation further stigmatization. Men assess menstruation as negative, debilitating, and performance inhibiting (Brooks-Gunn & Ruble, 1986; Marván et al., 2005) and menstruating and premenstrual women as unstable, difficult to deal with, moody, and demanding (Marván, Islas, Vela, Chrisler, & Warren, 2008; Peranovic & Bentley, 2017). A serious consequence of the stigmatization of menstruation is that the stereotypical view of menstruating women as physically or mentally debilitated can conflate illness, disability, and mental instability with being a woman (Chrisler & Caplan, 2002).

Menstruation is similar to hidden stigmas in that one's status is only revealed through disclosure or discovery (e.g., leakage of menstrual blood through clothing; Johnston-Robledo & Chrisler, 2013). Because of the fear surrounding menstrual blood leakage (Lee, 1994), some women have reported going to great lengths to conceal their menstrual status such as choosing baggier clothing to more reliably conceal menstrual status, and avoiding activities like swimming for fear of making this status known (Oxley, 1998). The design and advertising of menstrual hygiene products further perpetuate the stigma of secrecy and embarrassment surrounding menstruation, through a focus on invisibility under one's clothes, discrete disposal and packaging, an emphasis on improving "freshness" and the use of blue (rather than red) liquid in commercial demonstrations (Coutts & Berg, 1993; Merskin, 1999).

Menstrual Management

Menstrual management refers to the set of practices a person can engage in to physically cope with menstruation (Sumpter & Torondel, 2013). This includes a variety of practices such as concealing menstruation, removing menses from the body, preventing menses from touching or staining clothing, or avoiding school, work, or other situations (Sumpter & Torondel, 2013). Menstrual management varies across people, depending on personal preferences, cultural beliefs, access to resources, economic status, and knowledge of menstrual management techniques (Kaur et al., 2018; Sumpter & Torondel, 2013). A number of products have been developed to aid in menstrual management (Kaur et al., 2018; Planned Parenthood, 2018), but the price of these products can inhibit their usage (Kaur et al., 2018). Not only can menstrual management be financially costly, it also requires time; menstruators need additional restroom time--beyond the usual toilet use—during each visit to the restroom for menstrual management, but they also need more frequent use of the restroom to avoid leakage and, more importantly, unsanitary conditions. The consequences for improper menstrual management can be considerable. For example, infections such as toxic shock syndrome and reproductive tract infections can occur when menstrual management is not conducted in a timely manner (Anand, Singh, & Unisa, 2015); toxic shock syndrome can be life threatening (Mayo Clinic, 2017).

Menstrual Disorders

There are many menstrual disorders, but we review four and their potential effects on workers here. The first two, premenstrual syndrome (PMS) and premenstrual dysphoric disorder (PMDD), typically present symptoms during the luteal phase of the menstrual cycle (i.e., after ovulation and before menstruation) and typically subside with the onset of menses. PMS is common, experienced by 20–40% of premenopausal menstruators (Mishell, 2005). PMS symptoms include depression, anxiety, irritability, confusion, withdrawal, breast tenderness, abdominal bloating, headache, and swelling of extremities (American College of Obstetricians and Gynecologists [ACOG], 2015a). PMDD is essentially a more severe form of PMS, such that symptoms must be severe enough to disrupt daily functioning over a period of time; PMDD affects 3–8% of premenopausal menstruators (Halbreich, Borenstein, Terry, & Kahn, 2003). The third disorder, dysmenorrhea, is pain associated with menstruation (ACOG, 2015b). In studies of premenopausal women, 40%–90% reported menstrual pain (Aktaş, 2015; Burnett et al., 2005; Jones, 2004), while 17% reported pain that was severe enough to inhibit work and school (Burnett et al., 2005). Finally, endometriosis occurs when uterine lining tissue is found outside of the uterus (e.g., around the fallopian tubes, ovaries, bladder, or other internal organs). The symptoms of endometriosis are chronic pelvic pain (especially during menses), heavy menstrual bleeding, and pain during sexual intercourse, bowel movements, or urination (ACOG, 2018). Endometrial tissue outside the uterus responds to hormonal changes across the menstrual cycle like tissue inside the uterus: by breaking down and bleeding during the menses phase of the menstrual cycle. This process can cause lesions and scar tissue to form in the areas where this tissue is found, further exacerbating pain experiences.

Although the research is limited on the effects of menstrual disorders in the workplace, the evidence suggests that they are problematic for work productivity. For example, severity and number of endometriosis symptoms are positively related to presenteeism and absenteeism; endometriosis sufferers averaged 5.3 hours of presenteeism and 1.1 hours of absenteeism at work over the course of one week (Soliman et al., 2017). Some studies have demonstrated a relationship between dysmenorrhea and work stress (László, Győrffy, Ádám, Csoboth, & Kopp, 2008; László & Kopp, 2009), although other studies have not (Gordley, Lemasters, Simpson, & Yiin, 2000). Among PMDD sufferers, the most commonly experienced symptoms at work were concentration problems, self-doubt, fatigue, tearfulness, feelings of paranoia, social outbursts, a difficulty engaging in social interactions, and a sensitivity to the work environment; these symptoms were related to employee absenteeism and presenteeism during the luteal phase of the menstrual cycle (Hardy & Hardie, 2017). Interestingly, PMDD sufferers also reported guilt and an engagement in overcompensation behaviors (e.g., bringing work home, working longer hours) when PMDD symptoms subside with the onset of menses (Hardy & Hardie, 2017).

Whereas some of these menstrual disorders could fall under the Americans with Disabilities Act (ADA), others might not meet ADA criteria. Additionally, these disorders can be difficult to diagnose for a variety of reasons, including their intermittent nature, lack of knowledge even among sufferers, and/or pathologizing of pain associated with menstrual cycles as hysterical and catastrophizing (Jones, 2016). Regardless, these disorders are prevalent enough that organizations should consider how to best manage their workers who experience these symptoms.

Trans and Nonbinary Persons and Menstruation

It is not only cisgender women who menstruate; most (but not all) people who were assigned female at birth—including transmen and some nonbinary persons—are physically capable of menstruation. Trans and nonbinary people who are passing as cisgender might be concerned that menstrual matters will expose their gender status. Whereas some people who are capable of menstruating use hormone therapies that suppress menstruation, either purposefully or via a side effect of other trans health processes, others may choose trans health processes that do not affect their menstrual cycles at all (Chrisler et al., 2016). Trans and nonbinary persons who were assigned female at birth indicate that while it is generally easy to manage menstruation at home, it is significantly more difficult in work, school, or public places because of concerns about leaks as well as being seen or heard with menstrual hygiene products (Chrisler et al., 2016). Menstruation also puts trans and nonbinary people in a dilemma over determining which sexed bathroom to use (Chrisler et al., 2016).

Research Questions for IO Psychology at the Menstruation-Workplace Interface

Because so little research has been done on menstruation and the workplace overall, and none in industrial-organizational psychology, nearly any research would advance relevant fields on this topic. Here, we describe a few research topics that should be explored, but this list is meant as an inspirational starting point rather than an explicit research agenda.

First, there are a number of basic descriptive questions that should be addressed about the workplace-menstruation interface. For example, IO psychologists should examine whether and how menstrual disorders and symptomology influence turnover. One question to examine is the extent to which it is menstrual syndromes themselves or the workplaces structures and reactions that do not accommodate them that predict turnover (i.e., incremental prediction or relative dominance models). Another basic question would be to determine how menstrual hygiene is managed in different types of organizations and organizational settings. Factors such as the job-gender context of a workgroup (Gutek, 1985), access to bathroom breaks, cleanliness and privacy of bathroom areas, and organizational culture in the realms of diversity and inclusion, privacy, and autonomy could all be relevant to understanding how menstruation is managed in the workplace.

IO psychology can contribute to the literature on menstruation by bringing to bear our expertise on workplace processes and how people experience and behave in the workplace. For example, people can minimize the time they spend menstruating through medical techniques (e.g., continuous use of hormonal contraceptives). IO psychology can contribute to this by examining work-related factors that could influence whether people engage in menstrual suppression. There may be occupational factors that influence this decision; for example, jobs in which people have to be engaged for long periods of time without break (e.g., soldiers, emergency room doctors) might believe that their occupations necessitate menstrual suppression for effective performance. There might also be workplace factors that influence menstrual suppression choices, such as managerial supportiveness of menstrual hygiene needs or job-gender context (Gutek, 1985). Further, considering the globalization of work and corporations and the availability of international travel, the extent to which people engage in person in countries or cultures that have different menstrual hygiene practices readily available and different menstrual attitudes could influence menstrual suppression choices.

Further, experience sampling methods would be particularly useful in understanding how menstruation and work interact because menstruation does not happen most of the time a person is at work. Thus, cross-sectional methods fail to disentangle specific times of menstruation (i.e., some number of days per month) from non-menstrual times. Even though people can retrospectively report their work-related experiences during menstrual and non-menstrual times, experience sampling has the advantage of capturing experiences as they unfold, which should minimize common method problems that arise from measurement occasion, retrospection, and comparison effects of menstrual versus non-menstrual times (Fisher & To, 2012). Experience sampling could examine topics such as variations across the menstrual cycle in attendance, performance (both actual and perceived), attention, interactions with others, and mood. An interesting research design would have both the target worker and a critical informer (e.g., supervisor, coworker) supply information about the dependent variables, but only the target workers would have information about their own menstrual cycles. Not only would such a design allow for the examination of possible effects of menstruation on key indicators of workplace effectiveness, it would also allow researchers to disentangle the extent to which performance decrements are perceived by the worker relative to actual (as rated by others) performance decrements because the other informants' reports would not be tainted by stereotypes about menstruating people.

Importantly, these research questions need to be addressed with an intersectional frame, particularly with an eye toward socioeconomic factors, cultural factors, and race/ethnicity. Socioeconomic factors are likely to be very important to understanding the menstruation-workplace interface because of the costs associated with menstrual hygiene, the greater autonomy experienced by workers in higher levels of the organizational hierarchy, and the precarity of work often associated with lower levels of the socioeconomic hierarchy. Cultural factors are important because they are linked to menstrual myths, hygiene practices, educational levels, and workplace participation. Within the United States in particular but also in other counties, racial/ethnic factors will also be important to study because racial/ethnic minorities are typically sanctioned more heavily for any deviance than their majority (White) counterparts; knowledge of this could cause divergence of behaviors and choices between minority and majority people who menstruate. These factors are important to understand how organizational and societal factors restrict or even produce individual choice and behavior.

PERIMENOPAUSE AND MENOPAUSE

Menopause is the last menstruation that a person experiences; a person is considered to be menopausal once 12 months have passed since their last menses (National Health Institute, 2017). Before menopause, people experience perimenopause for several years, which includes changes in hormones that affect length of menstrual cycle and other bodily processes; these changes continue for a year following menopause. Perimenopause usually lasts 7 years, with menopause typically occurring between the ages of 45 and 55 (National Health Institute, 2017). Although symptoms can vary widely across perimenopausal people, common perimenopause symptoms include vasomotor (e.g., hot flashes, cold sweats, numbness and tingling), psychological (e.g., tiredness, irritability, forgetfulness, difficulty concentrating), somatic (e.g., headaches and bodily aches, sleeplessness, weight gain, loss of appetite, urinary elimination urgency), and menstrual (e.g., unpredictable—including both more frequent and less frequent than monthly—and/or heavy bleeding) components (National Institutes of Health, 2017; Neugarten & Kraines, 1965; Perz, 1997).

Approximately 80% of the civilian noninstitutional population between the ages of 45 and 54 in the U.S. participates in the labor force, with 88.3% of men and 74.5% of women in that age range in the labor force (Bureau of Labor Statistics, 2017). Thus, most people experiencing perimenopause are active in the workforce. The proportion of perimenopausal individuals in the workforce has been increasing (Griffiths et al., 2016). Thus, it is clear that perimenopause and menopause are important topics for organizations and organizational sciences.

Stigma and Stereotypes

Menopause is stigmatized because it is related to menstruation and because it is a sign that a person is aging or old in societies that value youth and attractiveness (Ballard, Elston, & Gabe, 2009; Chrisler, 2011;

McCrea, 1983; Nosek, Kennedy, & Gudmundsdottir, 2010). It is also stigmatized because of the myth that menopausal people are asexual, in a society that values sexuality (Hinchliff & Gott, 2008). It is produced by and reifies the sexism and ageism in society (McCrea, 1983). Stereotypes of perimenopausal people are generally negative and include concepts such as incompetence (Hardy, Hunter, & Griffiths, 2017), old and irritable (Marván et al., 2008), and moody (Marcus-Newhall, Thompson, & Thomas, 2001).

Like menstruation, perimenopause, and menopause are hidden stigmas that can be discovered. Some symptoms, such as tiredness, difficulty concentrating, and headaches, can be hidden or are common enough among all people that they can be attributed to other causes. However, the developmental timing of these symptoms along with their comorbidity might make them more difficult to attribute elsewhere. Other symptoms are not as easily hidden, most notably the prototypical perimenopause symptom: hot flashes. Because of the stigma associated with menopause, perimenopausal workers are likely to be motivated to manage (i.e., conceal) their symptoms in the workplace (Kittell, Mansfield, & Voda, 1998; Reynolds, 1999).

Management of Perimenopausal Symptoms

Perimenopausal symptoms can occur at any time, so some occur during the workday in the workplace. Some perimenopausal management strategies are individual-level, such as exercise, changes in diet, seeking information, or social support (Griffiths, MacLennan, & Hassard, 2013). However, other management strategies have considerable work and interpersonal components. For example, some perimenopausal people have to rearrange work hours or take some time off of work to manage symptoms (Griffiths et al., 2013).

The management of hot flashes is a prime example of how individual, interpersonal, and work factors all play a role in addressing perimenopausal symptoms. At the individual level, hot flashes can be managed by wearing layers of clothing that can be added or removed depending on individual temperature or by using a small fan when needed (Griffiths et al., 2013). However, not every job allows for this kind of personal accommodation. Jobs where uniforms or personal protective gear are required prevent the use of layered clothing. Some job environments could render personal fans unsafe (e.g., operating rooms, assembly lines), unsanitary (e.g., food service), ineffective (e.g., large, open spaces), or unusable because they impede work (e.g., assembly lines). Further, most people are unable to control the temperature of their work environment, which can intensify hot flashes (Griffiths et al., 2013). Additionally, managing temperatures or opening windows in shared workspaces requires negotiation and can create interpersonal difficulties at work (Griffiths et al., 2013).

Disclosure of perimenopause might make it easier for people to manage their symptoms, but disclosure is not common in the workplace (Griffiths et al., 2013; Hammam, Abbas, & Hunter, 2012). Disclosure would allow for managers and coworkers to accommodate employees' perimenopausal symptoms. Note, however, that the Americans with Disabilities Act does not consider menopause to be a disability (Whetzel, n.d.). Disclosure is also hampered by the communication taboo surrounding menstruation (Hammam et al., 2012; Houppert, 1999; Kissling, 1996a, 1996b). Further, workers find it more difficult to disclose perimenopause symptoms to managers and coworkers who are younger and/or male than to those who are older and/or female (Griffiths et al., 2013; Reynolds, 1999), consistent with research indicating men's general distaste for knowledge about menstruation (Forbes et al., 2003; Marván et al., 2005; Marván et al., 2014; Peranovic & Bentley, 2017; Roberts et al., 2002; Wong et al., 2013). Finally, disclosure is unlikely because it affirms a stigmatized identity.

Trans and Nonbinary People and Menopause

Menopause and perimenopause are a challenge for trans and nonbinary people to navigate. Transmen experience perimenopause and menopause on timelines akin to ciswomen if they do not engage in gender confirmation surgery that removes ovaries. For transmen, the process of disclosing perimenopausal symptoms is likely more difficult than for ciswomen because it also involves disclosing their identity. Transwomen experience a different dilemma. Because they were assigned male at birth and usually do not have internal reproductive organs that are part of the menstrual cycle, transwomen do not experience menopause. However, this becomes an issue when transwomen reach the age when they would be experiencing menopause if they were ciswomen and if they wish to pass as ciswomen. Transwomen can navigate this issue by either avoiding workplace conversations about menopause or faking menopausal symptoms in order to engage socially with other menopausal employees. However, this requires that transwomen engage in inauthentic experiences, which is damaging to well-being.

Research Questions at the Perimenopause-Workplace Interface

Although management training is important to all three issues raised in this chapter, it is addressed here because of the long-term, ongoing, and dynamic nature of perimenopause; while all three issues will require multiple disclosures, the other two issues are often cyclical (menstruation) or somewhat scheduled (infertility treatment). Perimenopause, on the other hand, is marked by irregularity, so workers will need to regularly check in with supervisors in order to manage their perimenopausal needs. Managers should be trained to respond to these disclosures appropriately, both in terms of interpersonal interactions and managerial decision making. Additionally, managers should be trained to engage in active accommodations, encouraging the worker to communicate on an as-needed basis for their current concerns. Managers should also maintain the worker's privacy around accommodations as best as possible.

What is not known yet is what kind of managerial training would be useful for these issues. It is clear from the review above that many people understand very little about menstruation and perimenopause, and this is especially true for cismen, and that cismen are particularly uncomfortable talking about menstruation and menopause. So, it seems that training for some basic knowledge about menstruation and perimenopause is in order. Additionally, positively responding to menstrual and perimenopause needs and variability would likely require some training (Kalinoski, Steele-Johnson, Peyton, Leas, Steinke, & Bowling, 2013). Research should examine what types of managerial interventions best result in more positive perimenopausal and menstrual experiences in the workplace.

As with menstruation, experience sampling methods would result in a better understanding of the perimenopause-work interface because of its ability to capture day-to-day experiences and changes of perimenopausal people. There is considerable uncertainty during perimenopause, with irregular menstruation and other symptoms. Thus, perimenopausal people are never certain what they might experience on any day, so a standard accommodation is not likely to meet their needs. Instead, different days will require different accommodations, so understanding how people determine their needs, how they communicate those needs, and how managers respond to those needs as they arise is necessary.

INFERTILITY

Infertility is a couple's inability to conceive. Within couples in which conception is a biological possibility (i.e., any couple in which one partner could produce sperm and the other could produce ova and menstruate), either or both partners can be the cause of the infertility (Balasch & Gratacós, 2011; Hull et al., 1985; Thonneau et al., 1999). Infertility naturally occurs among cisgender homosexual couples, although it is possible that either or both members of the couple have high fecundity (i.e., ability to contribute to conception); that is, infertility is a couple-level problem as well as often an individual problem. However, regardless of the causes of infertility within the couple, infertility treatments always involve the intended gestational carrier.

A wide variety of infertility treatments (often called assisted reproductive technology [ART]) exist. These range from superovulation (e.g., the drug Clomid) to intrauterine insemination (a.k.a., artificial insemination) to *in vitro* fertilization (IVF). Many of these treatments are stressful and time consuming (Cushing, 2010). For example, in the most common IVF approach, hormone therapies are used to induce superovulation in the intended gestational carrier, who then uses additional hormone therapies to prepare the uterus for implantation and hopeful pregnancy; this process requires that the intended gestational carrier attend multiple monitoring visits to adjust therapeutic hormone levels and to administer those therapies on a complex and constrained timetable (Cousineau & Domar, 2007; Finamore, Seifer, Ananth, & Leiblum, 2007; Mayo Clinic, 2018; Quigley, 2009). Other ARTs, even those that are less complex than IVF, can be time consuming and require frequent visits to the doctor (Finamore et al., 2007). However, because infertility treatments require precise timing that often evolves over the course of the treatment, it is extremely difficult to pinpoint exactly when an individual will need to be available for treatment (Hayes, 2010; Quigley, 2009).

Both ART and fertility preservation (i.e., medical techniques to save and store reproductive materials) are quite costly. The cryopreservation of sperm costs approximately $2,000 to $3,000 over a five-year period (Gorton & Grubb, 2014) and the cryopreservation for an ovulation cycle costs approximately $5,000 to $15,000 (Polly & Polly, 2014). A complete IVF cycle can cost approximately $12,000 to $15,000, although other treatments, such as superovulation medication, can be considerably less expensive (Cousineau & Domar, 2007). Infertility treatments are generally not designated an "Essential Health Benefit" covered by the Affordable Care Act in the United States (Curtis, 2018). Each state can decide whether to mandate insurance coverage, and most do not (Curtis, 2018; Griel, McQuillan, & Slauson-Blevins, 2011). Thus, roughly 70% of the people in the US who pursue IVF end up in debt (Curtis, 2018). In England, the National Health Service (NHS) recommends that intended gestational carriers have three rounds of IVF if they are under 40 and meet other criteria, but budgetary cuts to the NHS has limited IVF provision in recent years (Marsh, 2018). Infertility has been found to be a disability under the ADA (*Bragdon v. Abbott*, 1998) as it clearly interferes with a major life activity (i.e., reproducing), so workplaces covered by the ADA in the United States are required by law to provide reasonable accommodations for it, such as allowing work absences to attend infertility treatments (Sato, 2001). Interestingly, it is lawful for organizations to not cover infertility treatments in their health care plans so long as those plans are not discriminatory (i.e., access to treatment does not depend on other factors, such as fertility status; Sato, 2001).

Stigma of Infertility

Stigma regarding infertility arises from pronatalism, which is the idea that societies are in favor of parenthood, that parenthood is normative, and that structures are in place to encourage birth and parenting, including laws and churches; it pathologizes childlessness (Letherby, 1999; Miall, 1985; Whiteford & Gonzalez, 1995). Infertility stigma also arises from the production-reproduction divide (Acker, 1990) and from the considerable mythologizing that fertility problems are caused primarily by the female partner (Cousineau & Domar, 2007; Whiteford & Gonzalez, 1995). Unsurprisingly, women report more stress and more stigma regarding infertility than men do (Griel, 1997; Griel et al., 2010; Slade, O'Neill, Simpson, & Lashen, 2007).

Stigma regarding infertility includes two interrelated issues. The first is the childlessness stigma (Lampman & Dowling, 1995; Letherby, 1999; Miall, 1985). This stigma marks childlessness, in and of itself, as problematic. Second is infertility stigma. Infertility is perceived as a kind of defectiveness across a variety of cultures (Cousineau & Domar, 2007; Whiteford & Gonzalez, 1995). Because infertility is not associated with obvious physical symptoms or features, it is considered to be a "secret stigma" that is known only to the individuals themselves, unless disclosed to others (Griel, McQuillian, & Slauson-Blevins, 2011; Whiteford & Gonzalez, 1995).

Other Symptoms of Infertility and Infertility Treatment

Beyond the inability to achieve or maintain pregnancy, infertility has a number of effects on people. Infertility has been associated with emotional suffering (Cousineau & Domar, 2007) and psychological distress (Griel, Slauson-Blevins, & McQuillan, 2010), including feelings of worthlessness, loss, inadequacy, grief, depression, anxiety, and disrupted identity and life course plans (see Griel et al., 2010, for a review). The stress experiences of women with infertility have been compared to chronic illnesses like cancer, cardiac disease, and hypertension (Domar, Zuttermeister, & Friedman, 1993; McCarthy & Chiu, 2011). The distress of infertility is long lasting (Griel, McQuillan, Lowry, & Shreffler, 2011; Wirtberg, Moller, Hogstrom, Tronstad, & Lalos, 2007).

Many infertility treatments have side effects that are similar to the symptoms of menstruation and perimenopause. This is because many infertility treatments, especially for the intended gestational carrier, include hormone therapies that mimic or exacerbate the hormonal fluctuations in a menstrual cycle or in perimenopause. Symptoms include cramping, bloating, aches and discomfort throughout the body, vaginal bleeding, headaches, moodiness, and nausea (Mayo Clinic, 2018). Like menstrual and perimenopausal symptoms, these symptoms from infertility treatment require time and privacy to manage.

Management of Infertility and Infertility Treatments

While Cousineau and Domar (2007) asserted that couples who decide to pursue medical treatment for infertility have to significantly adjust their lifestyle, the intended gestational carrier will indisputably require more time away from work than the other partner would (Quigley, 2009). Many workers, especially the intended gestational carrier, who wish to undergo infertility treatments are left with a Catch-22: ask for a reduced or more flexible work schedule (and risk being seen as less committed to work and career) or give up the notion of pursuing infertility treatments and becoming a parent (Hayes, 2010). This is likely to be especially pronounced for ciswomen, as both mothers and women are already seen as less competent and committed workers (Acker, 1990, 2006; Bernard & Correll, 2010).

When people disclose to their employers that they are going through infertility treatments, "they must reveal both [their] desire to have a child and [their] inability to do so without recourse to expensive and time-consuming artificial treatment" (Hayes, 2010, p. 1310). Because IVF is not always successful, an individual may have to undergo several rounds before successfully having a child, which can be seen as a strain on an organization's resources (Hayes, 2010). Thus, legal scholars have indicated that there are two main employment risks for women who choose to undergo IVF: (a) being terminated for excessive absenteeism due to the infertility treatments, and (b) being denied insurance coverage for the infertility treatments (Cushing, 2010; Deardorff, 2011; Hayes, 2010). It is not yet a matter of settled law as to whether infertility treatments are covered by the Pregnancy Discrimination Act or the ADA, but some court decisions and in some appellate regions, infertility treatments are seen as gender specific and thus treating people differently due to their infertility treatment status is a form of sex discrimination (Cushing, 2010; Hayes, 2010; Johnson, 2010; Quigley, 2009).

Trans and Nonbinary People and Infertility

A large proportion—40 to 50%—of the transgender individuals living in the U.S. have a desire to have children (De Sutter, Kira, Verschoor, & Hotimsky, 2002; Obedin-Maliver, & Makadon, 2016; Tornello & Bos, 2017; Wierckx et al., 2012). However, trans and nonbinary people have a more challenging road to pregnancy than cispersons and some of these challenges intersect with the workplace.

Efforts to become a biological parent can disclose trans and nonbinary people's gender identities that had previously been hidden. For trans and nonbinary persons who use hormone therapies to support their gender health, becoming a biological parent could require that they stop using their health therapies (dickey, Ducheny, & Ehrbar, 2016; Goldman et al., 2017), which could result in changes to a number of personal characteristics such as facial hair, voice, face shape, and body shape. For transpersons who suppressed puberty and disrupted the development of secondary sex characteristics (Edwards-Leeper, Leibowitz, & Sangganjanavanich, 2016), efforts to become a biological parent could cause those secondary sex characteristics to develop.

Additionally, transpersons can transition at any age. Some transition as adults while they are in the workplace, and some transition choices can permanently affect their ability to create biological children (dickey et al., 2016). For these people, it might be necessary to preserve their reproductive materials before or during the transition process (Goldman et al., 2017), which could increase their medical costs and time away from work above and beyond those needed for transition alone.

Further, the costs for ART are likely to be higher for trans and nonbinary people compared to cispersons (dickey et al., 2016; Holley & Pasch, 2015). Most ART services are targeted towards cisgender women with cisgender men as partners (Holley & Pasch, 2015). Many insurance policies that provide coverage for ART require a diagnosis of infertility or clauses requiring the use of a spouse's gametes (Johnson, 2012; Rank, 2010). Transpersons often fall outside of the coverage set by insurance providers.

Research Questions at the Infertility-Workplace Interface

As with both menstruation and perimenopause, very little research has been done on infertility and the sociostructural aspects of the workplace overall, and none in industrial-organizational psychology. Thus again, nearly any research would advance relevant fields on this topic.

One important question is the differential experiences of the intended gestational carrier and their partners in how they are treated when requesting accommodations for infertility treatments. The intended gestational partner always has higher (sometimes considerably higher) treatment time than their partners do. Although the ADA requires that allowing time off for these appointments be treated as accommodations, it is clear that a number of factors go into decisions to grant accommodations (Carpenter & Paetzold, 2013) and not every request for accommodation is met straightforwardly. Thus, research should examine what factors of the request, the requestor, and the evaluator of the request are relevant to accommodation decisions. For example, considering how common infertility is, it may be that the person evaluating the accommodation request has also experienced infertility; it is likely that these evaluators are more likely to grant the accommodation. However, the non-gestational partner may wish to accompany the intended gestational partner to medical appointments, even if they are not medically required to be there. It is possible that these requests, which are not legally covered accommodations, have a different pattern of factors related to their success or failure.

An interesting problem for people who wish to obtain accommodations for infertility treatment is that they would be required to disclose their need for treatment to some members of the organization. Thus, they would have to make an invisible stigma visible; simultaneously, they would be obtaining an additional stigma of disability. Further, trans and nonbinary persons, people in same-sex partnerships, and others could also be disclosing potentially stigmatizing statuses. This is an important avenue for research for both understanding infertility in the workplace and for stigma disclosure researchers. For example, who is disclosed to and how disclosure occurs are important questions. Such research should not focus exclusively on individual factors, as there are likely to be organizational policies and practices that influence to whom and how people disclose.

ORGANIZATIONAL ACCOMMODATIONS

In this section of the chapter, we review responses that organizations can make to support people who are facing infertility, menstruating, or going through perimenopause. Considering the gendered nature of organizations (Acker, 1990, 2006, 2012), these suggestions are much more radical than they seem. The gendered nature of organizations make these accommodations seem unneeded; if the need is acknowledged, it is likely to be weighed against other organizational factors (e.g., cost) and abandoned at the first resistance. Thus, engaging in these kinds of changes will require sustained effort on the part of organizations.

Better Restroom Design

One of the most straightforward ways that organizations can support persons who menstruate, are going through perimenopause, or are going through infertility treatments is to design better restroom facilities (Herman, 2013). Good restroom facilities should be single stall (or single room), have a stall door that goes from ceiling to floor, and contain its own sink. Ideally, these facilities should also be wheelchair accessible and designed for use for people with mobility challenges (e.g., grab bars). These kinds of facilities are useful to all people, regardless of disability status, gender identity, menstruation status, or other factors. They also have the advantage of minimizing problems with queueing at sex-segregated bathrooms when there are disproportionate numbers of users. They are also useful for the private management of other conditions, such as the need to use injected medications (e.g., insulin) in the workplace or by clients and customers (e.g., in restaurants).

In the particular context of this chapter, these restroom designs provide menstruators the opportunity to conceal their menstrual status and to complete their menstrual management practices (e.g., disposal, handwashing) in private (Griffiths et al., 2016). These designs also allow transmen to use the restroom without having to choose between the facility that matches their gender identity and the facility that provides discreet menstrual hygiene product disposal. Further, these designs provide trans and nonbinary people the opportunity to keep their bodily features private, whether that is motivated by not being outed or not being ogled by others who are inappropriately curious about their bodies. It also should reduce verbal harassment at and denial of use of the bathroom for trans and nonbinary persons (Herman, 2013). Further, given the violence that occurs against transpersons (Lombardi, Wilchins, Priesing, & Malouf, 2002; Stotzer, 2009), good restroom designs are a wise investment for organizations as it provides additional safety for trans and nonbinary persons from others who wish to do them harm (Herman, 2013). Good restroom design also alleviates stress for transpersons (Herman, 2013). Inclusive restroom design will send a signal to trans and nonbinary employees, menstruators, and perimenopausal people that they are supported and welcome in the work environment, which should ultimately improve employee retention and productivity.

Access to Menstrual Hygiene Products

Organizations should ensure that all employees, regardless of perceived gender, have access to menstrual hygiene products. Many, but not all, women's restrooms in Western nations provide machines that dispense menstrual hygiene products for a fee. Access to these resources can be particularly useful in situations where menses begins unexpectedly or when an individual has run out of their own products. Nevertheless, in order for these machines to be truly useful they should be affordably priced for all employees and consistently stocked with a variety of hygiene product types. In addition, machines dispensing menstrual management products should be placed in all restrooms or in areas where all people can discreetly access them.

In developing countries, menstrual management is more challenging. Access to commercial menstrual hygiene products might be limited, either through availability or cost. These individuals may choose other means of menstrual leak protection or choose to forgo protection. Additionally, restroom facilities may be more difficult to access or not suitably designed for menstrual management practices. This prevents women's full participation in the workplace. Organizations that want to build human capital capacity in developing nations would be wise to partner with non-governmental organizations to provide menstrual hygiene products to women and girls in order to encourage women's participation in the labor force and girls' participation in schooling.

Work Accommodations and Flexibility

Good bathroom facilities and access to appropriate products is not enough; people must also have the opportunity to use them. They also need work flexibility to attend infertility treatments or manage their menstrual or perimenopausal symptoms. Accommodating employees with these needs should reduce absenteeism and presenteeism (Geukes, van Aalst, Robroek, Laven, & Oosterhof, 2016).

Flexibility at the workplace. Some jobs and/or organizations place restrictions on the frequency or length of breaks that employees can take, which can inhibit menstruators from completing menstrual management practices as needed. These practices are essential for personal hygiene and comfort. When menstruating employees are denied or limited restroom breaks, they may experience menstrual leaks. Menstruation—particularly, menstruation during perimenopause—can be unpredictable in both timing and heaviness of menses, so employees might need more breaks to manage menstruation in the face of this uncertainty. The frequency and length of needed breaks will vary across people, within people at different days during menstruation, and within people at different times in their lives, so it is not possible to make a recommendation as to what a "right number" of breaks would be. However, it is certainly within the realm of possibility that for some people, a 15 minute break every 2 hours would be necessary—although for some people it could be more often. Although these breaks might seem costly to management, the distractedness and worry regarding menstrual concealment that menstruators experience (Lee, 1994) can also be costly in the workplace.

Breaks are often considered costly to organizations when employees are paid hourly because the Fair Labor Standards Act (FLSA) requires that short breaks be paid and included in the calculation for overtime eligibility (US. Department of Labor, n.d.). However, these costs are not calculated for salaried workers because (a) they are often not eligible for overtime via the FLSA and (b) they are usually paid to complete their work as needed and not to be present at specific times. Thus, the focus on reducing breaks is a classist concern, motivated by the organization's desire for profit rather than concerns for worker well-being. This is a short-sighted view of profit, as it focuses on the daily cost of work rather than the overall return on organizational investment in its workers. Replacing workers is incredibly costly (Duffield, Roche, Homer, Buchan, & Dimitrelis, 2014; Glebbeek & Bax, 2004), so providing some accommodations in order to retain good workers is a wise investment.

Additionally, some symptoms of menstruation, perimenopause, and infertility treatments are uncomfortable. Organizations should be willing to engage in conversations concerning accommodations to the workplace that can make working while experiencing this discomfort more tolerable. This might include simple solutions like allowing employees to use heating pads to deal with cramping, to take breaks and short walks, or to do 10 minutes of relaxation exercises, or ensuring access to toilets, cold drinking water, and temperature control in the workspace (Dickerson, Mazyck, & Hunter, 2003; Griffiths et al., 2016).

What accommodations are easily provided depend in part on the organizational setting. For example, it might be easy for universities, hospitals, and large corporations to provide resting spaces with fans and heating pads, but it might not be easy for restaurants, warehouses, and manufacturing plants to do so because of the limited private space available within the building. Instead, restaurants, warehouses, and manufacturing plants might need to focus on increased access to toilets and increased break times. However, such organizations might also consider how to provide private space for temporary rest, because a huge portion of the working population will need such accommodations at some time and because the replacement costs of workers—especially good workers—is likely to be higher in the long run than creating these spaces or providing breaks.

Flexible work arrangements. Flexible work arrangements are opportunities to have flexibility in where and when work in completed (Allen, Johnson, Kiburz, & Shockley, 2013). These differ from flexibility in the workplace (above), whereby the idea is to give people who are onsite and on schedule some flexibility around when and how often they take breaks, use restroom facilities, and the like. Flexible work arrangements, on the other hand, refer to flexibility in when people are onsite, if they are onsite at all.

Although flexible work arrangements have a modest effect on work-family conflict (Allen et al., 2013), they are often touted as a potential accommodation for disabilities (Erickson, von Schrader, Bruyère, & VanLooy, 2014). Flexible work arrangements have been suggested as accommodations for menstrual and perimenopausal symptoms (Griffiths et al., 2016; Hammam et al., 2012). Flexible work arrangements would obviously reduce absenteeism and tardiness associated with infertility treatments. Unfortunately, there are many jobs in which some flexible work arrangements cannot be used (e.g., waitstaff cannot work from home), so offering these arrangements would only be useful in situations in which people could actually use them.

Health Care Plans

In the United States, health care plans are often tied to employment. Although there are some minimum requirements for health plans (Rosenbaum, 2011), health care plans and the benefits they provide vary considerably. Organizations can select plans that provide comprehensive reproductive (including infertility) and trans health coverage. Not only can this be a competitive advantage in recruiting people to organizations (Weller, 2017), it is also sends a signal about who is valued and what organizational values are. Additionally, good healthcare should reduce absenteeism and presenteeism.

Organizational Support

One of the biggest steps that organizations can make is ensuring that managers are knowledgeable and supportive of menstrual, menopausal, and infertility issues (Griffiths et al., 2013). Unfortunately, managers do not want information about employee experiences of hormonal issues and may be unsympathetic to requested accommodations for menstrual disorders (Hardy & Hardie, 2017). The resistance of managers to learn about menstrual health may be due to the greater likelihood of men holding these positions (Bureau of Labor Statistics, 2018) and their negative attitudes towards menstruation (Forbes et al., 2003; Marván et al., 2005, Roberts et al., 2002), lack of menstrual education (Marván et al., 2005), and view of menstruation as "none of men's business" (Peranovic & Bentley, 2017).

An initial step to breaking the taboo surrounding the discussion of menstruation can be providing managers with information about reproductive health and disorders and their intersection with the workplace (Hardy, Griffiths, & Hunter, 2017) as well as information about the experiences of trans and nonbinary workers. Managers can reduce the stigma surrounding these issues by remaining open to talking about these issues with employees in non-judgmental ways (Griffiths et al., 2013; Hardy & Hardie, 2017; Hardy et al., 2017). Organizations may also wish to seek training for managers regarding how to communicate with employees about these topics in ways that minimize discomfort and increase empathy towards the employee (Hardy et al., 2017). Managers should also seek to build a culture within the organization that is not tolerant of derogatory or stereotypical remarks about menstruation or menstruating people.

SOCIETAL CHANGES

In addition to organizational support for menstruation, menopause, and infertility, society-level changes are needed to alleviate some of the challenges listed herein. IO psychologists should consider how to advocate for these changes as individuals and as a field of professionals who are experts in human behavior, human capital, and analysis of fairness. IO advocacy is still in its infancy, so any positive change in these directions should make measurable differences for people.

Pregnancy Discrimination Act and/or ADA Classification and Accommodation

One of the primary ways to effect change at a societal level is to classify reproductive disorders and severe symptomology such as dysmenorrhea, infertility, and perimenopause as disabilities that require accommodation via the ADA and/or as covered by the Pregnancy Discrimination Act (PDA). This would force organizations to provide reasonable accommodations, such as modified attendance rules, extra sick leave and/or personal time off, and changes in working conditions such as the provision of cooling devices or extra breaks.

Interestingly, it is difficult to imagine that the ADA as it is currently written would cover menstruation or menopause because neither impairs a "major life activity" such as reading, walking, or communicating. It's possible that some severe menstrual disorders could do so, but generally they do not. Additionally, many symptoms of both menstruation and menopause are managed via personal mitigating factors, which are explicitly excluded from accommodation in the ADA (e.g., workplaces do not need to provide eyeglasses for the farsighted). Note, however, that menopause might occur because of an underlying condition that could be classified as a disability (e.g., hysterectomy following cancer treatment), so that would be accommodated even if menopause itself is not. The PDA, on the other hand, covers all processes related to pregnancy and childbirth, which should include both menstruation and menopause. Notably, pregnancy is considered a temporary disability under the PDA. It may be possible to view perimenopause as a temporary disability like pregnancy and to accommodate it therein. Menstruation is not a temporary disability because it is recurrent but not constant and because the time period over which menstruation occurs is long (i.e., decades). Thus, how menstrual problems are considered under ADA or PDA should be considered carefully, but there may be other disabilities (e.g., migraine) that are similar in recurrence, inconsistency, and temporality.

Of course, organizations are able to accommodate people even when there is no legal disability in place. This was part of our suggestions for organizational action and noted that such accommodations could be a competitive advantage for organizations. However, leaving such accommodations to organizations and their agents, rather than mandating them at a societal level, means that people will sometimes luck into accommodations when they are in the right kind of organization with the right kind of manager. Additionally, such accommodations will be more likely for people who have greater power, whether formal or personal, because they have greater ability to advocate for themselves and greater freedom of economic movement and support.

Eliminate the Tampon Tax

Organizational scientists should encourage the elimination of sales tax on menstrual hygiene products. Most states in the United States include tampons, sanitary napkins, and other menstrual hygiene products among their taxable goods (i.e., sales tax at the point-of-sale), despite the fact that most states also have many goods that are not taxed due to their necessity (Larimer, 2016). For example, many (but not all) foods are tax-exempt. Most states tax toilet paper, which is also a hygiene necessity in the United States. However, all people use toilet paper; this tax does not differentially affect people who menstruate. Thus, the tampon tax is an example of a "pink tax" (Ngabirano, 2017) but in this case it is institutionalized and government-sanctioned rather than one of the many general mark-ups in price for consumer goods that are created and marketed for women.

Changes in Health Care Coverage

In the United States, health care coverage is generally private and associated with employment, but not every worker is provided health insurance by their employer. Even when employees have health insurance, infertility treatments are often not covered (Curtis, 2018; Griel McQuillan, & Slauson-Blevins, 2011). Further, menstrual cups, tampons, sanitary pads, and other menstrual hygiene products are not considered medical devices nor are they eligible for medical expenditure reimbursements from pretax healthcare spending accounts.

Simply, all of this should change. IO psychologists should advocate for health care coverage—at the organizational level and the societal level—so that infertility treatments and menstrual hygiene products are covered by health insurance. The investment in people who experience infertility and menstruation—by alleviating economic costs and stress—should result in a healthier society.

Free Menstrual Hygiene Products[3]

Menstrual hygiene products are expensive. Some are more expensive at the outset but less expensive per use over time (e.g., menstrual cups) whereas others are cheaper but more costly over time (e.g., tampons and sanitary pads). Considering the societal-level expectations that menstruation should be private and hidden, as well as the societal-level expectations for cleanliness, menstrual hygiene is not a luxury but a necessity for all menstruators. Menstrual hygiene is expensive and particularly challenging for people in low socioeconomic brackets. For people who experience precarious housing, it is even more challenging because not only is hygiene expensive, but also the products must be maintained and carted from one housing situation to another.

Further, there is no parallel product that people who will not ever menstruate (i.e., people assigned male at birth; people who have no uterus and no ovaries) have to purchase. Both menstruators and never-menstruators will need other hygiene products (e.g., toilet paper, soap, shampoo); both menstruators and never-menstruators need or use clothing or equipment that are different due to gender but arguably parallel (e.g., gendered sports clothing such as athletic cups and sports bras). But there is no parallel for never-menstruators for menstrual hygiene products.

Thus, menstrual hygiene is essentially a tax, costing people who menstruate both money and time that people who never menstruate will never pay. As a field, IO psychology is invested in equity and equality, both in opportunity and in outcomes, and should advocate for equal and/or equitable treatment in our organizations and in society. Menstrual hygiene products are a need for people who menstruate and never for people who don't, so in this case the equitable treatment is to provide free menstrual hygiene products to those who need them.

This suggestion might seem antithetical to capitalist notions that underlie organizational sciences, which generally work with and study persons and places engaged in for-profit enterprises. But if a society does not fully subsidize menstrual hygiene products, then it is saying that only people who *earn* these products can use them; you have to be able to afford them to have them. This is a decidedly anti-woman and classist position, one that should not persist.

ADDITIONAL RESEARCH QUESTIONS

We close this chapter with a few thoughts about research directions on these topics. As this is an understudied topic, it is important to consider qualitative work to examine the experiences of people before jumping into quantitative work. Additionally, because of the cyclical and/or changing nature of these experiences, experience sampling approaches might be particularly useful.

Evaluating Practical Solutions

In this chapter, we recommended a number of practical solutions that could help people manage menstruation, perimenopause symptoms, and infertility treatments. Some of these are based on empirical evidence that has already tested the specific solution for these specific problems, but others are either suggestions that employees have made in surveys or extrapolations from broader occupational health initiatives. Thus, it is as yet unclear as to whether these solutions will improve the lived experiences of people who are menstruating, experiencing menopause, or undergoing infertility treatments.

One critical issue to resolve is determining the appropriate criterion measures for evaluating recommended solutions. It seems likely that successful interventions would reduce employee stress levels, increase employee health, and reduce employee absence and tardiness. It is also possible that there would be increases in employee attitudes, like job satisfaction, as well as increases in organizational commitment, both of which would reduce turnover (Griffeth., Hom, & Gaertner, 2000; Meyer, Stanley, Hershcovitch, & Topolnytsky, 2002).

Research should also examine effects at the group and organizational level. For example, it is possible that improving the workplace regarding menstruation, menopause, and infertility will create better team functioning, organizational productivity, organizational reputation, and ultimately organizational profitability. Importantly, research should investigate the extent to which these group- and organizational-level effects were due to improved individual performance or due to a decrease in sexism, anti-trans prejudice, and other discriminatory systems at the organizational level (Crenshaw, 1989, 1995). Because organizations are part and parcel of society, they cannot fully eradicate hegemonic masculinity within themselves, but organizations are likely to vary on the extent to which they attempt to dismantle these power structures. Those organizations that more effectively and extensively push back against these interrelated systems of oppression are more likely to have more equitable organizations, which could affect organizational functioning, above and beyond the direct performance and attitude effects from the individuals who are managing their menstruation, perimenopause, and infertility treatments.

What Model Is Appropriate?

While it is clear that these topics—menstruation, perimenopause, and infertility treatments—fall into the general realm of occupational health, it is not clear what kinds of philosophical and theoretical models should be applied to these issues. On one hand, stigma is clearly a relevant topic, which raises the specter of disclosure and discrimination models (Clair, Beatty, & MacLean, 2005). Much of this chapter focused on the taboos and need for privacy surrounding menstruation, perimenopause, and infertility treatments, so disclosure, stigma, and discrimination are clearly important factors at least for the people who are experiencing these reproductivity-related events. Additionally, stigma, discrimination, and disclosure models are important when considering the experiences of trans and nonbinary people and their heightened need for privacy to protect their identities. This kind of model would conceptualize menstruation, menopause, infertility treatments, and trans and nonbinary identities as hidden stigmas that can become visible and that people are generally motivated to keep hidden because of the negative consequences that they expect (or know) that they will experience if these characteristics become known.

However, there are other approaches that could be applied to these issues to further explicate workers' experiences. Work-life balance (Allen et al., 2000; Allen & Martin, 2017), for example, has some parallels with managing menstruation, perimenopause, and infertility. This is evident throughout the chapter whereby some of the solutions for these issues parallel those for work-life balance. Additionally, this is evident when considering the permeability of the work-life boundary and how one domain can affect the other (e.g., sleeplessness at home leads to lower productivity at work; poor performance at work leads to overwork at home). This kind of model would posit that menstruation, perimenopause, and infertility treatments are life domain experiences that interfere with work domain experiences (and, to a lesser extent, vice versa), how this boundary-crossing affects individual functioning, and how organizations can support people during these events.

Models of disability in the workplace also seem relevant. This is evident throughout this chapter, where we refer to accommodations for symptoms and laws that govern the disability-workplace relationship. Even though many of these experiences and symptoms do not meet the criteria for the ADA, there may be utility in conceptualizing them as subclinical disabilities that require some material support from the organization. This kind of model would posit menstruation, perimenopause, and infertility treatments as a factor that limits an employee's ability to contribute in a workplace that is not designed for them and their particular situation, but could more fully participate and perform when some reasonable accommodations are made.

This is not to suggest that there is a single model for examining menstruation, perimenopause, and infertility in the workplace. Instead, it is likely that all of these models, and probably others, are relevant. It is essential that researchers recognize which of these models is applicable to the particular problem they are addressing, so they appropriate variables are measured and/or interventions are designed.

CONCLUSION

This chapter provides a brief overview of some of the reproduction-related experiences of workers and how they affect their workplace experiences. The need to manage menstruation, perimenopause, and infertility treatments in the workplace is high, yet the attention it has received in IO psychology and other organizational sciences is low. Herein, we have provided information about managing menstruation, perimenopause, and infertility, risks that this poses to trans and nonbinary people, some practical solutions that organizations can undertake, and some research questions that should be addressed. We hope that this chapter begins a new subfield of IO psychology, whereby menstruation, perimenopause, and infertility treatments are seen as important, common, and worthy of study.

NOTES

1. Several key terms need to be defined. The gender binary references the idea that there are two genders (and two biological sexes): male and female. Cisgender (or cis) describes people whose gender identity matches their assigned sex. Transgender (or trans) describes people whose gender identity is the opposite, on the gender binary of male/female, of their assigned sex. However, there are a variety situations in which the gender binary is insufficient to describe a person's identity, biology, or experiences. For example, intersex persons have reproductive systems that do not neatly fit into "female" or "male" descriptors; this could occur through genes, internal organs/gonads, external organs, hormones, or any combination therein. Gender nonbinary persons (sometimes called gender nonconforming, gender creative, or gender fluid) do not identify exclusively with either component of the received gender binary; this is a catch-all category and can include people who identify with both male and female identities, or neither. Although not satisfactory as it erases the wide variety of experiences of people, we will refer to all persons whose identities and/or biology do not match the gender binary as nonbinary.
2. Not all transpersons are motivated to pass as cispersons. On the other hand, considering the violence that transpeople experience (Lombardi, Wilchins, Priesing, & Malouf, 2002; Stotzer, 2009), many people are likely to be motivated to do so.
3. We thank Mikki Hebl for this suggestion.

REFERENCES

Acker, J. (1990). Heirarchies, jobs, bodies: A theory of gendered organizations. *Gender & Society, 4*, 139–158.

Acker, J. (2006). Inequality regimes: Gender, class, and race in organizations. *Gender & Society, 20*(4), 441–464.

Acker, J. (2012). Gendered organizations and intersectionality: Problems and possibilities. *Equality, Diversity and Inclusion: An International Journal,* 214–224.

Aktaş, D. (2015). Prevalence and factors affecting dysmenorrhea in female university students: Effect on general comfort level. *Pain Management Nursing, 16*(4), 534–543.

Allen, T. D., Johnson, R. C., Kiburz, K. M., & Shockley, K. M. (2013). Work–family conflict and flexible work arrangements: Deconstructing flexibility. *Personnel psychology, 66*(2), 345–376.

Allen, T. D., & Martin, A. (2017). The work-family interface: A retrospective look at 20 years of research in JOHP. *Journal of Occupational Health Psychology, 22,* 259–272.

Allen, T. D., Herst, D. E. L., Bruck, C. S., & Sutton, M. (2000). Consequences associated with work-to-family conflict: A review and agenda for future research. *Journal of Occupational Health Psychology, 5,* 278–308.

American College of Obstetricians and Gynecologists. (2015a). Premenstrual Syndrome (PMS). Retrieved from https://www.acog.org/Patients/FAQs/Premenstrual-Syndrome-PMS?IsMobileSet=false

American College of Obstetricians and Gynecologists. (2015b). Dysmenorrhea: Painful periods. Retrieved from https://www.acog.org/Patients/FAQs/Dysmenorrhea-Painful-Periods?IsMobileSet=false

American College of Obstetricians and Gynecologists. (2018). Endometriosis. Retrieved from https://www.acog.org/Patients/FAQs/Endometriosis?IsMobileSet=false

Anand, E., Singh, J., & Unisa, S. (2015). Menstrual hygiene practices and its association with reproductive tract infections and abnormal vaginal discharge among women in India. *Sexual & Reproductive Healthcare, 6*(4), 249–254.

Avellar, S., & Smock, P. J. (2003). Has the price of motherhood declined over time? A cross-cohort comparison of the motherhood wage penalty. *Journal of Marriage and Family, 65*(3), 597–607.

Balasch, J., & Gratacós, E. (2011). Delayed childbearing: effects on fertility and the outcome of pregnancy. *Fetal diagnosis and therapy, 29*(4), 263–273.

Ballard, K. D., Elston, M. A., & Gabe, J. (2009). Private and public ageing in the UK the transition through the menopause. *Current Sociology, 57*(2), 269–290.

Barron, T. (2017, October 11). 800 million women and girls are on their period right now--let's talk about it. *International Business Times [online].* Retrieved October, 24, 2018, from https://www.ibtimes.co.uk/800-million-women-girls-are-their-period-right-now-lets-talk-about-it-1642606

Benard, S., & Correll, S. J. (2010). Normative discrimination and the motherhood penalty. *Gender & Society, 24*(5), 616–646.

Bragdon v. Abbott. (1998). 524 U.S. 624.

Britton, D. M., & Logan, L. (2008). Gendered organizations: Progress and prospects. *Sociology Compass, 2*(1), 107–121.

Brooks-Gunn, J., & Ruble, D. N. (1986). Men's and women's attitudes and beliefs about the menstrual cycle. *Sex Roles, 14*(5–6), 287–299.

Buckley, T., & Gottlieb, A. (Eds.). (1988). *Blood magic: The anthropology of menstruation.* Berkeley, CA: University of California Press.

Budig, M. J., & Hodges, M. J. (2010). Differences in disadvantage: Variation in the motherhood penalty across White women's earnings distribution. *American Sociological Review, 75*(5), 705–728.

Bureau of Labor Statistics. (2017). Employment status of the civilian noninstitutional population by age, sex, and race. Retrieved from https://www.bls.gov/cps/cpsaat03.pdf

Bureau of Labor Statistics. (2018). Employed persons by detailed occupation, sex, race, and Hispanic or Latino ethnicity. Retrieved December, 6, 2018, from https://www.bls.gov/cps/cpsaat11.htm

Burnett, M. A., Antao, V., Black, A., Feldman, K., Grenville, A., Lea, R., ... & Robert, M. (2005). Prevalence of primary dysmenorrhea in Canada. *Journal of Obstetrics and Gynaecology Canada, 27*(8), 765–770.

Carpenter, N. C., & Paetzold, R. L. (2013). An examination of factors influencing responses to requests for disability accommodations. *Rehabilitation Psychology, 58*(1), 18–27.

Chandler, M. A. (2017a, August 24). Federal prisons must now provide free tampons and pads to incarcerated women. *The Washington Post* [online]. Retrieved November, 9, 2018, from https://www.washingtonpost.com/local/social-issues/federal-prisons-must-provide-free-tampons-and-pads-to-incarcerated-women/2017/08/23/a9e0e928-8694-11e7-961d-2f373b3977ee_story.html?utm_term=.16ebe1190d23

Chandler, M. A. (2017b, September 11). This woman said she was fired for leaking menstrual blood at work. The ACLU is suing for discrimination. *The Washington Post* [online]. Retrieved November, 9, 2018 from, https://www.washingtonpost.com/local/social-issues/ga-woman-said-she-was-fired-for-leaking-during-her-period-at-work-the-aclu-is-suing-for-discrimination/2017/09/08/50fab924-8d97-11e7-8df5-c2e5cf46c1e2_story.html?utm_term=.b700f2961dd3

Chrisler, J. C. (2011). Leaks, lumps, and lines: Stigma and women's bodies. *Psychology of Women Quarterly, 35*(2), 202–214.

Chrisler, J. C., & Caplan, P. (2002). The strange case of Dr Jekyll and Ms Hyde: How PMS became a cultural phenomenon and a psychiatric disorder. *Annual Review of Sex Research, 13*, 274–306.

Chrisler, J. C., Gorman, J. A., Manion, J., Murgo, M., Barney, A., Adams-Clark, A., … McGrath, M. (2016). Queer periods: Attitudes toward and experiences with menstruation in the masculine of centre and transgender community. *Culture, Health & Sexuality, 18*(11), 1238–1250.

Clair, J. A., Beatty, J. E., & MacLean, T. L. (2005). Out of sight but not out of mind: Managing invisible social identities in the workplace. *Academy of Management Review, 30*(1), 78–95.

Connell, R. W. (2005). *Masculinities*. Cambridge, England: Polity.

Connell, R. W. (1985). Theorising gender. *Sociology, 19*(2), 260–272. doi:10.1177/0038038585019002008

Connell, R. W., & Messerschmidt, J. W. (2005). Hegemonic masculinity: Rethinking the concept. *Gender & Society, 19*(6), 829–859.

Correll, S. J., Benard, S., & Paik, I. (2007). Getting a job: Is there a motherhood penalty? *American Journal of Sociology, 112*(5), 1297–1338.

Cousineau, T. M., & Domar, A. D. (2007). Psychological impact of infertility. *Best Practice & Research Clinical Obstetrics and Gynaecology, 21*, 293–308.

Coutts, L. B., & Berg, D. H. (1993). The portrayal of the menstruating woman in menstrual product advertisements. *Health Care for Women International, 14*(2), 179–191.

Crenshaw, K. (1989). Demarginalizing the intersection of race and sex: A Black feminist critique of antidiscrimination doctrine, feminist theory and antiracist politics. *University of Chicago Legal Forum, 139*.

Crenshaw, K. (1995). *Critical race theory: The key writings that formed the movement*. New York, NY: New Press.

Curtis, M. (2018). Inconceivable: How barriers to infertility treatment for low-income women amount to reproductive suppression. *Georgetown Journal on Poverty Law and Policy, 25*, 323–342.

Cushing, K. (2010). Facing reality: The Pregnancy Discrimination Act falls short for women undergoing infertility treatment. *Seton Hall Law Review, 40,* 1697–1731.

De Sutter, P., Kira, K., Verschoor, A., & Hotimsky, A. (2002). The desire to have children and the preservation of fertility in transsexual women: A survey. *International Journal of Transgenderism, 6,* 183–185.

Deardorff, M. D. (2011). Beyond pregnancy: Litigating infertility, contraception, and breastfeeding in the workplace. *Journal of Women, Politics & Policy, 32,* 52–72.

Delaney, J., Lupton, M. J., & Toth, E. (1988). *The curse: A cultural history of menstruation.* Champaign, IL:University of Illinois Press.

Dickerson, L. M., Mazyck, P. J., & Hunter, M. H. (2003). Premenstrual syndrome. *American family physician, 67*(8), 1743–1752.

dickey, l. m., Ducheny, K. M., & Ehrbar, R. D. (2016). Family creation options for transgender and gender nonconforming people. *Psychology of Sexual Orientation and Gender Diversity, 3,* 173–179.

Domar, A. D., Zuttermeister, P. C., & Friedman, R. (1993). The psychological impact of infertility: A comparison with patients with other medical conditions. *Journal of Psychosomatic Obstetrics and Gynaecology, 14,* 45–52.

Duffield, C.M., Roche, M.A., Homer, C., Buchan, J., & Dimitrelis, S. (2014). A comparative review of nurse turnover rates and costs across countries. *Journal of Advanced Nursing, 70,* 2703–2712.

Dunnavant, N. C., & Roberts, T. A. (2013). Restriction and renewal, pollution and power, constraint and community: The paradoxes of religious women's experiences of menstruation. *Sex Roles, 68*(1-2), 121–131.

Edwards-Leeper, L., Leibowitz, S., & Sangganjanavanich, V. F. (2016). Affirmative practice with transgender and gender nonconforming youth: Expanding the model. *Psychology of Sexual Orientation and Gender Diversity, 3*(2), 165–172.

Erickson, W. A., von Schrader, S., Bruyère, S. M., & VanLooy, S. A. (2014). The employment environment: Employer perspectives, policies, and practices regarding the employment of persons with disabilities. *Rehabilitation Counseling Bulletin, 57*(4), 195–208.

Finamore, P. S., Seifer, D. B., Ananth, C. V., & Leiblum, S. R. (2007). Social concerns of women undergoing infertility treatment. *Fertility and Sterility, 88,* 817–821.

Fisher, C. D., & To, M. L. (2012). Using experience sampling methodology in organizational behavior. *Journal of Organizational Behavior, 33*(7), 865–877.

Forbes, G. B., Adams-Curtis, L. E., White, K. B., & Holmgren, K. M. (2003). The role of hostile and benevolent sexism in women's and men's perceptions of the menstruating woman. *Psychology of Women Quarterly, 27,* 58–63.

Geukes, M., van Aalst, M. P., Robroek, S. J. W., Laven, J. S. E., & Oosterhof, H. (2016). The impact of menopause on work ability in women with severe menopausal symptoms. *Maturitas, 90,* 3–8.

Glebbeek, A. C., & Bax, E. H. (2004). Is high employee turnover really harmful? An empirical test using company records. *Academy of Management Journal, 47,* 277–286.

Goldman, R. H., Kaser, D. J., Missmer, S. A., Farland, L. V., Ashby, R. K., & Ginsburg, E. S. (2017). Fertility treatment for the transgender community: A public opinion study. *Journal of Assisted Reproduction and Genetics, 34*, 1457–1467.

Gordley, L. B., Lemasters, G., Simpson, S. R., & Yiin, J. H. (2000). Menstrual disorders and occupational, stress, and racial factors among military personnel. *Journal of occupational and environmental medicine, 42*(9), 871–881.

Gorton, R. N., & Grubb, H. M. (2014). General, sexual, and reproductive health. In L. Erickson-Schroth (Ed.), Trans bodies, trans selves: A resource for the transgender community (pp. 215–240). New York, NY: Oxford University Press.

Greil, A. L. (1991). *Not yet pregnant: Infertile couples in contemporary America*. New Brunswick, NJ: Rutgers University Press.

Griel, A. L. (1997). Infertility and psychological distress: A critical review of the literature. *Social Science & Medicine, 45*, 1679–1704.

Griel, A. L., McQuillan, J., Lowry, M., & Shreffler, K. M. (2011). Infertility treatment and fertility-specific distress: A longitudinal analysis of a population-based sample of U.S. women. *Social Science & Medicine, 73*, 87–94.

Griel, A., McQuillan, J., & Slauson-Blevins, K. (2011). The social construction of infertility. *Sociology Compass, 5*, 736–746.

Griel, A. L., Slauson-Blevins, K., & McQuillan, J. (2010). The experience of infertility: A review of recent literature. *Sociology of Health and Illness, 32*, 140–162.

Griffeth, R. W., Hom, P. W., & Gaertner, S. (2000). A meta-analysis of antecedents and correlates of employee turnover: Update, moderator tests, and research implications for the next millennium. *Journal of management, 26*(3), 463–488.

Griffiths, A., Ceausu, I., Depypere, H., Lambrinoudaki, I., Mueck, A., Pérez-López, F. R., ... Rees, M. (2016). EMAS recommendations for conditions in the workplace for menopausal women. *Maturitas, 85*, 79–81.

Griffiths, A., MacLennan, S. J., & Hassard, J. (2013). Menopause and work: An electronic survey of employees' attitudes in the UK. *Maturitas, 76*, 155–159.

Gutek, B. A. (1985). *Sex and the workplace*. New York, NY: Jossey-Bass.

Guterman, M., Mehta, P., & Gibbs, M. (2008). Menstrual taboos among major religions. *The Internet Journal of World Health and Societal Politics, 5*(2), 1–7.

Habersham, R. (2017, November 16). Woman settles with employer she says fired her for getting period at work. *The Atlanta Journal-Constitution* [online]: https://www.ajc.com/news/crime--law/woman-settles-with-employer-she-says-fired-her-for-getting-period-work/afsPqA1kEa6mz0erIGMNaO/

Halbreich, U., Borenstein, J., Terry, P., & Kahn, L. S. (2003). The prevalence, impairment, impact, and burden of premenstrual dysphoric disorder (PMS/ PMDD). *Psychoneuroendocrinology, 28*(Supp3), 1–23.

Hammam, R. A., Abbas, R. A., & Hunter, M. S. (2012). Menopause and work–the experience of middle-aged female teaching staff in an Egyptian governmental faculty of medicine. *Maturitas, 71*(3), 294–300.

Hardy, C., & Hardie, J. (2017). Exploring premenstrual dysphoric disorder (PMDD) in the work context: A qualitative study. *Journal of Psychosomatic Obstetrics & Gynecology, 38*(4), 292–300.

Hardy, C., Griffiths, A., & Hunter, M. S. (2017). What do working menopausal women want? A qualitative investigation into women's perspectives on employer and line manager support. *Maturitas, 101*, 37–41.

Hayes, J. (2010). Female infertility in the workplace: Understanding the scope of the Pregnancy Discrimination Act. *Connecticut Law Review, 42*, 1299–1335.

Held, A. (2018, February 15). Arizona department of corrections changes sanitary pad policy following backlash. *NPR* [online]. Retrieved November, 9, 2018, from https://www.npr.org/sections/thetwo-way/2018/02/15/586134335/arizona-department-of-corrections-changes-sanitary-pad-policy-following-backlash

Herman, J. L. (2013). Gendered restrooms and minority stress: The public regulation of gender and its impact on transgender people's lives. *Journal of Public Management & Social Policy, 19*(1), 65.

Hillard, P. A. (2014). Menstrual suppression: Current perspectives. *International Journal of Women's Health, 6*, 631–637.

Hinchliff, S., & Gott, M. (2008). Challenging social myths and stereotypes of women and aging: Heterosexual women talk about sex. *Journal of Women & Aging, 20*(1-2), 65–81.

Hodges, M. J., & Budig, M. J. (2010). Who gets the daddy bonus? Organizational hegemonic masculinity and the impact of fatherhood on earnings. *Gender & Society, 24*(6), 717–745.

Holley, S. R., & Pasch, L. A. (2015). Counseling lesbian, gay, bisexual and transgender patients. In S. N. Covington (Ed.), *Fertility counseling: Clinical guide and case studies* (pp. 180–196). Cambridge, England: Cambridge University Press.

Houppert, K. (1999). *The curse: Confronting the last unmentionable taboo: Menstruation.* New York, NY: Macmillan.

Hull, M. G., Glazener, C. M., Kelly, N. J., Conway, D. I., Foster, P. A., Hinton, R. A., ... & Desai, K. M. (1985). Population study of causes, treatment, and outcome of infertility. *Br Med J (Clin Res Ed), 291*(6510), 1693–1697.

Johnson, K. (2010). Charting infertility in the workplace: An analysis of *Hall v. Nalco* and the Seventh Circuit's recognition of sex discrimination based on in vitro fertilization. *DePaul Law Review, 59*, 1283–1321.

Johnson, K. M. (2012). Excluding lesbian and single women? An analysis of U.S. fertility clinic websites. *Women's Studies International Forum, 35*, 394–402.

Johnston-Robledo, I., & Chrisler, J. C. (2013). The menstrual mark: Menstruation as social stigma. *Sex Roles, 68*(1–2), 9–18.

Jones, A. E. (2004). Managing the pain of primary and secondary dysmenorrhoea. *Nursing Times, 100*(10), 40–43.

Jones, C. E. (2016). The pain of endo existence: Toward a feminist disability studies reading of endometriosis. *Hypatia, 31*(3), 554–571.

Kalinoski, Z. T., Steele-Johnson, D., Peyton, E. J., Leas, K. A., Steinke, J., & Bowling, N. A. (2013). A meta-analytic evaluation of diversity training outcomes. *Journal of Organizational Behavior, 34*, 1076–1104.

Kaur, R., Kaur, K., & Kaur, R. (2018). Menstrual Hygiene, management, and waste disposal: Practices and challenges faced by girls/women of developing countries. *Journal of Environmental and Public Health, 2018*, 1–9.

Keller, E. F. (1985). *Reflections on gender and science*, New Haven, CT, Yale University Press.

King, E. B., & Botsford, W. E. (2009). Managing pregnancy disclosures: Understanding and overcoming the challenges of expectant motherhood at work. *Human Resource Management Review, 19*(4), 314–323.

Kissling, E. A. (1996a). Bleeding out Loud: Communication about menstruation. *Feminism & Psychology, 6*(4), 481–504.

Kissling, E.A. (1996b). "That's just a basic teen-age rule": Girls' linguistic strategies for managing the menstrual communication taboo. *Journal of Applied Communication Research, 24*, 292–309.

Kittell, L. A., Mansfield, P. K., & Voda, A. M. (1998). Keeping up appearances: The basic social process of the menopausal transition. *Qualitative Health Research, 8*(5), 618–633.

Lampman, C., & Dowling, G. S. (1995). Attitudes toward voluntary and involuntary childlessness. *Basic and Applied Social Psychology, 17*, 213–222.

Larimer, S. (2016, January 8). The 'tampon tax,' explained. *The Washington Post* [online]. Retrieved March, 25, 2018, from https://www.washingtonpost.com/news/wonk/wp/2016/01/08/the-tampon-tax-explained/?utm_term=.7b4abea4de7c

László, K. D., Győrffy, Z., Ádám, S., Csoboth, C., & Kopp, M. S. (2008). Work-related stress factors and menstrual pain: A nation-wide representative study. *Journal of Psychosomatic Obstetrics & Gynecology, 29*(2), 133–138.

László, K. D., & Kopp, M. S. (2009). Effort-reward imbalance and overcommitment at work are associated with painful menstruation: Results from the Hungarostudy Epidemiological Panel 2006. *Journal of Occupational and Environmental Medicine, 51*(2), 157–163.

Lee, J. (1994). Menarche and the (hetero)sexualization of the female body. *Gender & Society, 8*(3), 343–362.

Leslie, J. (1991). *Roles and rituals for Hindu women*. Madison, NJ: Fairleigh Dickinson University Press.

Letherby, G. (1999). Other than mother and mothers as others: The experience of motherhood and non-motherhood in relation to 'infertility' and 'involuntary childlessness'. *Women's Studies International Forum, 22*, 359–372.

Lombardi, E. L., Wilchins, R. A., Priesing, D., & Malouf, D. (2002). Gender violence: Transgender experiences with violence and discrimination. *Journal of Homosexuality, 42*(1), 89–101.

Maghen, Z. (1999). Close encounters: some preliminary observations on the transmission of impurity in early Sunnī jurisprudence. *Islamic Law and Society, 6*, 348–392.

Marcus-Newhall, A., Thompson, S., & Thomas, C. (2001). Examining a gender stereotype: Menopausal women. *Journal of Applied Social Psychology, 31*(4), 698–719.

Marsh, S. (2018, June 29). IVF services slashed in England as NSH bosses cut costs. *The Guardian* [online]. Retrieved December, 6, 2018, from https://www.theguardian.com/society/2018/jun/29/ivf-cycles-restricted-england-nhs-advisers-ignored

Marván, M. L., Cortés-Iniestra, S., & González, R. (2005). Beliefs about and attitudes toward menstruation among young and middle-aged Mexicans. *Sex Roles, 53*(3–4), 273–279.

Marván, M. L, Vázquez-Toboada, R., & Chrisler, J. C. (2014). Ambivalent sexism, attitudes towards menstruation and menstrual cycle-related symptoms. *International Journal of Psychology, 49*(4), 280–287.

Marván, M. L., Islas, M., Vela, L., Chrisler, J. C., & Warren, E. A. (2008). Stereotypes of women in different stages of their reproductive life: Data from Mexico and the United States. *Health Care for Women International, 29*, 673–687.

Mascarenhas, M. N., Flaxman, S. R., Boerma, T., Vanderpoel, S., & Stevens, G. A. (2012). National, regional, and global trends in infertility prevalence since 1990: a systematic analysis of 277 health surveys. *PLoS medicine, 9*(12), e1001356.

Mayo Clinic. (2017). Toxic Shock Syndrome. Retrieved from https://www.mayoclinic.org/diseases-conditions/toxic-shock-syndrome/symptoms-causes/syc-20355384

Mayo Clinic. (2018). In Vitro Fertilization. Retrieved December, 6, 2018, from https://www.mayoclinic.org/tests-procedures/in-vitro-fertilization/about/pac-20384716

McCarthy, M. P., & Chiu, S.-H. (2011). Differences in women's psychological well-being based on infertility treatment choice and outcome. *Journal of Midwifery & Women's Health, 56*, 475–480.

McCrea, F. B. (1983). The politics of menopause: The "discovery" of a deficiency disease. *Social Problems, 31*(1), 111–123.

McIntosh, P. (2004). White privilege: Unpacking the invisible knapsack. *Race, Class, and Gender in the United States, 6*, 188–192.

McIntosh, P. (2007). White privilege and male privilege. *Race, Ethnicity and Gender: Selected Readings*, 377–385.

Merskin, D. (1999). Adolescence, advertising, and the ideology of menstruation. *Sex Roles, 40*(11–12), 941–957.

Meyer, J. P., Stanley, D. J., Herscovitch, L., & Topolnytsky, L. (2002). Affective, continuance, and normative commitment to the organization: A meta-analysis of antecedents, correlates, and consequences. *Journal of vocational behavior, 61*(1), 20–52.

Miall, C. E. (1985). Perceptions of informal sanctioning and the stigma of involuntary childlessness. *Deviant Behavior, 6*, 383-403.

Mishell, D.R., Jr. (2005). Premenstrual disorders: Epidemiology and disease burden. *The American Journal of Managed Care, 11*(16), S473–S479.

Murphy, T. F. (2010). The ethics of helping transgender men and women have children. *Perspectives in Biology and Medicine, 53*, 46–60.

National Health Institute. (2017). What is menopause? Retrieved from https://www.nia.nih.gov/health/what-menopause

Neugarten, B. L., & Kraines, R. J. (1965). "Menopausal symptoms" in women of various ages. *Psychosomatic Medicine, 27*(3), 266–273.

Ngabirano, A-M. (2017, March 27). 'Pink Tax' forces women to pay more than men. *USA Today* [online]. Retrieved March, 31, 2019, from https://www.usatoday.

com/story/money/business/2017/03/27/pink-tax-forces-women-pay-more-than-men/99462846/

Nosek, M., Kennedy, H. P., & Gudmundsdottir, M. (2010). Silence, stigma, and shame a postmodern analysis of distress during menopause. *Advances in Nursing Science, 33*(3), E24–E36.

Obedin-Maliver, J., & Makadon, H. J. (2016). Transgender men and pregnancy. *Obstetric Medicine, 9,* 4–8.

Oxley, T. (1998). Menstrual management: An exploratory study. *Feminism & Psychology, 8*(2), 185–191.

Peranovic, T., & Bentley, B. (2017). Men and menstruation: A qualitative exploration of beliefs, attitudes and experiences. *Sex Roles, 77*(1–2), 113–124.

Perz, J. M. (1997). Development of the menopause symptom list: a factor analytic study of menopause associated symptoms. *Women & Health, 25*(1), 53–69.

Planned Parenthood. (2018). Menstruation. Retrieved from https://www.plannedparenthood.org/learn/health-and-wellness/menstruation

Polly, K., & Polly, R. G. (2014). Parenting. In L. Erickson-Schroth (Ed.), *Trans bodies, trans selves: A resource for the transgender community* (pp. 390–405). New York, NY: Oxford University Press.

Quigley, M. (2009). Fired for wanting a child: Why infertility treatment is within the scope of the Pregnancy Discrimination Act. *Michigan State Law Review, 2009,* 755–788.

Rank, N. (2010). Barriers for access to assisted reproductive technologies by lesbian women: the search for parity within the healthcare system. *Houston Journal of Health Law & Policy, 10,* 115-146.

Reynolds, F. (1999) Distress and coping with hot flushes at work: Implications for counsellors in occupational settings, *Counselling Psychology Quarterly, 12*(4), 353–361

Roberts, T.-A., Goldenberg, J. L., Power, C., & Pyszczynski, T. (2002). "Feminine protection": The effects of menstruation on attitudes towards women. *Psychology of Women Quarterly, 26*(2), 131–139.

Rosenbaum, S. (2011). The Patient Protection and Affordable Care Act: Implications for public health policy and practice. *Public Health Reports, 126*(1), 130–135.

Rothenberg, P. S. (2008). *White Privilege.* Macmillan.

Sato, S. (2001). A Little Bit Disabled: Infertility and the Americans with Disabilities Act. *NYU Journal of Legislation & Public Policy, 5,* 189–215.

Slade, P., O'Neill, C., Simpson, A. J., & Lashen, H. (2007). The relationship between perceived stigma, disclosure patterns, support and distress in new attendees at an infertility clinic. *Human Reproduction, 22,* 2309–2317.

Soliman, A. M., Coyne, K. S., Gries, K. S., Castelli-Haley, J., Snabes, M. C., & Surrey, E. S. (2017). The effect of endometriosis symptoms on absenteeism and presenteeism in the workplace and at home. *Journal of Managed Care & Specialty Pharmacy, 23*(7), 745–754.

Sommer, M., Chandraratna, S., Cavill, S., Mahon, T., & Phillips-Howard, P. (2016). Managing menstruation in the workplace: An overlooked issue in low-and middle-income countries. *International Journal for Equity in Health, 15*(1), 86.

Steinberg, J. (1997). From a "pot of filth" to a "hedge of roses" (and back): changing theorizations of menstruation in Judaism. *Journal of Feminist Studies in Religion, 13*, 5–26.

Stotzer, R. L. (2009). Violence against transgender people: A review of United States data. *Aggression and Violent Behavior, 14*(3), 170–179.

Sumpter, C. & Torondel, B. (2013). A systematic review of the health social effects of menstrual hygiene management. *PLOS ONE, 8*(4), 1–15.

Thonneau, P., Marchand, S., Tallec, A., Ferial, M. L., Ducot, B., Lansac, J., ... & Spira, A. (1991). Incidence and main causes of infertility in a resident population (1 850 000) of three French regions (1988–1989). *Human reproduction, 6*(6), 811–816.

Tornello, S. L., & Bos, H. (2017). Parenting intentions among transgender individuals. *LGBT Health, 4*, 115–120.

U.S. Department of Labor. (n.d.). Breaks and meal periods. Retrieved March, 31, 2019, from https://www.dol.gov/general/topic/workhours/breaks

Weller, C. (2017, September 17). What you need to know about egg-freezing, the hot new perk at Google, Apple, and Facebook. *Business Insider* [online]. Retrieved December, 6, 2018, from https://www.businessinsider.com/egg-freezing-at-facebook-apple-google-hot-new-perk-2017-9

Whetzel, M. (n.d.). Is menospause a disability under the ADA? *Job Accommodation Network, 9* [online]. Retrieved December, 6, 2018, from https://askjan.org/publications/consultants-corner/vol09iss01.cfm

Whiteford, L. M., & Gonzalez, L. (1995). Stigma: The hidden burden of infertility. *Social Science & Medicine, 40*, 27–36.

Wierckx, K., Van Caenegem, E., Pennings, G., Elaut, E., Dedecker, D., Van de Peer, F., ..., & T'sjoen, G. (2011). Reproductive wish in transsexual men. *Human Reproduction, 27*, 483–487.

Williams, C. L., Muller, C., & Kilanski, K. (2012). Gendered organizations in the new economy. *Gender & Society, 26*(4), 549–573.

Wirtberg, I., Moller, A., Hogstrom, L., Tronstad, S. E., & Lalos, A. (2007). Life 20 years after unsuccessful infertility treatment. *Human Reproduction, 22*, 598–604.

Wong, W. C., Li, M. K., Chan, W. Y. V., Choi, Y. Y., Fong, C. H. S., Lam, K. W. K., ... Yeung, T. Y. (2013). A cross-sectional study of the beliefs and attitudes towards menstruation of Chinese undergraduate males and females in Hong Kong. *Journal of Clinical Nursing, 22*(23–24), 3320–3327.

CHAPTER 4

UNDERSTANDING INTERSECTIONAL ANALYSES

Rifat Kamasak
Bahçeşehir University

Mustafa F. Ozbilgin
Brunel University

Meltem Yavuz
Istanbul University

All human beings are intersectional. Every individual has a gender, an ethnicity, an age, a class position, a sexual orientation, a belief system, and a disability status, among many other categories of difference. In this chapter we define intersectionality as the unique way that categories of difference such as gender, ethnicity, sexual orientation, and others, overlap and sometimes contradict with each other and ultimately shape an individual or an organization's identity, choices, and chances (e.g., Corrington, Nittrouer, Trump-Steele, & Hebl, 2018; Dennissen, Benschop, & Van den Brink, 2018a; Holvino, 2010, 2012; Ozbilgin, Beauregard, Tatli, & Bell, 2011; Roberson, 2018). Intersectionality is often defined at the individual level as "the interaction between various categories of difference in individual lives, social practices, institutional arrangements, and cultural ideologies and the outcomes of these interactions in terms of power" (Davis, 2008,

Pushing Our Understanding of Diversity in Organizations, pp. 91–113

p. 68). Starting from the 1990s, the use of the intersectional approach has gained momentum in order to analyse the complex interactions of demographic differences and social identities in the fields of social sciences and humanities (Acker, 2006; Baglama, 2018; Belkhir & Ball, 1993; Mueller, 2016). All significant works on intersectionality identify a number of challenges associated with its operationalization, and complexity in exploring the dynamics and consequences of intersectionality (e.g., Crenshaw, 1991; Kabeer, 2010; Kelan, 2014; King, Mohr, Peddie, Jones, & Kendra, 2017; Mik-Meyer, 2015; Okazawa-Rey, 2017; Wijeyesinghe & Jones, 2014). In this chapter, we focus on three distinct challenges facing intersectional analyses: notably the challenge of its individual focus, the challenge of operationalization and the challenge of essentialism in categories of difference.

One of the main reasons for conducting intersectional analyses is that considering multiple categories of difference allows analyses of social reality closer to achieve veracity (Healy et al., 2018; Holvino, 2010; McCall, 2005). In her well-regarded work, Acker (2006, 2011) explored the identity categories that individuals possessed and noticed that interaction of different identity categories of difference and diversity, particularly gender, ethnicity and class, complicated the life experiences and struggles of individuals. Similarly, Holvino (2010), who accounts for the possession of multiple identities, suggests that experiences of a White woman can be different than that of a Black woman who works in the same male dominated work environment. Thus, the significance of the variance between patterns of life experiences that were created by one identity category alone (i.e., gender) and the interaction of different identity categories (i.e., gender and race) led theorists and practitioners to examine the intersections of several categories for a better understanding of inequalities and multiple forms of discrimination (Taylor, 2009; Winker & Degele, 2011; Ulus, 2018). The addition of each unique and embedded identity category sheds light to new blind spots in the phenomena being investigated. Indeed, the popularity of intersectional analysis emerges from its ability to address the blind spots generated by the embedded and intertwined identity categories in diversity studies (Mahalingam, 2007; Ozbilgin et al., 2011; Walby, Armstrong, & Strid, 2012). Therefore, the intersectional approach is "well situated [in diversity area] and opened up a robust and meaningful way forward for the future research in the field" (Ozbilgin et al., 2011, p. 186). Despite its well charted and now mature territory intersectional analyses continues to face the three challenges we listed.

Predictions on the future of workforce diversity suggests that number of people from atypical backgrounds will become more common in workplaces and in leadership positions of the 21st century (Alcázar, Fernández, & Gardey, 2013; Roberson & Park, 2007; Shore et al., 2011). Futurology in the field of workplace demography predicts that diversity and intersectionality will gain further significance in shaping management and leadership decisions into the future (Triandis, 2003). Resultantly, there is growing awareness that intersectional analysis, if taken up effectively by corporate leaders, may help organizations to future proof and capture the predicted rise of diversity and intersectionality and implement significant changes in how they manage workforce diversity (Moorosi, 2014). In fact, business and management scholars are not alone in focusing on intersectionality. Intersectional approach has been used broadly in social sciences from law and politics to sociology, behavioral sciences, and psychology because of the promise and challenges it brings to wide domains of social research (Christensen & Jensen, 2012; Gamson & Moon, 2004; Goff, Thomas, & Jackson, 2008; Shields, 2008). Building on Hancock's (2007) suggestions about intersectional approach as a useful research paradigm rather than a simple normative-theoretical argument, Dhamoon (2011) states that "intersectionality can be applied to populations beyond those with inter-secting marginalised identities" (p. 230).

Although intersectional study is becoming commonplace across sub-disciplines of social sciences and humanities, intersectional analyses faces a number of challenges (Kerner, 2012; Marfelt, 2016; Tatli & Ozbilgin, 2012b). In this chapter, we address the three challenges facing intersectional analyses. First, the challenge of individualization, Second the challenge of operationalization. Third, the challenge of essentialism. We address these three challenges by offering three distinct solutions: First, we offer intersec-tional encounters as theoretical expansion, and explicate the encounter of individual and institutional intersections through the concepts of intersec-tional hostility and intersectional solidarity. Second, we examine the range of approaches that are used to engage in intersectional analyses focusing on studies of categories of difference that are covered, exploring cumula-tive versus idiosyncratic treatment of intersections. We offer relational and multilevel perspective as a way to free intersectional analyses from single level studies and objective-subjective divide in its current formulations. Third, we note that intersectional analyses is often essentialized as the categories differences are considered fixed and static, despite context and history. Falling into the trap of essentialism, we witness the instrumental-ization of supposedly essential differences and their intersections in the extant literature. In order to counteract the essentialist tendency in inter-sectional analysis, we introduce the concept of synchronicity and explore the dynamic emergence of new categories or intersectionality and explore the possibility of framing intersectionality as the energy in unplanned and acausal forms of intersectional encounters and togetherness. To capture such emergence, we allude to emic intersections and explore their utility in intersectional analyses. In the Table 4.1 we summarize the conceptual universe of this chapter in terms of key definition and examples.

Table 4.1.
Key Concepts, Definitions and Examples in Intersectional Analysis

Concept	Definition	Example
Intersectionality	Intersectionality is the unique way that categories of difference such as gender ethnicity, sexual orientation and others, overlap and sometimes contradict with each other and ultimately shape an individual or an organisations' identity, choices and chances.	An organizational culture with a male dominated and heteronormative intersectionality would make it very difficult for a lesbian woman to come out and experience authenticity at work.
Individual intersections	The interactions of different sociodemographic categories which shape positive or negative life experiences of an individual in different contexts.	"Pale, male, stale" is a colloquial expression which refers to the privileged intersections that White, conservative men enjoy in positions to power and influence in English speaking countries.
Institutional intersections	The taken for granted institutional practices, processes, norms and structures that can perpetuate inequalities.	In universities with middle class ethos which are White dominated, a White student from a low income family may still face difficulties in terms of entry and attainment.
Macro contextual intersections	Societal practices, ideologies, structures, and norms related to local or global culture that legitimate inequality regimes.	A gay man may be prosecuted and persecuted in a country where religious structure and laws are homophobic, when being a man is afforded privileges.
Intersectional solidarity	The emerging situation where intersectional identities of individuals were complemented and supported by institutional practices.	A female worker with disabilities could experience solidarity with colleagues in a gender egalitarian and disability friendly workplace.
Intersectional hostility	The emerging situation where intersectional identities of individuals conflicted with institutional practices and a tension was created.	A gay refugee may experience intersectional hostility in a homophobic and racist community.

(Table continues on next page)

Table 4.1.

Key Concepts, Definitions and Examples in Intersectional Analysis (Continued)

Concept	Definition	Example
Relational and multilevel intersectionality	Intersectional analysis which takes into account the interplay between categories at macro-societal (ie. sociocultural norms), meso-organizational (ie. work practices in organizations) and micro-individual (ie. multiple identities of individuals) levels.	Understanding a White, working class women's experience in a middle class White male dominated organization requires us to understand the specific context. This experience would not be the same in two different teams, two different sectors or two different countries such as Britain and the United States because of the differences in history of gender, ethnic and class relations at these micro, meso and macro levels.
Cumulative intersections	A method adding categories of disadvantage in a summative fashion in order to understand multiple forms of disadvantage.	Black women experience both gender and ethnic discrimination which has a cumulative impact.
Idiosyncratic intersections	A method of considering each intersectional inequalities as unique rather than cumulative.	Chinese women have higher economic activity rates than White men in the United Kingdom. This presents a surprising contrast to cumulative effects that one would expect.
Synchronicity	Energy in or utility of acausal togetherness between people which involves cognitive and behavioral alignment.	Individuals may sometimes benefit from alignment or "in sync" with others in interpersonal relationships even when this is not intended.
Etic intersections	Etic intersections are categories of difference that are covered by empirical studies of diversity. These typically include gender, ethnicity, age, sexual orientation, class, disability, among others.	Gender, ethnicity and class are the most typical categories of difference that are covered as etic intersections.
Emic intersections	Emic intersections are salient categories of difference that emerge from the local setting and that have not been covered by previous studies.	Passport holders versus others and tribal ties are two emic categories of intersection which is not typically covered in studies of intersectionality but emerge as salient in some contexts.

TRANSCENDING THE CHALLENGE OF INDIVIDUALIZATION OF INTERSECTIONALITY: INTERSECTIONAL ENCOUNTERS BETWEEN INDIVIDUAL AND INSTITUTIONAL INTERSECTIONS

There is a tendency in intersectional analyses to focus on individual intersections. Intersections do not only reside in individuals but also in institutions (Campbell, 2016; Tatli & Ozbilgin, 2012a; Tatli, Ozturk, & Woo, 2017). Individual intersections are studied well in the diversity management literature. These studies (e.g., Atewologun & Sealy, 2014; Finkelstein, Ryan, & King, 2013; Kaplan, Sabin, & Smaller-Swift, 2009; Ozturk & Tatli, 2016; West & Fenstermaker, 1995; Wright, 2016) are generally grounded on sociodemographic categories of difference and the interactions of these differences (i.e., gender, class, race, sexual orientation, age, occupational status, education, religion, disability, ethnicity) which shape positive or negative life experiences of an individual in different contexts. The contribution of the studies based on individual level of analysis is undeniable as individual level intersectional analysis is foundational if we need to understand how social identity and life choices operate.

Beyond individual intersections, organizations, and institutions have also intersections, that is, they have processes, structures, routines, and functions that generate intersectional impact as they favor some individual intersections and discourage others (Omanović, 2009; Roberson, 2013). For example, it is well documented that historically institutions of work privilege White, able bodied, middle class, heterosexual men, and disadvantage others who do not fit the norm. As such an institution can be gendered, ethicized, racialized, sexualized, and classed (Tatli et al., 2017). Similarly, macro national and sectoral contexts offer climates, cultures, regulatory structures that privilege or disadvantage certain intersections in individuals (Barron & Hebl, 2010; Bowleg, 2012).Thus, individual experiences are intersectional in nature and intersectional experience permeates everything that individuals do at work and in domains outside work. Similarly, individual, institutional and macro level intersections do interplay and generate interesting outcomes for individuals.

Intersectionality is a social and relational phenomenon which is inherent in practices, structures, processes and norms in various institutional contexts such as family, society, school, employment, law, and politics (Syed & Ozbilgin, 2009; Tatli, 2011). Institutional intersections might result in differentiated outcomes for individuals with different identities, thus intersectional analyses which ignore the interaction of individual intersections and institutional intersections may fail to adequately represent life courses of people. In parallel, Castro and Holvino (2016) who highlight the necessity of looking at the intersections of individuals and institutions to capture the complex reality, defines intersectionality as "a way of thinking that understands [individual] categories of social difference as interlocking and mutually constitutive at the micro level of individual experience and at the macro level of institutional and societal structures and cultural ideologies" (p. 329).

A number of studies (i.e., Healy, Bradley, & Forson, 2011; Khattab & Modood, 2018; Muhr & Sløk-Andersen, 2017; Tatli & Ozbilgin, 2012b; Tatli et al., 2017; Wright, 2013, 2016; Zanoni & Janssens, 2007) that examine the real life experiences of individuals through intersections both at the individual and institutional levels has increased in the literature. For example, Healy et al. (2011) conducted an empirical intersectional study on 152 Bangladeshi, Caribbean, and Pakistani women working in the public sector to explore life experiences of women with ethnic origins. Healy and her colleagues take ethnicity, gender and religion as individuals' identities on board in combination with interrelated practices, structures, policies, processes, actions, and meanings of institutions (Acker, 2006) to explore how they interact to shape the multiple dimensions of women and result in, reproduce and maintain inequalities. They found several institutional processes such as promotion and workplace interaction which intersect with individual identity categories and produce inequalities.

Similarly, the study by Castro and Holvino (2016) explored the intersections of gender, class, and racio-ethnicity at the individual level and how they interacted with the institutional structures in specific sociocultural contexts. The study which included 37 managers and staff members from professional service firms in Mexico revealed that when individual identity categories intersected with the institutional structures and cultural scripts of the sociocultural context, different types of inequalities other than those created by merely individual level constructs were produced. Shifting from a single dimensional analysis to a multidimensional analysis did not only yield differentiated outcomes of inequalities that were shaped by institutional intersections, but it also broadened the horizons of researchers to better understand intersectional phenomena in unique socioeconomic contexts (Ozeren & Aydin, 2016; Ozturk & Ozbilgin, 2015).

At the point when an individual encounters an institution, what we call an intersectional encounter takes place (King & Cortina, 2010; Rodriguez, Holvino, Fletcher, & Nkomo, 2016; Tatli & Ozbilgin, 2012b). A gendered, ethicized, and sexualized institution reacts to the particular intersections of an individual. The result would present a duality or a paradox in an intersectional encounter: intersectional hostility may occur if the individual intersections collide with institutional intersections. For example, a lesbian woman may experience intersectional hostility in a homophobic and/or sexist workplace. When there is complementarity between intersections, there could be intersectional solidarity. For example, a Black woman could experience solidarity with colleagues in a gender and ethnicity inclusive institution. Figure 4.1 outlines our proposed vision of intersectional analyses, which moves it from its individual level exploration and exposes the possibilities of institutional intersections and intersectional encounters which can yield both hostility and solidarity. We envisage that inclusive workplace practices are about addressing institutional intersections by making workplaces more inclusive so that the intersectional encounters can move from intersectional hostility to intersectional solidarity.

TRANSCENDING THE CHALLENGE OF OPERATIONALIZATION: METHODOLOGICAL EXPANSION AND RELATIONAL STUDY OF INTERSECTIONS

Studies of intersectionality have evolved from the field of law (Crenshaw, 1991). Intersectional analysis is widely adopted as a way to analyse disadvantage (Eveline, Bacchi, & Binns, 2009; Tatli et al., 2017) and more recently privilege (Atewologun & Sealy, 2014; Janssens & Zanoni, 2014; Tatli & Ozbilgin, 2012b) at the intersections of social and economic backgrounds of individuals. Intersectional is widely studied with individual level data (i.e., Farough, 2006; Knapp, 2005; Kuriloff & Reichert, 2003) and more recently it is used to explore institutional level intersections (Campbell, 2016; Castro & Holvino, 2016; Dennissen, Benschop, & Van den Brink, 2018b; Ozturk & Tatli, 2016). Since intersectionality "serves as one such multidimensional conceptualization of diversity" (Marfelt, 2010, p. 32), unique research approaches utilizing multidimensional conceptualizations of diversity are needed (Ozbilgin et al., 2011; Roberson, 2013). In exploring intersections, individual level cross-sectional data (i.e., Knapp, 2005; Wright, 2013) is frequently collected. The institutional level data often took the form of meso level data examining work processes and outcomes measures (Acker, 2006). The field of intersectional analyses suffers from operationalization. Many of the constructs and categories of difference do not travel internationally (Tatli et al., 2017).

There are two common treatment of intersectional disadvantage and privilege. The most common approach is the cumulative approach which is underpinned by the assumption that multiple categories of disadvantage add up in a cumulative fashion and lead to greater disadvantage than single category of disadvantage. For example, the work of Woodhams, Lupton, and Cowling (2015) shows the cumulative disadvantage in pay by gender, ethnicity and other criteria. The second approach to intersectionality is idiosyncratic. Idiosyncratic intersectionality refers to an approach which is underpinned by the fact that each intersection is unique and

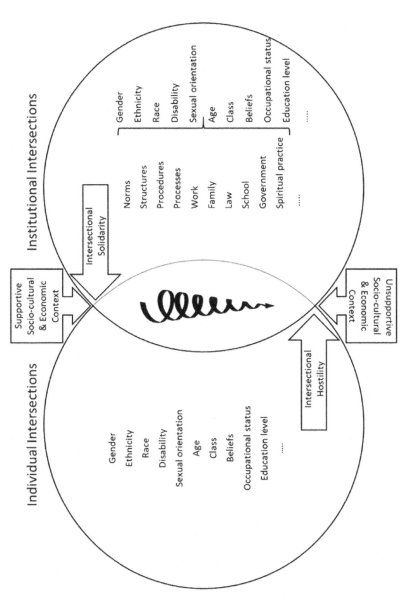

Figure 4.1. Individual and institutional intersections: moving from intersectional hostility to intersectional solidarity

sometimes intersections of multiple disadvantage do not lead to cumulative but unique and surprising outcomes (Tatli & Ozbilgin, 2012b).

In fact, these two approaches call support for the intersectional designs that use multilevel data (Winker & Degele, 2011) such as individual, institutional, and sectoral or national and more grounded ways of intersectional analysis (Marfelt, 2010; Metcalfe & Woodhams, 2012). In line with these propositions, for example, Tatli and Ozbilgin (2012b) carried out an intersectional research on the arts and cultural sector in the United Kingdom. The study explored intersectional encounters between individuals and institutions at the sectoral level, identifying idiosyncratic rather than cumulative disadvantage in the creative and cultural industry. Atewologun and Mahalingam (2018) call for reflexivity in studies of intersectionality as cumulative approaches to intersectionality underplay the unique nature of each intersection.

In order to transcend the challenge of operationalization, we suggest the use of relational and multilevel approach to intersectionality. Relational approach dates back to the relational semiotics work of Ferdinand de Saussure (1983) and explains any concepts has meaning only in its specific multilevel context and in relation to other concepts and the field of relations in which it is embedded. Relationality is widely used as a way to study organisations (Kyriakidou & Ozbilgin, 2006; Ozbilgin & Vassilopoulou, 2018; Hennekam, Tahssain-Gay, & Syed, 2017).

Relational approach could help the field of intersectionality overcome its challenge of operationalization in two distinct ways. There is a tendency to explore intersectionality at the micro-individual level as explored in the earlier section. Yet, this leaves the intersectional analyses anemic in terms of its relational context, the meaning it has it its specific setting, for example, the meaning of intersectional experience for a specific team, in a unique organization with a particular ethos or in different national or cultural settings with historical differences. Relational analyses of intersectionality offers a multilevel approach to intersectionality in which intersectional experience can be studied and practiced at the micro-individual, meso-institutional and macro-national levels. As such, bringing the historicity and context specificity, intersectional analyses could be embedded and given more robust meaning in a specific context. Using relational approach and its multilevel, contextually enriched take, intersectional analyses can provide depth and meaning to the variance of chances and choices in intersectional analyses (Ozbilgin & Vassilopoulou, 2018; Syed, Ali, & Hennekam, 2018). The challenge of operationalisation therefore is the challenge of contextualisation through relational and multilevel approaches to an extent. If the intersectional analyses could be contextualized in its particular context, it needs to be operationalized in a way which captures the context each time.

Second, and more importantly, operationalization of intersectionality presents a challenge because often intersectionality is considered a property of the individual. It is however, as we illustrated a property of meso-level institutions and macro-level national and cultural qualities. Therefore, operationalization becomes challenging if only individual intersections were targeted through change interventions. Use of multilevel relational approach expands the focus of responsibility for change from individual awareness raising to institutional and national change interventions that target how institutions and countries operate, how they are perceived in relation to intersections of difference and what they could do to accommodate intersecting differences and combat intersecting inequalities. Figure 4.2 outlines how intersectional encounters can be viewed from the perspective of multilevel relationality.

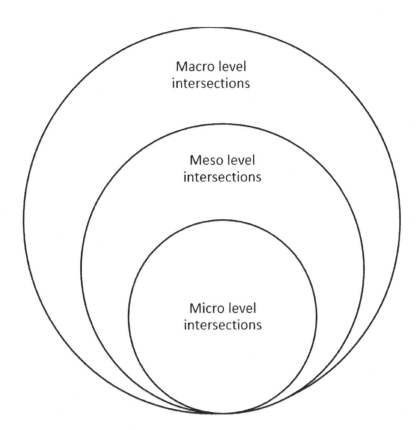

Figure 4.2.   Relational multilevel framework for intersectional encounters and intersectional analysis.

THE CHALLENGE OF ESSENTIALISM IN INTERSECTIONS: INTERSECTIONAL SYNCHRONICITY AND EMIC INTERSECTIONS

The intersectional approach has been criticized in terms of being too static and following a heavy structuralist approach that might hinder emergence of new directions for the phenomena under investigation. A number of researchers (i.e., Boogaard & Roggeband, 2010; Carastathis, 2016; Lykke, 2010; McCall, 2005; Staunaes & Søndegaard, 2011) suggest that the intersectional approach should rely less on a methodological enquiry where identities are fixed. Lykke (2010) expresses this situation through a traffic jam metaphor which compared intersectionality "to the roads (as opposed to the traffic) that meet at an intersection, but ... go in separate directions before and after this meeting" (p. 73). Similarly, Staunaes and Søndegaard (2011) bring the question into minds that "one can inquire whether the intersection takes place between entities that are already fixed? Or is it the place that creates the entities?" (p. 53).

An intersectional approach uses the categories of difference which it hopes to dissolve in an ideal world. Categories, that is, gender, ethnicity, class, sexual orientation should not form the basis of discrimination and exclusion at work. Yet they do. One challenge that faces intersectional analyses is that it tackles categories of difference that it aims to dissolve and by doing so it runs the risk of essentializing these categories (McCall, 2005; Prasad, 2012; Walby et al., 2012). Essentialism is a way of treating a demographic difference, such as gender, ethnicity, race, class, or sexual orientation, as unchanging and fixed (Marfelt, 2016; Richardson, 2007). It is a trap that some social science research fall by identifying traits and connecting these traits with categories of people (McCall, 2005; Ozbilgin & Tatli, 2012b; Prasad, 2012). For example, some of the studies which explain the unique contribution of women, minority ethnic groups and LGBTI+ individuals, without recognizing that women, minority ethnic groups and LGBTI+ individuals are not monolithic and homogenous groups, fall into this trap. It is important to recognize that there is dynamism and heterogeneity among these groups, and not only across these groups. Essentialism presents a divisive perspective which does not consider the possibility of complementarity among different identity groups (Miles & Torres, 2007; Prasad, 2012; Verkuyten & Brug, 2004). In order to counteract the essentialist tendency in intersectional analyses we propose synchronicity, a dynamic concept which does not perceive categories of difference as fixed and sees possibilities of coexistence in juxtapositions or difference.

Synchronicity is a concept introduced by Karl Jung (1944/2010) who defined it as energy in acausal togetherness. For intersectionality, synchronicity has a number of benefits. First, the challenge of essentialism in intersectional analyses means that categories of differences are considered fixed. As such some literature on intersectionality may search for ways to fix or to garner utility from such fixed set of differences. Remarkable example of such an essentialist approach would be the treatment of migrant women in the literature which either proposes ways of integration or examine the utility and the business case for migrant women. If we take a synchronicity approach however we do not attempt at identifying a business case for but argue for the existence of a fundamental and inalienable utility in togetherness and coexistence of people (Cambray & Rosen, 2009). Acausal coexistence which is inherent in synchronicity (Aziz, 1990; Roehlke, 1988) combats the essentialist tendency of intersectional analyses that forces it garner evidence for business benefits of multiple forms of diversity which causes precarity for intersectional interventions as the business case arguments merely work for some categories under certain conditions and at certain times. The planned and essentializing properties of intersectional analyses makes it vulnerable and precarious when diversity and inclusion are contested by business rationales and when intersectional encounters cannot be planned.

In contemporary framing of intersectionality, categories of differences are considered together often as juxtapositions (Cole, 2009; Fine & Burns, 2003). The assumption in such a framing is one of conflict or cumulative cases of oppression (Marfelt, 2016; Yuval-Davis, 2011). Synchronicity can help us move from the potential conflict between categories to seeing possibilities of complementarity, moving from intersectional hostility to intersectional solidarity (Cambray, 2019). Seeing possibilities of complementarity and solidarity between categories of difference rather than focusing on hostility can free up the potential benefits envisaged in synchronicity.

With synchronicity, what becomes important is the emergence of intersectional categories of difference (Cambray, 2004; Tatli & Ozbilgin, 2012a). Such emergence of salient categories that do not subscribe to fixed and settled categories of difference is treated under different themes. For example, the notion of emic intersections makes it possible to examine and analyze beyond those categories of difference which are covered by the extant literature.

One obvious case where synchronicity and emic approach becomes relevant is the case of intersectionality of refugees and displaced individuals at work. Most categories of intersectionality are well planned. For example, there is myriad of literature on intersection of gender and ethnicity. Thus, institutional interventions can be crafted in a planned fashion on these categories. Unprecedented patterns of migration internationally renders intersections which involve refugees and displaced individuals particularly challenging in terms of planning. Synchronicity approach allows rooms for unplanned togetherness and combats the kneejerk, ill thought, often deregatory, and dehumanizing treatment of emergent forms of intersectionality such as in the case of refugees, by welcoming such acausal coexistence as a sources of energy and as helpful, and beneficial (Atmanspacher & Fach, 2016; Fach, 2014).

In terms of their fit with current structures of work and professions, displaced individuals and refugees are often treated as dirt in the well-oiled machinery of modern societies as they fail to fit in with routines, systems and structures in their new host environments (Brotman & Lee, 2011; Lee & Brotman, 2013; Mahalingam, Balan, & Haritatos, 2008; Pöge, Strasser, & Rommel, 2018). Because refugees are perceived as a threat to the well-planned work and social institutions (Bredström, 2003; Knappert, Kornau, & Figengül, 2018; Qvist, 2017). In fact, it is increasingly inconceivable in modern daily lives to allow room for acausal togetherness. There are many social and economic benefits to efficient and effective integration of refugees and displaced individuals (Hesse, Kreutzer, & Diehl, 2018; Zhou, 2000). Synchronicity as a concept frames such possibilities of garnering energy and benefits from chance and acausal togetherness (Bright, 1997; Main, 2006; Yiassemides, 2011) such as collaboration, teamwork and other forms of coexistence for refugees and settled workers (Butcher, 2011; Laskowski, 2018). Welcoming approach of synchronicity allows for individuals whose intersections clash with the systems and structures to engage and to seek legitimate coexistence, without being dehumanised. Such engagement is only possible with active listening of their demands and integration of their differences to codesign of processes and systems. If the unplanned others are allowed to contribute, the system will not perceive them as a threat and sustain a relationship of togetherness with the unplanned others. Therefore, synchronicity presents an opportunity for togetherness without a cause in advanced societies which have come to resist change and unplanned outsiders.

CONCLUSION

Intersectional analyses are taking root in social sciences with significant impact on social policies such as human rights, equality, welfare, and integration and corporate policy on management of diversity. Yet intersectional analysis is experiencing a number of challenges. In this chapter, we examined three significant challenges facing intersectional analyses in the field of diversity management and offer three corresponding solutions in order to transcend these challenges.

We first debated where intersections reside, locating the intersectional analysis at the individual micro level in the mainstream literature, following the original theorisation by Crenshaw. We explicated that intersectionality does not only exist at the micro individual level but manifests also at meso institutional and macro societal levels. At the meso level, institutions have their own intersections in line with Acker's theorization. At the macro level, there is the broad national and international context in which large number of actors such as social movements, governments, trade unions and employers among others in the field of diversity and equality play roles in setting the regulatory context of intersecting categories of difference.

Reflecting on the consequences of locating intersectional analyses at the individual level, we discussed the possibility of locating intersections in systems, institutions, and structures and in encounters between individuals and institutions. Moving from individual to systemic treatment of intersections, the chapter introduced four concepts: institutional intersections, intersectional hostility, intersectional solidarity, and intersectional encounters. We illustrated the ways to transcend individualism of intersectionality with Figure 4.1 that outlines our conceptual universe and noted that institutions need to change in order to move from intersectional hostility towards experiences of intersectional solidarity at their intersectional encounters with individuals.

Intersectional analyses suffer from the problem of operationalization. There are many applications of intersectional analyses. Yet, there is not an agreed way or a consensus in terms of data, methods, and frames. Yet, there are some complexities around difficulties in data collection and identification of appropriate measures that can transcend a variety of differences. In order to overcome difficulties of operationalization, we discussed intersectional analyses and levels of data collection that combine cumulative and idiosyncratic outcomes. We also introduced the relational ontology which can help intersectionality scholars connect their intersectional analysis and approach to the specific requirements of the macro context, meso institutional arrangements and micro level identities. We note that intersections emerge and gain meaning at the interface of these three levels. Developing robust ways to analyze intersections should start with an appreciation of the context or the relational web of meanings that shape what intersectionality means in any specific locality. In doing so, the chapter connected workforce diversity with social movements and highlighted how problems often associated with operationalizing intersections may be overcome by taking a relational approach to intersectionality.

Intersectional analysis is also critiqued for essentializing difference, as it may fall into the trap of fixing categories of difference and failing to consider possibilities of complementarity and togetherness across fault lines. We propose synchronicity as a way to move the debate on intersectionality forward. Synchronicity is similar notion to emic approach to diversity as it allows for reading the locally salient categories of difference and seek possibilities of utility in coexistence of differences.

There are many practical and policy implications of this chapter. Primarily, in diversity management, we can increase personal awareness and competence for dealing with individual intersections. Yet, organizations do have a responsibility in transforming their own intersections so that they can move from intersectional hostility towards solidarity in their intersectional encounters with individuals. Intersectional analyses cannot be performed on the individual level alone. Intersectional analyses can inform organizational efforts and interventions to change. Yet institutional practices, processes and outcomes can change so could the intersectional inequalities that are entrenched within those intersections. Therefore, policy efforts should not simply focus on training and education but also organizational design and change.

Human capital approaches, with the underpinning assumption that individuals will achieve equality if they have equal amount of human capital, have been the dominant paradigms for organizational change interventions, which leads them to focus on training and education rather than change of systems and structures of work. Yet it is insufficient to change people through training and education alone. Systems, structures and processes should change as they lead to differential outcomes across intersectional lines. Similarly, at the macro level there is a role for national governments, social movements and international agencies to regulate better the intersections inherent in cultures and laws that govern chances and choices of workers.

REFERENCES

Acker, J. (2006). Inequality regimes: gender, class, and race in organizations. *Gender & Society, 20*, 441–464.

Acker, J. (2011). Theorizing gender, race, and class in organizations. In Jeanes, E., Knights, D., & Martin, P. Y. (Eds.) *Handbook of gender, work and organization* (pp. 65–80). Chichester, England: Wiley.

Alcázar, M., F., Fernández, M. R. P., & Sánchez Gardey, G. (2013). Workforce diversity in strategic human resource management models: A critical review of the literature and implications for future research. *Cross Cultural Management: An International Journal, 20*(1), 39–49.

Atewologun, D., & Mahalingam, R. (2018). Intersectional reflexivity: Methodological challenges and possibilities for qualitative equality, diversity, and inclusion research. In R. Bendl, L. Booysen, & J. Pringle (Eds.), *Handbook of research methods on diversity management, equality, and inclusion at work*. Cheltenham, England: Edward Elgar.

Atewologun, D., & Sealy, R. (2014). Experiencing privilege at ethnic, gender and senior intersections. *Journal of Managerial Psychology, 29*, 423–439.

Atmanspacher, H., & Fach, W. (2016). Synchronistic mind-matter correlations in therapeutic practice: A commentary on Connolly (2015). *Journal of Analytical Psychology, 61*(1), 79–85.

Aziz, R. C. G. (1990). *Jung's Psychology of Religion and Synchronicity*. New York, NY: State University of New York Press.

Baglama, S. H. (2018). *The resurrection of the spectre: A Marxist analysis of race, class and alienation in the post-war British novel*. Berlin, Germany: Peter Lang.

Barron, L. G., & Hebl, M. (2010). Reducing "acceptable" stigmatization through legislation. *Social Issues and Policy Review, 4*(1), 1–30.

Belkhir, J. G., & Ball, M. (1993). Integrating race, sex and class in our disciplines. *Race, Sex and Class, 1*, 3–11.

Boogaard, B., & Roggeband, C. (2010). Paradoxes of intersectionality: Theorizing inequality in the Dutch police force through structure and agency. *Organization, 17*(1), 53–75.

Bowleg, L. (2012). The problem with the phrase women and minorities: Intersectionality—an important theoretical framework for public health. *American Journal of Public Health, 102*(7), 1267–1273.

Bredström, A. (2003). Gendered racism and the production of cultural difference: Media representations and identity work among" immigrant youth" in contemporary Sweden. *Nora: Nordic Journal of Women's Studies, 11*(2), 78–88.

Bright, G. (1997). Synchronicity as a basis for analytical attitude. *Journal of Analytical Psychology, 42*(4), 613–635.

Brotman, S., & Lee, E. (2011). Exploring gender and sexuality through the lens of intersectionality: Sexual minority refugees in Canada. *Canadian Social Work Review, 28*(1), 151–156.

Butcher, M. (2011). *Managing cultural change*. London, England: Routledge.

Cambray, J. (2004). Synchronicity as emergence. In *Analytical Psychology* (pp. 235–260). London, England: Routledge.

Cambray, J. (2019). Enlightenment and individuation: Syncretism, synchronicity and beyond. *Journal of Analytical Psychology, 64*(1), 53–72.

Cambray, J., & Rosen, D. H. (2009). Empathy and the analytic field. In *Synchronicity: Nature and Psyche in an Interconnected Universe* (pp. 68–88). College Station, TX: Texas A&M University Press.

Campbell, R. (2016). "It's the way that you do it:" Developing an ethical framework for community psychology. *American Journal of Community Psychology, 58*, 294–302.

Carastathis, A. (2016). *Intersectionality: Origins, contestations, horizons*. Lincoln, NE: University of Nebraska Press.

Castro, M. R., & Holvino, E. (2016). Applying intersectionality in organizations: Inequality markers, cultural scripts and advancement practices in a professional service firm. *Gender, Work and Organization, 23*, 328–347.

Christensen, A. D., & Jensen, S. Q. (2012). Doing intersectional analysis: Methodological implications for qualitative research. *NORA-Nordic Journal of Feminist and Gender Research, 20*(2), 109–125.

Cole, E. R. (2009). Intersectionality and research in psychology. *American Psychologist*, *64*, 170–180.

Corrington, A., Nittrouer, C. L., Trump-Steele, R. C. E., & Hebl, M. (2018). Letting him B: A study on the intersection of gender and sexual orientation in the workplace. *Journal of Vocational Behaviour*. https://doi.org/10.1016/j.jvb.2018.10.005

Crenshaw, K. (1991). Mapping the margins: Intersectionality, identity politics and violence against women of color. *Stanford Law Review*, *43*, 1241–1299.

Davis, K. (2008). Intersectionality as buzzword: A sociology of science perspective on what makes a feminist theory successful. *Feminist Theory*, *9*, 67–85.

Dennissen, M., Benschop, Y., & Van den Brink, M. (2018a). Rethinking diversity management: An intersectional analysis of diversity networks. *Organization Studies*, doi:10.1177/0170840618800103.

Dennissen, M., Benschop, Y., & Van den Brink, M. (2018b). Diversity networks: Networking for equality? *British Journal of Management*. doi:10.1111/1467-8551.12321.

Dhamoon, R. K. (2011). Considerations on mainstreaming intersectionality. *Political Research Quarterly*, *64*(1), 230–243.

Eveline, J., Bacchi, C., & Binns, J. (2009). Gender mainstreaming versus diversity mainstreaming: Methodology as emancipatory politics. *Gender, Work and Organization*, *16*, 198–216.

Fach, W. (2014). Complementary aspects of mind-matter correlations in exceptional human experiences. In H. Atmanspacher & C. Fuchs (Eds.), *The Pauli-jung conjecture and its impact today*. Exeter, England: Imprint Academic.

Farough, S. D. (2006). Believing is seeing: The matrix of vision and White masculinities. *Journal of Contemporary Ethnography*, *35*, 51–83.

Fine, M., & Burns, A. (2003). Class notes: Toward a critical psychology of class and schooling. *Journal of Social Issues*, *59*(4), 841–860.

Finkelstein, L. M., Ryan, K. M., & King, E. B. (2013). What do the young (old) people think of me? Content and accuracy of age-based metastereotypes. *European Journal of Work and Organizational Psychology*, *22*(6), 633–657.

Gamson, J., & Moon, D. (2004). The sociology of sexualities: Queer and beyond. *Annual Review of Sociology*, *30*, 47–64.

Goff, P. A., Thomas, M. A., & Jackson, M. C. (2008). "Ain't I a woman?": Towards an intersectional approach to person perception and group-based harms. *Sex Roles*, *59*(5–6), 392–403.

Hancock, A.-M. (2007). When multiplication doesn't equal quick addition: Examining intersectionality as a research paradigm. *Perspectives on Politics*, *5*(1), 63–79.

Healy, G., Bradley, H., & Forson, C. (2011). Intersectional sensibilities in analysing inequality regimes in public sector organizations. *Gender, Work and Organization*, *18*, 467–487.

Healy, G., Tatli, A., Ipek, G., Ozturk, M., Seierstad, C., & Wright, T. (2018). In the steps of Joan Acker: A journey in researching inequality regimes and intersectional inequalities. *Gender, Work and Organization*, *Special Issue*, 1–15.

Hennekam, S., Tahssain-Gay, L., & Syed, J. (2017). Contextualising diversity management in the Middle East and North Africa: A relational perspective. *Human Resource Management Journal, 27*(3), 459–476.

Hesse, A., Kreutzer, K., & Diehl, M. R. (2018). Dynamics of institutional logics in a cross-sector social partnership: The case of refugee integration in Germany. *Journal of Business Ethics.* https://doi.org/10.1007/s10551-017-3775-0.

Holvino, E. (2010). Intersections: The simultaneity of race, gender and class in organization studies. *Gender Work and Organization, 17,* 248–277.

Holvino, E. (2012). Time, space and social justice in the age of globalization: Research and applications on the simultaneity of differences. *Practising Social Change, 5,* 4–11.

Janssens, M., & Zanoni, P. (2014). Alternative diversity management: Organizational practices fostering ethnic equality at work. *Scandinavian Journal of Management, 30,* 317–331.

Jung, C. G. (2010). *Synchronicity: An acausal connecting principle.* (From Vol. 8. of the collected works of CG Jung) (New in paper). Chicago, IL: Princeton University Press.

Kabeer, N. (2010). Can the MDGs provide a pathway to social justice? The challenge of intersecting inequalities. In I. Ortiz, L. M. Daniels, & S. Engilbertsdóttir (Eds.), *Child poverty and inequality* (pp. 57–63). New York, NY: United Nations Children's Fund (UNICEF), Division of Policy and Practice.

Kaplan, M. M., Sabin, E., & Smaller-Swift, S. (2009). *The Catalyst guide to employee resource groups* (Vol. 1). New York, NY: Catalyst.

Kelan, E. K. (2014). From biological clocks to unspeakable inequalities: The intersectional positioning of young professionals. *British Journal of Management, 25*(4), 790–804.

Kerner, I. (2012). Questions of intersectionality: Reflections on the current debate in German gender studies. *European Journal of Women's Studies, 19*(2), 203–218.

Khattab, N., & Modood, T. (2018). Accounting for British Muslim's educational attainment: Gender differences and the impact of expectations. *British Journal of Sociology of Education, 39,* 242–259.

King, E. B., & Cortina, J. M. (2010). The social and economic imperative of lesbian, gay, bisexual, and transgendered supportive organizational policies. *Industrial and Organizational Psychology, 3*(1), 69–78.

King, E. B., Mohr, J. J., Peddie, C. I., Jones, K. P., & Kendra, M. (2017). Predictors of identity management: An exploratory experience-sampling study of lesbian, gay, and bisexual workers. *Journal of Management, 43,* 476–502.

Knapp, G. A. (2005). Race, class, gender. *European Journal of Women's Studies, 12,* 249–265.

Knappert, L., Kornau, A., & Figengül, M. (2018). Refugees' exclusion at work and the intersection with gender: Insights from the Turkish-Syrian border. *Journal of Vocational Behavior, 105,* 62–82.

Kuriloff, P., & Reichert, M. (2003). Boys of class, boys of color: Negotiating the academic and social geography of an elite independent school. *Journal of Social Issues, 59,* 751–770.

Kyriakidou, O., & Ozbilgin, M. (Eds.). (2006). *Relational perspectives in organizational studies: A research companion.* Cheltenham, England: Edward Elgar.

Laskowski, K. (2018). *From entitlement to capabilities: Shifting the narrative of response to displaced populations in urban settings* (Unpublished PhD thesis). New York, NY: Fordham University.

Lee, E., & Brotman, S. (2013). SPEAK OUT! Structural intersectionality and anti-oppressive practice with LGBTQ refugees in Canada. *Canadian Social Work Review, 30*(2), 157–183.

Lykke, N. (2010). *Feminist studies: A guide to intersectional theory, methodology and writing*. New York, NY: Routledge.

Mahalingam, R. (2007). Culture, power and psychology of marginality. In A. Fuligni (Ed.), *Contesting stereotypes and creating identities: Social categories, social identities, and educational participation* (pp. 42–65). New York, NY: SAGE.

Mahalingam, R., Balan, S., & Haritatos, J. (2008). Engendering immigrant psychology: An intersectionality perspective. *Sex Roles, 59*(5–6), 326–336.

Main, R. (2006). The social significance of synchronicity. *Psychoanalysis, Culture & Society, 11*(1), 36–53.

Marfelt, M. M. (2016). Grounded intersectionality: Key tensions, a methodological framework, and implications for diversity research. *Equality, Diversity and Inclusion: An International Journal, 35*, 31–47.

McCall, L. (2005). The complexity of intersectionality. *Signs: Journal of Women in Culture and Society, 30*, 1771–1800.

Metcalfe, B., & Woodhams, C. (2012). Introduction: New directions in gender, diversity and organization theorizing—Re-imagining feminist post-colonialism, transnationalism and geographies of power. *International Journal of Management Reviews, 14*, 123–140.

Mik-Meyer, N. (2015). Gender and disability: Feminizing male employees with visible impairments in Danish work organizations. *Gender, Work and Organization, 22*, 579–595.

Miles, R., & Torres, R. (2007). Does 'race' matter: Transatlantic perspectives on racism and 'race relations'. In Gupta T. D., James, C. E., Maaka, R. C. A., Galabuzi, G. E., & C. Andersen (Eds.), *Race and racialization: Essential readings* (pp. 65–73). Toronto, Cananda: Canadian Scholars' Press.

Moorosi, P. (2014). Constructing a leader's identity through a leadership development programme: An intersectional analysis. *Educational Management Administration & Leadership, 42*(6), 792–807.

Mueller, U. (2016). Lost in representation? Feminist identity economics and women's agency in India's local governments. *Feminist Economics, 22*, 158–182.

Muhr, S. L., & Sløk-Andersen, B. (2017). Exclusion and inclusion in the Danish Military: A historical analysis of the construction and consequences of a gendered organizational narrative. *Journal of Organizational Change Management, 30*, 367–379.

Okazawa-Rey, M. (2017). A "Nation-ized" intersectional analysis: The politics of transnational campus unity. *New Directions for Student Services, 157*, 81–90.

Omanović, V. (2009). Diversity and its management as a dialectical process: Encountering Sweden and the US. *Scandinavian Journal of Management, 25*(4), 352–362.

Ozbilgin, M., Beauregard, T. A., Tatli, A., & Bell, M. P. (2011). Work-life, diversity and intersectionality: A critical review and research agenda. *International Journal of Management Reviews, 13,* 177–198.

Ozbilgin M., & Vassilopoulou J. (2018) Relational methods in organization studies: A critical overview. In M. Ciesielska & D. Jemielniak (Eds.), *Qualitative methodologies in organization studies.* Cham: Palgrave Macmillan,

Ozeren, E., & Aydin, E. (2016). What does being LGBT mean in the workplace? A comparison of LGBT equality in Turkey and the UK. In A. Klarsfeld, E. S. Ng, L. A. E. Booysen, L. C. Christiansen, & B. Kuvaas (Eds.), *Research handbook of international and comparative perspectives on diversity management* (pp. 199–226), London, England: Edward Elgar.

Ozturk, M. B., & Ozbilgin, M. (2015). From cradle to grave: The lifecycle of compulsory heterosexuality across the institutions of patriarchy in Turkey. In Colgan, F. and Rumens, N. (Eds.), *Sexual Orientation at Work: Contemporary Issues and Perspective* (pp. 152–165), London, England: Routledge.

Ozturk, M. B., & Tatli, A. (2016). Gender identity inclusion in the workplace: Broadening diversity management research and practice through the case of transgender employees in the UK. *International Journal of Human Resource Management, 27,* 781–802.

Pöge, K., Strasser, S., & Rommel, A. (2018). Perspectives of LGBTIQ migrants, refugees and ethnic minorities for the development of a gender-sensitive and intersectional health reporting in Germany. *European Journal of Public Health.* https://doi.org/10.1093/eurpub/cky213.79328

Prasad, A. (2012). Beyond analytical dichotomies. *Human Relations, 65*(5), 567–595.

Qvist, M. (2017). Meta-governance and network formation in collaborative spaces of uncertainty: The case of Swedish refugee integration policy. *Public Administration, 95*(2), 498–511.

Richardson, D. (2007). Patterned fluidities: (Re)imagining the relationship between gender and sexuality. *Sociology, 41*(3), 457–474.

Roberson, Q. M. (2013). *The Oxford handbook of diversity and work.* New York, NY: Oxford University Press.

Roberson, Q. M. (2018). Diversity in the workplace: A review, synthesis, and future research agenda. *Annual Review of Organizational Psychology and Organizational Behavior.* https://doi.org/10.1146/annurev-orgpsych-012218-015243

Roberson, Q. M., & Park, H. J. (2007). Examining the link between diversity and firm performance: The effects of diversity reputation and leader racial diversity. *Group & Organization Management, 32*(5), 548–568.

Rodriguez, J. K., Holvino, E., Fletcher, J. K., & Nkomo, S. M. (2016). The theory and praxis of intersectionality in work and organisations: Where do we go from here? *Gender, Work & Organization, 23*(3), 201–222.

Roehlke, H. (1988). Critical incidents in counselor development: Examples of Jung's concept of synchronicity. *Journal of Counseling & Development, 67*(2), 133–134.

Saussure, F. D. (1983). Course in general linguistics. 1916. (Roy Harris, Trans.). London, England: Duckworth.

Shields, S. A. (2008). Gender: An intersectionality perspective. *Sex roles, 59*(5–6), 301–311.

Shore, L. M., Randel, A. E., Chung, B. G., Dean, M. A., Holcombe Ehrhart, K., & Singh, G. (2011). Inclusion and diversity in work groups: A review and model for future research. *Journal of management, 37*(4), 1262–1289.

Stauaes, D., & Søndegaard, D. M. (2011). Intersectionality: A theoretical adjustment. In R. Buikema, G. Griffin, & N. Lykke (Eds.). *Theories and methodologies in postgraduate feminist research: Researching differently* (pp. 45–59). New York, NY: Routledge.

Syed, J., & Ozbilgin, M. (2009). A relational framework for international transfer of diversity management practices. *The International Journal of Human Resource Management, 20*(12), 2435–2453.

Syed, J., Ali, F., & Hennekam, S. (2018). Gender equality in employment in Saudi Arabia: a relational perspective. *Career Development International, 23*(2), 163–177.

Tatli, A. (2011). A multi-layered exploration of the diversity management field: diversity discourses, practices and practitioners in the UK. *British Journal of Management, 22*(2), 238–253.

Tatli, A., & Ozbilgin, M. (2012b). Surprising intersectionalities of inequality and privilege: The case of the arts and cultural sector. *Equality, Diversity and Inclusion: An International Journal, 31*, 249–265.

Tatli, A., & Ozbilgin, M. F. (2012a). An emic approach to intersectional study of diversity at work: A Bourdieuan framing. *International Journal of Management Reviews, 14*, 180–200.

Tatli, A., Ozturk, M. B., & Woo, H. S. (2017). Individualization and marketization of responsibility for gender equality: The case of female managers in China. *Human Resource Management, 56*, 407-430.

Taylor, Y. (2009). Complexities and complications: Intersections of class and sexuality. *Journal of Lesbian Studies, 13*(2), 189–203.

Triandis, H. C. (2003). The future of workforce diversity in international organisations: A commentary. *Applied Psychology, 52*(3), 486-495.

Ulus, E. (2018). White fantasy, White betrayals: On neoliberal feminism in the US presidential election process. *Ephemera, 18*(1), 163–181.

Verkuyten, M., & Brug, P. (2004). Multiculturalism and group status: The role of ethnic identification, group essentialism and protestant ethic. *European Journal of Social Psychology, 34*(6), 647–661.

Walby, S., Armstrong, J., & Strid, S. (2012). Intersectionality: Multiple inequalities in social theory. *Sociology, 46*(2), 224–240.

West, C., & Fenstermaker, S. (1995). Doing difference. *Gender & Society, 9*, 8–37.

Wijeyesinghe, C. L., & Jones, S. R. (2014). Intersectionality, identity, and systems of power and inequality. In D. Mitchell, C. Y. Simmons, & L. A. Greyerbiehl (Eds.), *Intersectionality and higher education: Theory, research, and praxis* (pp. 9–19). New York, NY: Peter Lang.

Winker, G., & Degele, N. (2011). Intersectionality as multi-level analysis: Dealing with social inequality. *European Journal of Women's Studies, 18*, 51–66.

Woodhams, C., Lupton, B., & Cowling, M. (2015). The snowballing penalty effect: multiple disadvantage and pay. *British Journal of Management, 26*(1), 63–77.

Wright, T. (2013). Uncovering sexuality and gender: An intersectional examination of women's experience in UK construction. *Construction Management and Economics*, *31*, 832–844.

Wright, T. (2016). Women's experience of workplace interactions in male-dominated work: The intersections of gender, sexuality and occupational group. *Gender, Work and Organization*, *23*, 348–362.

Yiassemides, A. (2011). Chronos in synchronicity: Manifestations of the psychoid reality. *Journal of Analytical Psychology*, *56*(4), 451–471.

Zhou, M., & Bankston, C. L. (2000). *Straddling two social worlds: The experience of Vietnamese refugee children in the United States*. New York, NY: ERIC Clearinghouse on Urban Education.

Yuval-Davis, N. (2011). *The Politics of Belonging –Intersectional Contestations*. London, England: SAGE.

Zanoni, P., & Janssens, M. (2007) Minority employees engaging with (diversity) management: An analysis of control, agency, and micro-emancipation. *Journal of Management Studies*, *44*, 1371–1397.

CHAPTER 5

IDENTITY MANAGEMENT STRATEGIES OF LGB WORKERS WHO ARE RACIOETHNIC MINORITIES

Raymond N. C. Trau
Macquarie University

Brent J. Lyons
York University (Canada)

Due to the rising prevalence of lesbian, gay, and bisexual (LGB) people in the workplace and supportive policies and practices concerning sexual minorities in some contexts globally (Pichler & Ruggs, 2015), LGB workers are increasingly recognizing the benefits of disclosing their sexual identity at work. Mounting research evidence, that has primarily been conducted in Western and majority White countries (e.g., Australia, Canada, United Kingdom, United States), suggests that "coming out" is linked to positive work attitudes among LGB workers (Button, 2001; Griffith & Hebl, 2002; Ragins & Cornwell, 2001; Trau, 2015). However, scholars have noted that much of existing research in Western and majority White contexts has examined a perspective that positions White and middle-class individuals as the social norm. Thus, theorizing on identity management, or the

Pushing Our Understanding of Diversity in Organizations, pp. 115–133
Copyright © 2020 by Information Age Publishing
115

"strategic decisions individuals make regarding how they present their social identities to others" (Lyons, Wessel, Ghumman, Ryan, & Kim, 2014, p. 678), has not been sensitive to, and inclusive of, the experiences of racial and ethnic minorities of the LGB population.

The lived experiences of racial and ethnic minorities influence their identity management decisions, including how they learn about their sexual identity and their feelings toward being open about their sexual identity to others at work (Croteau, Anderson, & VanderWal, 2008; Villicana, Delucio, & Biernat, 2016). Despite previous models of identity management acknowledging that race, ethnicity, and culture play a role in identity management decisions, current understanding of the experience of sexual identity management of racial and ethnic minorities is limited.

Accordingly, in this chapter, we aim to generate new understanding about identity management of sexual minorities who are racial and ethnic minorities and who live and work in Western and majority White countries. Our arguments are informed by models of sexual identity development and we integrate perspectives of intersectionality and multicultural identities.

Intersectionality is defined "as overlapping social categories, such as race and gender, that are relevant to a specified individual or group's identity and create a unique experience that is separate and apart from its originating categories" (Rosette, de Leon, Koval, & Harrison, 2018, p. 3). Several important assumptions are commonly recognized with the analytical framework of intersectionality: (a) No social group is homogenous; (b) People and groups are located in terms of social structures, and power relations apply to social groups within those social structures; (c) Unique effects occur from identifying with more than one social group (Mahalingam, Balan, & Haritatos, 2008). The framework of intersectionality recognizes that multiple and overlapping identities are embedded within specific social, cultural, and interpersonal contexts, and create unique experiences for individuals who belong to multiple marginalized social groups. Being a member of two or more overlapping groups is more than the sum of being a member of either category, and individuals living with multiple devalued social identities often experience oppressions beyond those imposed by each identity separately. Drawing from the perspective of intersectionality, in this chapter we specifically speak to how LGB workers who are racial and ethnic minorities' unique experiences of sexual identity development impact their identity management decisions.

In addition to incorporating the perspective of intersectionality, we also incorporate the perspective of multicultural identities to address how cultural and community factors impact the sexual identity development and identity management decisions of LGB workers who are racial and ethnic minorities. Racial and ethnic minorities in majority White contexts oftentimes navigate multiple cultures: the culture associated with their race and ethnicity, including the values, beliefs, and customs associated with family and community, and the culture associated with the majority dominant White group. They are thus considered "multicultural" in that they experience, have knowledge of, and internalize multiple cultural identities (Fitzsimmons, 2013; Sanchez, Shih, & Wilton, 2014; Vora, Martin, Fitzsimmons, Pekerti, Lakshman, & Raheem, 2018). LGB workers who are racial and ethnic minorities can experience conflict between these identities, including misalignments between the values, beliefs, and expectations regarding LGB identity of their racial and ethnic communities and the values, beliefs, and expectations regarding LGB identity in the majority and dominant White culture.

In considering models of the sexual identity development that are socially and culturally sensitive and by integrating the perspectives of intersectionality and multicultural identities, we seek to better understand the identity management experiences of LGB workers who are racial and ethnic minorities (e.g., lesbian Black woman). In this chapter, we will describe how LGB workers who are racial and ethnic minorities experience identity management of their sexual minority identities in unique ways compared with LGB workers who are White (Purdie-Vaughns & Eibach, 2008). These differences are due to having multiple and overlapping devalued social groups and racial, ethnic, and cultural norms concerning, for example, family and community (Croteau et al., 2008). It is our argument that LGB workers who are racial and ethnic minorities are confronted with broader contextual (e.g., cultural and community) and internal (e.g., identity conflict) influences that complicate their identity management decisions.

For the remainder of this chapter, we use the term "racioethnicity" because it covers a range of identities across categories of racial and ethnic origins. Racial or ethnic minorities (e.g., African Americans, Hispanics, and Asians) represent a large proportion of the workforce in Western countries, such as the United States, United Kingdom, Canada, and Australia. Many studies have found similar psychological effects on well-being, belonging, behavior, and identity exploration among racial and ethnic minorities, and hence, scholars have argued for the utility of merging these aspects into a racioethnic construct (Sanchez, Shih, & Wilton, 2014).

We will first review the current frameworks and empirical research relating to identity management. Then we will discuss these previous frameworks and research in the context of perspectives of sexual identity development, intersectionality, and multicultural identities. We will conclude by discussing the implications of these issues for organizations and workplace interactions and provide directions for future research.

IDENTITY MANAGEMENT

LGB workers must make ongoing assessments and decisions as to whom, when, where, and how to disclose their sexual minority identity to others at work. One component of identity management is disclosure. Disclosure is defined as a process through which individuals express their personal and distinctive self-information to others (Goffman, 1963; Phillips, Rothbard, & Dumas, 2009), whereas identity management more broadly is about "how" individuals disclose or conceal (Lyons et al., 2014). In this section, we will first review existing frameworks and previous research on disclosure and then identity management.

Previous theory and research have suggested that disclosure is not a simple decision, but a decision that involves a cost-benefit analysis of what the disclosure means to the individual and their everyday experience (Clair, Beatty, & MacLean, 2005; Ragins, 2008). A cost-benefit analysis involves an assessment of the implications of the disclosure decision regarding psychological benefits, relationships with others, and career progressions. According to Chaudoir and Fisher's (2010) disclosure process model, the disclosure decisions of individuals who pursue *positive outcomes* are driven by possible rewards (e.g., better career opportunities) or positive psychological states (e.g., feeling good about being authentic). Conversely, the disclosure decisions of individuals who focus on avoiding *negative outcomes* are driven by a desire to avoid possible retributions (e.g., less promotion opportunities) or negative psychological states (e.g., social rejection or internal conflict).

Accordingly, disclosure goals—whether they are about approaching positive outcomes or avoiding negative outcomes—impact the likelihood of disclosure and concealment and the consequences of disclosing and concealing. On the positive side, individuals who view being open about their LGB identity as important may focus on behaviors directed at being authentic at work. They may disclose with the aim of fostering a positive impression of LGB people by creating opportunities for identity-related conversations with others (Creed & Scully, 2000; Roberts & Creary, 2012; Rumens, 2012). By disclosing, it is assumed that individuals are less likely to experience conflict between who they are (i.e., the private self) and who they are expected to be at work (Ragins, 2008).

In contrast, research suggests that LGB individuals who focus on negative outcomes, such as social rejection, are less likely to disclose (Chaudoir & Fisher, 2010; Meyer, 2003). Instead, they may conceal their identity or choose a less direct method of communicating information about their identity to minimize the possibility of rejection. It is argued that negative consequences of concealing an identity include stress associated with not being authentic and not receiving social support for the identity (Ragins, 2008).

Another consideration of previous research has been the consistency of one's disclosure between work and non-work domains. Some LGB workers may disclose their identity at work but not in their private lives (e.g., at home with family) and this inconsistency has been argued to be stressful and have negative consequences for well-being (Ragins, 2008). While consistent disclosure across domains is thought to be most optimal, Ragins does acknowledge that is only the case when both settings are supportive of the LGB identity.

In addition to making decisions about whether, to whom, and where to disclose, LGB workers make strategic decisions about "how" to disclose or conceal to manage impressions about their sexual identity to others—that is, they make identity management decisions. Among the earlier models of LGB identity management, Woods (1993) identified three major strategies adopted by gay men in the corporate environment: integrating, avoiding, and counterfeiting. The integrating strategy involves revealing the LGB identity in a subtle or overt way. Avoiding and counterfeiting strategies both involve an intention to conceal. The avoiding strategy involves avoiding opportunities that may reveal an individual's identity and includes avoiding the topic or not correcting false assumptions from others, whereas the counterfeiting strategy involves actively constructing a false identity, such as discussing past heterosexual relationships. Later, Button (2001) provided empirical evidence to support this model of identity management by lesbian and gay employees.

Since the establishment of the identity management framework by Woods (1993), several scholars have expanded on conceptualizations of different identity management strategies (see Clair, et al., 2005; Jones & King, 2014; Lyons, Pek, & Wessel, 2017; Ramarajan & Reid, 2013; Roberts, 2005; Shih, Young, & Bucher, 2013). These frameworks convey several different identity management strategies. One such strategy is signaling (Clair et al., 2005; Jones & King, 2014), which involves indirect disclosure through symbols and clues (e.g., place a picture of a partner at a work desk). An additional strategy is one that minimizes the importance of the stigmatized identity by disclosing and making the identity seem as though it has qualities like those of other more dominant identities. Another strategy is disclosure that differentiates the stigmatized identity from other more dominant identities and emphasizes its positive qualities (see Clair et al., 2005; Lyons et al., 2017; Roberts, 2005). Although research on the antecedents and consequences of different identity management strategies is in its infancy, in one recent paper Lynch and Rodell (2018) found that individuals receive more positive and less negative responses from coworkers when they adopt identity management strategies that embrace the positive of the stigmatized identity.

However, although extant theories of identity management are helpful in advancing understanding of the experiences of LGB workers, they have generally not been sensitive to the experiences of LGB workers who are racioethnic minorities except, to our knowledge, one exception. Lidderdale and colleagues (2007) detail a model, based on the social cognitive career theory, that illustrates how that the interaction between behavior, cognition, and context influences identity management strategies of LGB workers. Their model acknowledges that social group identities and cultural variables (such as race and ethnicity) influence how individuals learn about their sexual identity which in turn influences how they think about identity management. More specifically, for many LGB workers who are racioethnic minorities, cultural messages about sexual orientation stem from family and community, educational opportunities, socioeconomic environment, and representation (or lack thereof) in media and popular culture. These cultural messages are thought to limit the development of beliefs about positive outcomes of disclosure because racioethnic minorities are less likely to be exposed to positive messages about racioethnic minorities being out. In contrast, LGB individuals from the dominant group (e.g., Whites in Western countries) may have greater exposure to more positive 'coming out' messages and experiences via, for example, diverse representation in media and popular culture. Based on this model, we can see that learning experiences associated with one's racioethnic culture influence how LGB individuals who are racioethnic minorities view their identity and also their decisions about how to manage their LGB identity to others.

In sum, theoretical frameworks and previous research on identity management have taken numerous important steps toward understanding the experiences of LGB workers. Research has found that identity management strategies can have both positive and negative consequences, though research has found that disclosing in ways that embrace the identity leads to more positive outcomes than concealing or downplaying the identity. Previous research has also noted that disclosure is not wholly positive and concealing is not wholly negative: concealing or downplaying one's LGB identity can also shield against anti-LGB stigmatization and discrimination (Ragins, 2004). Scholars across several identity management frameworks also note that other social identities (e.g., race or ethnicity) to which LGB workers belong complicate affect identity management decisions (e.g., Clair et al., 2005; Jones & King, 2014; Phillips et al., 2009; Ragins, 2008), but extant theory and research on have just begun to unpack how and why race and ethnicity impact identity management decisions.

Lidderdale and colleagues (2007) explore the social and cultural factors as important for understanding LGB identity management decisions and they explicitly emphasize the importance of culture in individuals' development of their identity and beliefs about identity management. In order to build on the growing identity management literature, in the next section of this chapter we integrate models of sexual identity development with perspectives on intersectionality and multicultural identities to enrich understanding about how racioethnicity influences LGB workers' identity management decisions.

IDENTITY MANAGEMENT AND IDENTITY DEVELOPMENT: CHALLENGES FROM MULTICULTURAL IDENTITY AND INTERSECTIONALITY PERSPECTIVES

Models of sexual identity development articulate how cultural and social factors influence individuals' own beliefs about their identity and identity management. Cultural messages about sexual orientation, economic and educational opportunities, and community norms and practices influence how individuals learn about their sexual identity (Croteau et al., 2008; Lidderdale et al., 2007). LGB individuals progress through a series of developmental stages to reach a fully integrated gay identity that is fulfilling to their sense of self (Cass, 1984; McDonald, 1982; Sophie, 1986; Troiden, 1993). Each stage of sexual identity development has implications for how one thinks about their identity and their beliefs about identity management (Fukuyama & Ferguson, 2000). The general conclusion among these identity development models is that as individuals progress through stages in identity development they start to feel more positively about their LGB identity, feelings of anxiety stemming from stigma associated with their LGB identity are less intense and they are more likely to be open about their sexual identity to others. These identity development models highlight how identity management is a decision based on the individual's evaluation of their own personal pride regarding their LGB identity and how others around them also view the identity.

In a growing body of research, models of sexual identity development have been challenged (e.g., Fukuyama & Ferguson, 2000; Han, Proctor, & Choi, 2014; Villicana et al., 2016). This growing body of research has explicitly examined the sexual identity development from the perspectives of LGB individuals who are racioethnic minorities. The main criticism of early sexual identity development models is that they conceptualize sexual identity development within a White framework with little consideration of racioethnicity (Fukuyama & Ferguson, 2000; Villicana et al., 2016). These scholars acknowledge that the lived experience and culture associated with race and ethnicity may facilitate, hinder, or delay sexual identity development of LGB individuals who are racioethnic minorities. For example, in majority White and Western countries racioethnic minority individuals may be more likely to grow up experiencing prejudice and discrimination associated with their race and ethnicity and they may be less likely to anticipate positive outcomes of disclosure and identity management even if they have progressed to personally accepting their LGB identity. Expecting LGB individuals who are racioethnic minorities to develop and make similar identity management decisions as implied by the earlier models of sexual identity development overlooks how and why racioethnicity influences peoples' understanding, interpretation, learning, and efficacy regarding identity management (Croteau et al., 2008; Fukuyama & Ferguson, 2000; Greene, 1997; Loiacano, 1989). Individuals approach their identity management decisions according to their own circumstances, which include culture, family, and community, and these circumstances reflect additional factors impacting identity management, above and beyond concerns about authenticity and avoiding rejection which are prominent factors in current models of identity management.

Challenges From a Multicultural Identity Perspective

Scholars in the field of multicultural research have argued that identity development is complicated by multiple cultural identities (Fitzsimmons, 2013; Sanchez et al., 2014). Multicultural individuals vary in how they define their own identities and identify with the dominant culture (Vora et al., 2018). In this light, research focusing on racial and cultural identity development has found that racioethnic minorities, at some point in their lives, experience tension and conflict with their different cultural identities (Park, 1928; Sanchez et al., 2014), though the extent to which they experience tension and conflict varies with the extent to which they maintain the multiple identities as a part of their self-concept (Kang & Bodenhausen, 2015). On one extreme, assimilation occurs when multicultural individuals evolve toward identifying with the dominant (White) culture and lose their own racial or cultural identity (Sanchez et al., 2014). On the other end of the spectrum, however, some multicultural individuals may not wholly assimilate and instead preserve and identify with their own racioethnic cultural in addition to being influenced by the dominant culture (LaFromboise, Coleman, & Gerton, 1993). Multicultural individuals can identify with one, both, or neither cultures.

Identifying with more than one culture has several implications for LGB workers who are racioethnic minorities. These individuals are inevitably caught between multiple cultural identities and may experience identity confusion and rejection by their in-groups and out-groups. They must continuously negotiate a divergent set of norms, values, beliefs, and practices regarding LGB identity between the cultures to which they belong, as well as tackle the alignment between these cultural identities (Chen & Vollick, 2013; Greene & Croom, 2000; Villicana et al., 2016).

Navigating these multiple and possibly conflicting cultural identities involves a number of psychological challenges. Individuals may feel conflict with their racioethnic identity if heterosexism and homophobia are a part of their racioethnic culture. For example, previous research has found that Asian and Hispanic LGB individuals can feel that their sexual identity conflicts with cultural values and beliefs associated with their racioethnic community. For cultures such as Asian and Hispanic, the family is valued as the primary social unit and expects respect, obedience, and conformity to cultural values (Chung & Katayama, 1998; Villicana et al., 2016). Sexual identity violates gender roles and threatens the family system (Han, Proctor, & Choi, 2014). As a result, disclosure of one's sexual identity may be met stigma, shame, and rejection from family and as well as community members (Kulik, Bainbridge, & Cregan, 2008). Indeed, previous research indicates that LGB individuals who are racioethnic minorities are more likely to avoid disclosing when the values and beliefs of their community include disapproval of homosexuality (Han, 2009).

Rejection from family and community is particularly challenging and compounding for LGB workers who are racioethnic minorities because family and community represent critical sources of support and safety from racism (Greene & Croom, 2000; Loiacano, 1989; Villicana et al., 2016). As a consequence of these possible negative outcomes, some racioethnic workers may prefer to hide their sexual identity from people in their family and community. For some LGB workers who are racioethnic minorities they may opt to pass as heterosexual in the domain of family and community in order to maintain supportive relationships with family and friends, while they may opt to be open about their sexual identity at work (Sedlovskaya et al., 2013). Although this disclosure inconsistency across work and non-work domains may be a source of stress for LGB workers (Ragins, 2008), it may also be a necessary source of support for LGB workers who are racioethnic minorities who must also navigate the challenges of racism.

However, some LGB workers may choose to separate their racioethnic identity from their self-concept and thus choose not to abide by or resist against the cultural values, beliefs, and expectations associated with their racioethnicity. For these individuals, they would be open about their sexual identity in both work and non-work domains which may help reduce anxiety associated disclosure inconsistencies across domains (Ragins, 2008) but they may risk losing support from their family and community if values and beliefs are unsupportive of LGB identities.

Challenges From Intersectionality Perspectives

In addition to the complexities that LGB workers who are racioethnic minorities navigating complexities of multicultural identity, they may also experience a distinctive form of marginalization that is a result of multiple overlapping forms of oppression, including heterosexism from the dominant White culture and their racioethnic community (Fukuyama & Ferguson, 2000; Han et al., 2014; Loiacano, 1989), racial- or ethnic-based prejudice and discrimination by other White sexual minority individuals (Han et al., 2014; Harper, Jernewall, & Zea, 2004; Loiacano, 1989), and sexism experienced by lesbian women (Purdie-Vaughns & Eibach, 2008).

Purdie-Vaughns and Eibach (2008) highlight the importance of an intersectionality lens when understanding the identity management experiences of LGB individuals who are racioethnic minorities. Purdie-Vaughns and Eibach note that, in majority White and Western contexts, societal standards place White heterosexual men as the cultural norm and the experiences of racioethnic minorities who are LGB are treated as invisible, misrepresented, or de-emphasized. They argue that because men and heterosexuality are societal standards for gender and sexual identity, the prototypical racioethnic minority is a heterosexual man of color; because White and heterosexuality are societal standards for race and sexual identity, the prototypical woman is straight and White; and because men and Whiteness are societal standards for gender and race, the prototypical gay person is a White man.

Accordingly, extant theory and research on identity management that position 'coming out' as beneficial and concealment as detrimental are more reflective of the experiences of White gay men and lesbians but not the experiences of racial and ethnic minorities, such as Black gay men and lesbian women. For example, for some Black gay men, being on the "down low" (i.e., not being out to friends, family, or coworkers but maintaining same-sex relationships) allows them to assert masculinity, affirm racial identity, and distance from White gay culture that may not be inclusive of racioethnic minorities (Purdie-Vaughns & Eibach, 2008).

Thus, LGB workers who are racioethnic minorities are prone to experiencing exclusion, even if the organization in which they work incorporates practices (e.g., diversity training, employee resource groups, ally programs) that are presumably supportive of LGB-identified individuals. In these organizations, the experiences of gay White men and women are represented and attended to and the experiences of people of color are rendered invisible, de-emphasized, or misrepresented. To the extent that organizational practices encourage workers to be "out" and authentic about their sexual identity while at the same time not addressing racial prejudice and discrimination in the organization and cultural barriers of disclosing a LGB identity, in addition to racism within the LGB community, then these organizational practices are not likely to be inclusive of the experiences of LGB workers who are also racioethnic minorities. Indeed, racioethnic minorities often have limited experiences to learn about their intersectional identity (e.g., African American lesbian women) at work due to little visibility of similar others. Hence, LGB-supportive organizational practices may have little or no guidance in dealing with their unique experiences of racism within the LGB community and sexual-identity based oppression and it is this important for LFB-supportive organization practices to encourage conversations on the unique and diverse ways people can experience their LGB identity at work and the complexities underlying identity management decisions of LGB workers who are racioethnic minorities.

THEORETICAL IMPLICATIONS AND FUTURE DIRECTIONS

Throughout this chapter, we have reviewed theories and frameworks on identity management strategies, sexual identity development, multicultural identities, and intersectionality to capture the challenges experienced by LGB workers who are racioethnic minorities in managing their LGB identity at work. The current literature has provided a rich understanding of individual and contextual factors that contribute to identity management decisions of LGB workers.

Two overlapping themes are important to consider when attempting to understand the experiences of LGB workers who are racioethnic minorities. First, these individuals hold multiple and overlapping identities, and therefore, they need to grapple with, and negotiate among, these sometimes conflicting identities. Moreover, some of their cultural values and beliefs may clash with their LGB identities, and thus, there are costs to the disclosure to family and community. Second, LGB individuals have been historically marginalized because of racism, heterosexism, and sexism from both the LGB community and the broader dominant culture, and hence, they experience multiple forms of oppression that complicate their identity management decisions. Our discussion provides several workplace implications for LGB workers who are racioethnic minorities, their coworkers, and organizations.

Identity management decisions are challenging, yet a decision that one needs to make to respond to, and cope with, discrimination and exclusion (Clair et al., 2005; Ragins, 2008) and manage relationships with others (King, Reilly, & Hebl, 2008; Phillips et al., 2009) at work. When taking into account racial, ethnicity, and cultural factors, identity management is no longer a decision with purely individual or intrapersonal consequences, since it may involve a cost to relationships not only at work but also individuals' racioethnic culture, family, and community. The interplay between personal needs and cultural factors complicates the negotiation between that LGB workers who are racioethnic minorities engage in as they consider which identities to be included or excluded at work, both in an exclusionary, discriminatory environment and in a supportive LGB workplace environment (Ramarajan & Reid, 2013). Stigma theory posits that the environment influences how a stigma is incorporated into a person's self-concept (Crocker & Major, 1989; Jones et al., 1984) and people tend to drift away from groups and contexts that do not verify their identity (Swann et al., 2004) or exclude their identity (Petriglieri, 2011; Ramarajan & Reid, 2013). Hence the decision to include or exclude a particular identity among other identities is a big dilemma.

It is important to highlight that LGB-supportive policies and practices in organizations may pressure racioethnic minority individuals toward or away from their racioethnic group (Vora et al., 2018). Supportive LGB policies and practices may also assert inclusionary pressure on bringing their LGB identity to work, which may assert exclusionary pressure on their racioethnic identity when associated cultural values and beliefs do not align with the LGB identity. While some individuals might choose to comply with inclusionary pressure, other LGB workers who are racioethnic minorities might choose not to adapt to inclusionary norms and values of their organization (Creary, Caza, & Roberts, 2015; Ramarajan & Reid, 2013) by not disclosing their identity. As theorized by Lidderdale et al. (2007), many LGB individuals who are racioethnic minorities have had a long history of struggling with multiple forms of oppression, and hence, these individuals may be less likely to anticipate positive outcomes from being open about one's sexual identity at work, even if their current workplace climate encourages them to do so. This dilemma is perhaps even more problematic for those whose racioethnic identity is central to their self-concept but whose racioethnic identity is in conflict with their sexual minority identity. Hence, them "being out and proud" potentially means shifting away from their core identity of which racioethnicity is a part (Settles, 2004; Stryker & Serpe, 1994). Thus, there is much to be discovered about how organizational contexts affect the identity conflict between LGB and racioethnic identities, and future research could examine the differential effects of inclusionary or exclusionary pressures for various identities on identity management decisions and associated psychological and work outcomes.

Having multiple overlapping identities also has implications for interpersonal interactions within groups at work. LGB employees who are racioethnic minorities are often a minority at work and, therefore, they are more likely to be conscious of their distinctive identity. The lack of visibility or representation of similar others leads to a lack of emotional and developmental support for coping with their unique experiences (Trau, 2015). Individuals also face a dilemma in regard to how others evaluate their membership to sexual minority and racioethnic groups: When they behave in ways that affirm and embrace their sexual identity and racioethnic groups they risk experiencing prejudice and discrimination, but when they downplay or avoid their sexual identity and racioethnic groups they risk alienation from members of their in-group (Hogg, van Knippenberg, & Rast, 2012). Diverging pressures and expectations from different groups leads to the feeling of being a "misfit with one or the other" because of two or more conflicting identities, which in turn has implications for interactions with coworkers (Creary et al., 2015; Kang & Bodenhausen, 2015; Purdie-Vaughns & Eibach, 2008). For example, coworkers in an organization that values diversity may believe that enacting both LGB and racioethnic identities is beneficial to the team and organization, leading to an expectation that their LGB workers who are racioethnic minorities would bring both identities to work. However, the LGB worker who is a racioethnic minority may prefer to enact only one or none of these identities, and thus potentially constrain the individual's relationships with coworkers and risk being misunderstood. The multiple oppressions experienced by LGB workers who are racioethnic minorities lead to the feeling of being misunderstood and being viewed as a misfit by others (Purdie-Vaughns & Eibach, 2008). Future research could further explore how LGB workers who are racioethnic minorities navigate and negotiate their multiple identities through identity management strategies and the implications that these identity management strategies have for how their coworkers, who are members of out- and in-groups, perceive and interact with them.

It is important for researchers to recognize and capture the unique identity management experiences of LGB workers who are racioethnic minorities. Most of the existing frameworks on identity management place little emphasis on how racioethnic cultures can impact sexual identity development which has implications for identity management (Croteau et al., 2008). Empirical studies involving LGB people are predominantly of White, well-educated, relatively high-income earning individuals (i.e., educated and professional), and tend to emphasize positive outcomes associated with disclosure (Croteau et al., 2008). Similarly, the "coming out" narrative in the mainstream LGB community sends a similar message that "being out is good" and "staying in the closet is problematic" (Croteau et al., 2008; Purduie-Vaughns & Eibach, 2008). Such perspectives have been criticized as cultural bias, since some LGB workers who are racioethnic minorities, who have been mostly excluded in the literature, are struggling with poverty or low-paying jobs and experiencing multiple forms of oppressions, and therefore cannot afford to risk losing their job or alienating family and community members who provide economic and emotional support (Loiacano, 1989; Villicana et al., 2016). Their perspectives and experiences of identity management and their perceptions of the benefits of 'coming out' therefore extend beyond meeting individual needs, and for some, coming out is tied to collective interests (Villicana et al., 2016). Hence, future research could examine the role of considering collective interests (i.e., family and community) in order to better understand the cost-benefit analysis of disclosure and identity management at work.

Further, while much of the existing research focuses on disclosing or concealing one's sexual identity, little is known about the "signaling" strategy, which is an indirect and mostly nonverbal form of signaling sexual identity to others (Jones & King, 2014). This identity management strategy may be a more common and preferred method among racioethnic minorities way to disclose LGB identity to others, and more research is needed to understand the motives and approaches of signaling identity management strategies. Villicana et al. (2016) compared the coming-out experiences of gay White and Latino men and found that identification with the gay identity was positively related to verbal disclosure for the former but not for the latter. Further, they found that verbal disclosure was positively related to well-being for gay White men but not for gay Latino men. Together, these findings suggest that notions of healthy expression of the LGB identity are not shared across racioethnic cultural groups of gay men. Further, the existing identity management frameworks also emphasize that fully 'coming out' is a form of expressing one's true self, which is primarily based on the individualist cultural norms and values of the U.S. and other majority White and Western contexts (Villacana et al., 2016). LGB individuals who are racioethnic minorities might adopt a subtle approach to expressing their LGB identity and still feel authentic. Together, these unique perspectives and findings suggest future research could explore alternative perspectives and approaches to identity management decisions. Such knowledge would also be particularly helpful to understand how non-LGB coworkers can better recognize and affirm the diversity of ways in which racioethnic minorities express their LGB identities (Creary et al., 2015).

In conclusion, this chapter aimed to direct attention to understanding the interaction of LGB and racioethnic identities in identity management decisions of LGB workers who are racioethnic minorities. By integrating models of identity management, sexual identity development, multicultural identity and intersectionality, we begin to develop understanding about how these individuals need to negotiate among multiple identities, cultures, family, and community, work and non-work contexts when making identity management decisions. This discussion is timely and worthwhile, given the context of globalization and increasing diversity of modern workplaces. Clearly, further research is needed to better understand the identity management experiences of LGB workers who are racioethnic minorities and the implications for themselves, their coworkers, and organizations.

REFERENCES

Akerlund, M., & Cheung, M. (2000). Teaching beyond the deficit model. *Journal of Social Work Education, 36*(2), 279–292. doi:10.1080/10437797.2000.10779008

Ashforth, B. E., & Mael, F. (1989). Social identity theory and the organization. *Academy of Management Review, 14*, 20–39. doi:10.5465/amr.1989.4278999

Brewer, M. B. (1991). The social self: On being the same and different at the same time. *Personality and Social Psychology Bulletin, 17*, 475–482. doi:10.1177/0146167291175001

Brewer, M. B., & Chen, Y. (2007). Where (Who) are collectives in collectivism? Toward conceptual clarification of individualism and collectivism. *Psychological Review, 114*, 133–151. doi:10.1037/0033-295X.114.1.133

Brewer, M. B., & Gardner, W. (1996). Who is this "we"? Levels of collective identity and self representations. *Journal of Personality and Social Psychology, 71*, 83–93. doi:10.1037/0022-3514.71.1.83

Button, S. (2001). Organizational efforts to affirm sexual diversity: A cross-level examination. *Journal of Applied Psychology, 86*, 17–28. doi:10.1037/0021-9010.86.1.17

Cass, V. C. (1984). Homosexual identity formation: Testing a theoretical model. *Journal of Sex Research, 20*(2), 143–167. doi:10.1080/00224498409551214

Chaudoir, S. R., & Fisher, J. D. (2010). The disclosure process model: Understanding disclosure decision making and postdiscloure outcomes among people living with a concealable stigmatized identity *Psychological Bulletin, 136*, 236–256. doi:10.1037/a0018193

Chen, C. P., & Vollick, S. (2013). Multiple identities and career development of GLB immigrants. *Counselling Psychology Quarterly, 26*(2), 208–224. doi:10.10 80/09515070.2012.735892

Chung, Y. B., & Katayama, M. (1998). Ethnic and sexual identity development of Asian-American lesbian and gay adolescents. *Professional School Counseling, 1*(3), 21–25.

Clair, J. A., Beatty, J., & MacLean, T. (2005). Out of sight but not out of mind: Managing invisible social identities in the workplace. *Academy of Management Review, 30*, 78–95. doi:10.5465/amr.2005.15281431

Creary, S. J., Caza, B. B., & Roberts, L. M. (2015). Out of the box? How managing a subordinate's multiple identities affects the qualit of a manager-subordinate relationship.. *Academy of Management Review, 40*(4), 538–562. doi:10.5465/amr.2013.0101

Creed, W. E. D., & Scully, M. (2000). Songs of ourselves: Employee's deployment of social identity in the workplace encounters. *Journal of Management Inquiry, 9*, 391–413. doi:10.1177/105649260000900410

Croteau, J. M., Anderson, M. Z., & VanderWal, B. L. (2008). Models of workplace sexual identity disclosure and management: Reviewing and extending concepts. *Group and Organization Management, 33*, 532–565. doi:10.1177/1059601108321828

Croteau, J. M., Anderson, M. Z., & VanderWal, B. L. (2008). Models of workplace sexual identity disclosure and management: reviewing and extending concepts. *Group & Organization Management, 33*(5), 532–565. doi:10.1177/1059601108321828

Fitzsimmons, S. R. (2013). Multicultural employees: A framework for understanding how they contribute to organizations. *Academy of Management Review, 38*(4), 525–549. doi:10.5465/amr.2011.0234

Fukuyama, M. A., & Ferguson, A. D. (2000). Lesbian, gay, and bisexual people of color: Understanding cultural complexity and managing multiple oppressions. In *Handbook of counseling and psychotherapy with lesbian, gay, and bisexual clients.* (pp. 81–105). Washington, DC: American Psychological Association.

Goffman, E. (1963). *Stigma: Notes on the management of spoiled identity.* Eaglewood Cliffs, NJ: Prentice-Hall.

Greene, B. (1997). *Ethnic minority lesbians and gay men: Mental health and treatment issues.* Thousand Oaks, CA: SAGE.

Greene, B., & Croom, G. L. (2000). *Education, research, and practice in lesbian, gay, bisexual, and transgendered psychology a resource manual.* Thousand Oaks, CA: London, England: SAGE.

Griffith, K. H., & Hebl, M. R. (2002). The disclosure dilemma for gay men and lesbians: Coming out at work. *Journal of Applied Psychology, 87*, 1191–1199. doi:10.1037/0021-9010.87.6.1191

Han, C.-s. (2009). Introduction to the Special Issue on GLBTQ of Color. *Journal of Gay & Lesbian Social Services, 21*(2–3), 109–114. doi:10.1080/10538720902771826

Han, C.-S., Proctor, K., & Choi, K.-H. (2014). We pretend like sexuality doesn't exist: Managing homophobia in Gaysian America. *The Journal of Men's Studies, 22*(1), 53–63. doi:10.3149/jms.2201.53

Harper, G. W., Jernewall, N., & Zea, M. C. (2004). Giving voice to emerging science and theory for lesbian, gay, and bisexual people of color. *Cultural Diversity and Ethnic Minority Psychology, 10*(3), 187.

Hogg, M. A., & Terry, D. J. (2000). Social identity and self-categorization process in organizational context. *Academy of Management Review, 25*, 121–140.

Hogg, M. A., van Knippenberg, D., & Rast III, D. E. (2012). The social identity theory of leadership: Theoretical origins, research findings, and conceptual developments. *European Review of Social Psychology, 23*, 258–304.

Jones, K. P., & King, E. B. (2014). Managing concealable stigmas at work: A review and multilevel model. *Journal of Management, 40*, 1466–1494. doi:10.1111/1467-6486.00387

Kang, S. K., & Bodenhausen, G. V. (2015). Multiple Identities in Social Perception and Interaction: Challenges and Opportunities. *Annual Review of Psychology, 66*(1), 547–574. doi:10.1146/annurev-psych-010814-015025

Kang, S. K., & Bodenhausen, G. V. (2015). Multiple identities in social perception and interaction: challenges and opportunities. *Annual Review of Psychology, 66*(1), 547–574. doi:10.1146/annurev-psych-010814-015025

King, E. B., Reilly, C., & Hebl, M. R. (2008). The best and worst of times: Dual perspectives of coming out in the workplace. *Group and Organization Management, 33*, 566–601. doi:10.1177/1059601108321834

Kulik, C. T., Bainbridge, H., & Cregan, C. (2008). Known by the company we keep: Stigma by association effects in the workplace. *Academy of Management Review, 33*, 216–230.

LaFromboise, T., Coleman, H. L., & Gerton, J. (1993). Psychological impact of biculturalism: Evidence and theory. *Psychological Bulletin, 114*(3), 395.

Lidderdale, M. A., Croteau, J. M., Anderson, M. Z., Tovar-Murray, D., & Davis, J. M. (2007). Building lesbian, gay, and bisexual vocational psychology: a theoretical model of workplace sexual identity management. In *Handbook of counseling and psychotherapy with lesbian, gay, bisexual, and transgender clients* (2nd ed., pp. 245–270). Washington, DC: American Psychological Association.

Loiacano, D. K. (1989). Gay identity issues among Black Americans: Racism, homophobia, and the need for validation. *Journal of Counseling & Development, 68*(1), 21–25.

Lynch, J. W., & Rodell, J. B. (2018). Blend in or stand out? Interpersonal outcomes of managing concealable stigmas at work. *Journal of Applied Psychology, 103*(12), 1307–1323.

Lyons, B. J., Pek, S., & Wessel, J. L. (2017). Toward a "sunlit path": Stigma identity management as a source of localized social change through interaction. *Academy of Management Review, 42*(4), 618–636. doi:10.5465/amr.2015.0189

Lyons, B. J., Wessel, J. L., Ghumman, S. Ryan, A. M. & Kim, S. Y. (2014). Applying models of employee identity management across cultures: Christianity in the United States and South Korea. *Journal of Organizational Behavior, 35*, 678–704.

Mahalingam, R., Balan, S., & Haritatos, J. (2008). Engendering Immigrant Psychology: An Intersectionality Perspective. *Sex Roles, 59*(5), 326–336. doi:10.1007/s11199-008-9495-2

McDonald, G. J. (1982). Individual differences in the coming out process for gay men: Implications for theoretical models. *Journal of Homosexuality, 8*(1), 47–60. doi:10.1300/J082v08n01_05

Meyer, I. H. (2003). Prejudice, social stress, and mental health in lesbian, gay, and bisexual populations: Conceptual issues and research evidence. *Psychological Bulletin, 129*(5), 674–697. doi:10.1037/0033-2909.129.5.674

Park, R. E. (1928). Human migrations and the marginal man. *American Journal of Sociology, 33*, 881–893. doi:10.1086/214592

Petriglieri, J. L. (2011). Under threat: Responses to and the consequences of threats to individual identities. *Academy of Management Review, 36*(4), 641–662. doi:10.5465/amr.2009.0087

Phillips, K. W., Rothbard, N. P., & Dumas, T. L. (2009). To disclose or not to disclose? Status distance and self-disclosure in diverse environments. *Academy of Management Review, 34*, 710–732. doi:10.5465/AMR.2009.44886051

Pichler, S., & Ruggs, E. N. (2015). LGBT workers. In A. Collela & E. B. King (Eds.), *Oxford Handbook of Workplace Discrimination*. New York, NY: Oxford University Press.

Purdie-Vaughns, V., & Eibach, R. P. (2008). Intersectional invisibility: The distinctive advantages and disadvantages of multiple subordinate-group identities. *Sex Roles, 59*, 377–391.

Ragins, B. R. (2004). Sexual orientation in the workplace: The unique work and career experiences of gay, lesbian and bisexual workers. *Research in Personnel and Human Resource Management, 23*, 37–122. doi:10.1016/S0742-7301(04)23002-X

Ragins, B. R. (2008). Disclosure disconnected: Antecedents and consequences of disclosure invisible stigmas across life domains. *Academy of Management Review, 33*. doi:10.5465/AMR.2008.27752724

Ragins, B. R. (2008). Disclosure disconnected: Antecedents and consequences of disclosure invisible stigmas across life domains. *Academy of Management Review, 33*, 194–215.

Ragins, B. R., & Cornwell, J. M. (2001). Pink triangles: Antecedents and consequences of perceived workplace discrimination against gay and lesbian employees. *Journal of Applied Psychology, 86*, 1244–1261. doi:10.1037/0021-9010.86.6.1244

Ramarajan, L., & Reid, E. (2013). Shattering the myth of seperate worlds: Negotiating non-work identities at work. *Academy of Management Review, 38*, 621–644. doi:10.5465/amr.2011.0314

Roberts, L. M. (2005). Changing faces: Professional image construction in diverse organizational settings. *Academy of Management Review, 30*, 685–711. doi:10.5465/AMR.2005.18378873

Roberts, L. M., & Creary, S. J. (2012). Positive identity construction. In G. Spreitzer & K. Cameron (Eds.), *The Oxford handbook of positive organizational scholarship*. New York, NY: Oxford University Press. doi:10.1093/oxfordhb/9780199734610.013.0006

Rosette, A. S., Ponce de Leon, R., Koval, C. Z., & Harrison, D. A. (2018). Intersectionality: Connecting experiences of gender with race at work. *Research in Organizational Behavior, 38*, 1–22. https://doi.org/10.1016/j.riob.2018.12.002

Rumens, N. (2012). Queering cross-sex friendships: An analysis of gay and bisexual men's workplace friendships with heterosexual women. *Human Relations, 8*, 955–978. doi:10.1177/0018726712442427

Sanchez, D. T., Shih, M. J., & Wilton, L. S. (Producer). (2014). Exploring the identity autonomy perspective (IAP): An integrative theoretical approach to multicultural and multiracial identity. In *The Oxford Handbook of Multicultural Identity*. New York, NY: Oxford University Press.

Sedlovskaya, A., Purdie-Vaughs, V., Eibach, R. P., LaFrance, M., Romero-Canyas, R., & Camp, N. P. (2013). Internalizing the closet: Concealment heightens the cognitive distinction between public and private selves. *Journal of Personality and Social Psychology, 104*, 695–715. doi:10.1037/a0031179

Settles, I. H. (2004). When multiple identities interfere: The role of identity centrality. *Personality and Social Psychology Bulletin, 30*, 487–500. doi:10.1177/0146167203261885

Shih, M., Young, M. J., & Bucher, A. (2013). Working to reduce the effects of discrimination: Identity management strategies in organizations. *68*(3), 145–157.

Sophie, J. (1986). A critical examination of stage theories of lesbian identity development. *Journal of Homosexuality, 12*(2), 39–51. doi:10.1300/J082v12n02_03

Stryker, S., & Serpe, R. T. (1994). Identity salience and psychological centrality: Equivalent, overlapping and complementary concepts? *Social Psychology Quarterly, 57*, 16–35. doi:10.2307/2786972

Swann, W. B., Polzer, J., Seyle, D., & Ko, S. (2004). Finding value in diversity: Verification of personal and social self-views in diverse groups. *Academy of Management Review, 29*, 9–27. doi:10.5465/AMR.2004.11851702

Trau, R. N. C. (2015). The impact of discriminatory climate perceptions on the composition of interorganizational developmental networks, psychosocial support, and job and career attitudes of employees with an invisible stigma. *Human Resource Management, 54*, 345–366. doi:10.1002/hrm.21630

Troiden, R. R. (1993). *The formation of homosexual identities.* New York, NY: Columbia University Press.

Villicana, A. J., Delucio, K., & Biernat, M. (2016). "Coming out" among gay Latino and gay White men: implications of verbal disclosure for well-being. *Self and Identity, 15*(4), 468–487. doi:10.1080/15298868.2016.1156568

Vora, D., Martin, L., Fitzsimmons, S. R., Pekerti, A. A., Lakshman, C., & Raheem, S. (2018). Multiculturalism within individuals: A review, critique, and agenda for future research. *Journal of International Business Studies.* doi:10.1057/s41267-018-0191-3

Woods, J. D. (1993). *The corporate closet.* New York, NY: Free Press.

CHAPTER 6

ORGANIZATIONAL IDENTITY GROUP RELATIONS IN THE TRUMP ERA

An Asymmetric Model of Diversity and Inclusion Norm Violations

Alison M. Konrad
Western University

This chapter examines recent theory and research on identity group relations in organizations with the purpose of distinguishing between accounts that consider the impact of status differentials between identity groups and those which fail to do so. Making this distinction is important to the validity of diversity and inclusion (D&I) theorizing, and therefore, the usefulness of the field for predicting and explaining the emergence and impact of identity group dynamics in organizations. Developing valid and usable D&I theory is particularly important in contemporary times when some political leaders have chosen to inflame intergroup tensions with hateful rhetoric in order to garner and solidify a power base (Corrington & Hebl, 2018; Konrad, 2018). Sadly, these inflamed tensions enter work organizations with damaging consequences (Ferdman, 2018), such as impaired working relationships, weakened norms of workplace civility and devel-

Pushing Our Understanding of Diversity in Organizations, pp. 135–152
Copyright © 2020 by Information Age Publishing
135

opment of countercultural subgroups alienated from organizational D&I values. Tracing the processes through which such damage occurs may be valuable for identifying actions organizational leaders can take to limit these negative effects.

Making the distinction between high and low status identity groups in D&I scholarship is critical for recognizing the intergroup dynamics most likely to be damaging and difficult for leaders to manage. In particular, the intergroup processes resulting when high status groups assent to negative attitudes, beliefs, and behaviors toward low status groups are distinctively dynamic and self-perpetuating (Hekman, Johnson, Foo, & Yang, 2017; Ridgeway & Correll, 2006). These processes bring divisive societal-level political debates into the workplace to generate D&I norm violations, briefly defined as behaviors that violate the organization's D&I values and/ or damage the organization's D&I climate. These ugly dynamics threaten organizational efforts to enhance the status of historically marginalized groups by labeling those efforts as illegitimate.

In the next sections, I first draw upon a select set of articles published in top tier journals within the field of management and organizational studies to illustrate the conceptual and methodological effects of formally considering status as an analytical construct in D&I scholarship. Conceptually, D&I theorizing which takes status into consideration results in the development of asymmetric arguments identifying distinctive workplace processes experienced by high and low status identity groups. Methodologically, considering status alters D&I analyses in ways that allow researchers to test for possible intergroup differences in patterns of findings.

Next, based on substantial evidence for status effects, I apply and extend theory to explain workplace D&I norm violations generated by divisive political rhetoric exaggerating the threatening nature of low status identity groups. The analysis is inspired by the election of U.S. President Donald Trump in 2016, with attention to his core base of supporters. Given that President Trump has been able to maintain a consistent base of support whereby between 35 and 45% of the U.S. public approve of his presidential job performance (Gallup, 2018), understanding his appeal may help to illuminate troubling identity group dynamics extant in contemporary work organizations. Theory development in this area may be useful for identifying factors leaders can attend to and manage to prevent and mitigate potential D&I norm violations and their negative effects.

ORGANIZATIONAL IDENTITY GROUP DYNAMICS: RECENT EVIDENCE

Recent D&I scholarship shows a vibrant variety of theoretical and methodological approaches, generating a rich and growing understanding of identity group relations in work organizations. Many papers take a "symmetric" approach to theorizing whereby the experiences of high and low status groups are treated as similar, if not equivalent. Such work is beneficial for uncovering basic human tendencies driving intergroup relations that affect all identity groups. A growing number of other papers take an "asymmetric" approach (Chattopadhyay, 1999, 2003) by conceptualizing ways that the experiences of high and low status groups follow distinctive processes generating different outcomes. This work is vital for building knowledge of the interplay between identity group dynamics and status effects, which pose some of the greatest D&I challenges faced by organizational leaders.

The Symmetric Approach

While the theoretical foundation of D&I scholarship continues to develop and expand, at their core, symmetric approaches to D&I often draw upon similarity-attraction theory (Byrne, 1971), social identity theory (Tajfel & Turner, 1986), and/or the business case for diversity (Cox, 2001). Similarity-attraction theory began as an individualistic paradigm arguing that individuals are significantly more attracted to interacting with others whose attitudes, beliefs and values are similar to their own (Byrne, 1971). Social identity theory is a more collectivistic approach, arguing for the importance of the sense of self as a member of one or more groups of individuals, for instance, women, Canadians, or members of the Deaf community, called "identity groups." Individuals are biased in favor of viewing their own identity groups (in-groups) more positively than other groups (out-groups). Together, the similarity-attraction and social identity theory perspectives form what Harrison and Klein (2007) call the "separation" approach to D&I. The separation approach is based upon numerous findings showing that all identity groups, regardless of their status in society, show a preference for similar others who are members of the in-group and a bias against different others who are members of out-groups.

The business case for diversity argues that a demographically diverse human capital base can enhance organizational performance due to greater variety in knowledge, information, and perspectives. This variety potentially enhances creativity and problem solving as well as understanding of a diverse customer base (Cox, 2001; Cox & Blake, 1991). Harrison and Klein (2007) label this perspective the "variety" approach to D&I. The variety approach is based upon the value of diversity over homogeneity, regardless of whether a homogeneous organization must add low or high status group members in order to enhance its diversity.

D&I scholarship has integrated these views through assumptions and theorizing. D&I scholarship has often assumed that knowledge, attitudes, beliefs and values are more similar within identity groups than between them. This assumption has been contested (Lawrence, 1997), however, the notion that identity groups differ in work attitudes, beliefs and values has received weak to moderate empirical support (e.g., Greenhaus, Parasuraman, & Wormley, 1990; Konrad, Ritchie, Lieb, & Corrigall, 2000; Simons, Friedman, Liu, & McLean Parks, 2007; Twenge, 2010). A powerful example of theorizing combining these views is the categorization-elaboration model (CEM; van Knippenberg, De Dreu, & Homan, 2004) which indicates that diversity in teams leads to greater elaboration of information and perspectives for improved decision-making and performance, but only under the condition of low levels of categorization and identity threat. Also, the inclusion framework by Shore et al. (2011) argues that the sense of inclusion is highest in workplaces where individuals who are relatively unique in that they are demographically distinct from most others also experience a high level of belongingness because they are, "treated as an insider and also allowed/encouraged to retain uniqueness within the work group" (Figure 1, p. 1266).

The separation and variety approaches take a symmetric view of D&I because they are conceptually applicable to all identity groups and predict similar outcomes regardless of the status of the group(s) to which an individual belongs. To quote a D&I study recently published in a top-tier journal, "according to the categorization-elaboration model … any category of diversity can result in categorization processes and in-group bias" (Spoelma & Ellis, 2017, Abstract, p. 1344). In this approach, members of any identity group add variety to and potentially experience bias and discrimination from members of other groups through the same psychological and behavioral processes.

Several recently published top-tier articles take a symmetric approach. For example, Spoelma and Ellis (2017) theorize that members of work teams show in-group bias by considering ideas generated by in-group members to be more "truly creative and worth building upon" (p. 1346) than ideas generated by members of out-groups. The negative impact of this bias disappears when work teams are under threat of negative consequences for poor performance. Westphal and Shani (2016) find that members of the corporate elite focus on shared characteristics with high-status others prior to interacting with them. Furthermore, they find that this focus on shared qualities is particularly valuable for influencing high status individuals to recommend a demographically dissimilar colleague for a board appointment at another firm. Lindsey, Avery, Dawson, and King (2017) find that when management and employees have a higher level of ethnic similarity, employees are less likely to perceive themselves as experiencing interpersonal mistreatment at work, and that this effect is stronger for employees who are ethnically dissimilar to their supervisor and coworkers. All three of these studies propose processes through which shared identity group memberships create a foundation for positive social interaction at work, and these dynamics are described as symmetric or similar in form regardless of whether an individual is a member of a high or a low status identity group, that is, for women and men, White and non-White, persons with and without disabilities, and so forth.

Symmetric approaches to D&I emphasize how intergroup dynamics constitute human universals in that they are important to all members of work organizations, regardless of identity group status. As such, they illustrate how "everyone" is included in D&I values, goals, and initiatives, which is valuable for overcoming resistance to D&I (Thomas, 2008). Conceptually, symmetric approaches are intended to be generalizable across contexts and implicitly assume that historical intergroup inequalities need not be considered to understand the impact of diversity on workplace outcomes.

Methodologically, symmetric approaches measure diversity in ways that combine high and low status group members into the same analytic category (e.g., Nishii, 2013; Nishii & Mayer, 2009). For instance, the Blau index of heterogeneity is equivalent for teams that are 90% male and teams that are 90% female. The Euclidian distance measure is equivalent for a White manager who leads a team that is 90% Black and for a Black manager who leads a team that is 90% White. By treating these different situations as being the same in analysis, the symmetric approach obscures any differences between the experiences of high and low status groups that might be present in the data. It is possible to "test for" status effects by, for instance, examining whether gender moderates the impact of gender diversity using a multiplicative interaction term (e.g., female dummy variable × Blau index of gender diversity). However, interaction tests are notoriously low in statistical power (Aguinis, Beaty, Boik, & Pierce, 2005). Particularly in the case of larger, powerful business sectors where women and ethnic minorities tend to be found in low numbers, unequal sample sizes mean that such tests are likely to show nonsignificant findings even when real differences exist in the sample.

Furthermore, when samples include relatively small proportions of low status groups, "main effect" findings are likely to reflect traditional workplaces where high status identity groups are also higher in organizational status and power. The study of corporate elites by Westphal and Shani (2016), for instance, likely indicates the value of emphasizing shared characteristics with high status others for women and members of ethnic minority groups who are interacting with White men (the predominant configuration in the population) and may have relatively little relevance for White men interacting with high status women or ethnic minorities (as there are likely to be very few of these dyads in the sample).

While the symmetric approach is valuable for theoretical, methodological and practical reasons, it also raises the threat of cooptation by historically privileged groups. Theorizing that "everyone" experiences bias, discrimination and poorer social interactions when they are in the numerical minority creates space for a "White men, too" discourse. For instance, the findings cited in this section suggest that having one's ideas devalued in creative teams, having to cognitively search for similarities to high status others to gain a board appointment, and experiencing interpersonal mistreatment at work when your ethnic category does not match that of the predominating management group happens to everyone, "White men, too." While I have suggested that this type of conclusion is false for methodological reasons, the message that "we are all in the D&I boat together" is "palatable" for individuals who might otherwise find the D&I field difficult to "stomach."[1] As such, the separation and variety perspectives are highly likely to be included in D&I teaching and executive education because they are nonthreatening to high status groups, who tend to be the informal leaders in classrooms (Konrad, Radcliffe, & Shin, 2016; Konrad, Seidel, Lo, Bhardwaj, & Qureshi, 2017) and therefore have substantial voice concerning the acceptability of both the content being taught and the person doing the teaching.

The Asymmetric Approach

The asymmetric approach to D&I scholarship explicitly considers whether high and low status identity group members have distinct experiences in diverse work organizations. In the asymmetric approach, authors integrate theoretical perspectives on power, inequality, and D&I to predict that high and low status groups have different outcomes in diverse organizations and to articulate the different processes through which those outcomes occur. Research models and measurement in this perspective take what Harrison and Klein (2007) called the "disparity" approach to uncover inequalities between groups in access to productivity-enhancing resources and desirable workplace outcomes.

Ridgeway's (1991) status characteristics theory provides an important conceptual foundation for D&I scholarship taking the asymmetric approach (e.g., Abraham, 2017; Chatman & O'Reilly, 2004; Geddes & Konrad, 2003; Graham, Dust, & Ziegert, 2018). Status characteristics theory (Ridgeway, 1991; Ridgeway & Balkwell, 1997; Ridgeway & Correll, 2006) links a societal history of unequal access to productivity-enhancing resources between identity groups to expectations for individual identity group members' performance in task groups. A history of unequal access to resources such as high quality education, socialization for professional occupations, and munificent network connections creates inequalities between identity groups in their ability to add value in the workplace. These group-level differences in preparation generate a history of experiences where members of different identity groups systematically show different levels of contribution to task effectiveness in groups. Members of those identity groups with the most access to productivity-enhancing resources generally perform better and add greater value to task success than members of less privileged identity groups. Over time, people come to accord higher status to members of more productive identity groups and lower status to members of less productive groups based on expectations for their ability to add value to task teams. As performance-related stereotypes become attached to otherwise nominal categories such as male and female gender, White and visible minority racioethnicity, these categorizations come to be associated with high or low status. Ridgeway (1991) calls such categories, "status characteristics."

Furthermore, Ridgeway (1991; Ridgeway & Balkwell, 1997; Ridgeway & Correll, 2006) outlines the asymmetric team processes through which historically-determined status characteristics and their associated stereotypes are replicated and reinforced in organizations. She argues that the high performance expectations enjoyed by members of high status groups lead team leaders and members to provide them with more speaking time, assign them to more challenging tasks, and show positive bias in evaluating their ideas and actions. These tendencies provide members of high status identity groups with many opportunities to add value. Members of low status identity groups experience a different process in teams where they receive less speaking time, are more likely to be interrupted, are assigned to easier sub-tasks, and endure negative evaluation bias in assessments, all of which damage their ability to perform.

Some recent studies take an asymmetric approach to theorizing and research. For instance, Hekman et al. (2017) find that while raters penalize non-White or female leaders for engaging in diversity-valuing behaviors by giving them lower performance ratings, the ratings of White or male leaders are unaffected by such behaviors. They theorized that this asymmetric effect occurs because diversity-valuing behaviors make leaders' low-status racioethnicity or gender "instantly salient, thus activating negative stereotypes associated with their low-status category" (p. 773). Zapata, Carton, and Liu (2016) found that when leaders adhered to interpersonal justice rules, subordinates gave higher ratings to White leaders than to their racioethnic minority counterparts but showed no evaluation bias against leaders who violated interpersonal justice rules (i.e., rating White and non-White justice violators similarly negatively). These authors attributed their findings to the effect of stereotype inhibition, "Supervisors who violate interpersonal justice rules trigger subordinates to search for reasons why their supervisors are threatening them, causing subordinates to be more attuned to supervisors' individual characteristics, and therefore unlikely to use stereotypes when evaluating them" (Abstract, p. 1150). Pearce and Xu (2012) find that female supervisors show evaluation bias in favor of same-gender subordinates while male supervisors do not. They explain their findings by suggesting that, "those supervisors not occupying high-status demographic groups might be highly sensitive to the relative status loss implied by having subordinates in high-status demographic groups and may be motivated to defend their relative standing" (p. 375) by rating such subordinates more negatively.[2]

Methodologically, asymmetric D&I research measures diversity in ways that distinguish between members of high and low status groups in order to examine data for possible differences in experiences of workplace processes and outcomes, such as comparing men and women or examining relationships with the percentages of White and racioethnic minority employees. For example, McKay, Avery, and Morris (2008) found that a positive diversity climate increased the relative sales performance of Black and Hispanic employees, with the impact of reducing racioethnic performance disparities. Pugh, Dietz, Brief, and Wiley (2008) found that the relationship between percentage of racioethnic minorities in the workplace and diversity climate becomes more strongly positive as the percentage of racioethnic minorities in the surrounding community increased. Chattopadhyay, George, and Lawrence (2004) found that MBA students perceived their assigned project teams more clearly and positively when the teams had lower proportions of women and non-Australians, identified as low-status groups in the research context. A methodological challenge for the asymmetric approach to D&I continues to be the fact that many datasets show highly unequal frequency distributions with low proportions of low status identity groups, which reduce the power of statistical tests to detect real intergroup differences in workplace experiences. A potential solution to this statistical problem is randomly selecting a matching high-status group member for each of the members of low-status groups to create a balanced and matched sample, but this step is not often taken.

In summary, the asymmetric approach to D&I is essential for revealing workplace disparities in organizational processes and outcomes for high and low status identity groups. This approach acknowledges the ongoing impact of a history of unequal intergroup access to productivity-enhancing resources. Due to the positive expectations associated with membership in high status identity groups (Ridgeway, 1991), members of these groups show more positive workplace outcomes when in the numerical minority (e.g., glass escalators v. glass ceilings, Maume, 1999), enjoy considerably stronger in-group bias effects (Bettencourt, Dorr, Charlton, & Hume, 2001) and show less interest in building demographically diverse personal networks than members of low status identity groups do (Konrad et al., 2017). Altogether, substantial evidence supports the contention that identity group status has significant impact on processes and outcomes in a diverse workplace, with important implications for inclusion and effectiveness. Such effects are among the most difficult for leaders to manage because efforts to improve intergroup equity and equality in the workplace threaten the privileged status of historically predominant groups (Thomas, 2008).

ASYMMETRIC D&I NORM VIOLATION IN THE WORKPLACE

Since the election of President Donald Trump, aggression against low status identity groups has increased in U.S. society, as indicated by a 17% increase in hate crimes reported by the FBI in 2017 (Schneider, 2018). This behavior and the dynamics driving it infiltrate work organizations, resulting in challenging incidents of D&I norm violations that are difficult for leaders to manage. D&I norm violations, as behaviors that violate organizational D&I values and/or damage the organizational D&I climate, are a form of workplace aggression targeting individuals or groups because of their social identity group membership(s). As a form of workplace aggression, D&I norm violations are intentional acts that can be verbal or physical, passive or active, indirect or direct (Baron & Neuman, 1996), and include instances of workplace victimization targeting members of specific identity groups. Examples include sexual and gender harassment (Kabat-Farr & Cortina, 2014), racial and ethnic microaggressions (Lewis & Neville, 2015; Shenoy-Packer, 2015; Sue, Bucceri, Lin, Nadal, & Torino, 2009; Sue et al., 2007), and presentation of symbols and other physical manifestations of White supremacy (Liu & Pechenkina, 2016). D&I norm violations can also include acts of bullying (Salin, 2003), incivility (Andersson & Pearson, 1999), and social undermining (Duffy, Ganster, & Pagon, 2002) targeting specific social identity groups and/or their members. For instance, selective incivility, or, "low-intensity deviant behavior with ambiguous intent to harm the target, in violation of workplace norms for mutual respect" (Andersson & Pearson, 1999, p. 457) targeting individuals or groups because of their identity group membership(s) constitute D&I norm violations. Such acts violate the D&I values of respecting all identity groups, appreciating a variety of perspectives and knowledge bases, and promoting the expression of social identities in the workplace (Hajro, Gibson, & Pudelko, 2017). As such, they have the potential to damage the diversity climate in diverse work teams by harming fairness perceptions (McKay et al., 2008) and reducing participation in integrative, problem-solving discussions (Dwertmann, Nishii, & van Knippenberg, 2016).

As an example, in July, 2017, Google engineer James Damore shared a 10-page document that came to be known as a "manifesto" arguing that the lack of women in technology leadership is due in part to innate differences in the preferences and abilities of women and men (Redden & Davis, 2017, August 6). The document angered many female Google staff and presented Google's leaders with a challenge to the company's culture and D&I efforts. After protracted debate, the leadership team decided to terminate Mr. Damore for breaching the company's basic values and code of ethics by perpetuating gender stereotypes (Waters, 2017, August 8). In an e-mail to all employees explaining their response, CEO Sundar Pichai wrote that saying "a group of our colleagues have traits that make them less biologically suited to that work [i.e., the technology industry] is offensive and not OK" (Waters, 2017, August 8).

The phenomenon of D&I norm violation in response to relative status loss has received relatively little attention from management and organization studies scholars. Leaders in this area include Berdahl (2007), who documented that women with masculine (i.e., assertive, dominant and independent) personalities are relatively frequent targets of sexual harassment, and Aquino and Douglas (2003), who found that experiencing identity threat at work is a positive predictor of antisocial behavior toward other employees. Both of these studies showed that status loss predicts workplace aggression; specifically, the sexual harassment of women who threaten men's predominance with their strong personalities, and interpersonal aggression as a response to attacks on one's sense of competence, dignity, or self-worth.

Theory development is needed to help leaders prevent and manage incidents of D&I norm violations in response to the organizational advancement of members of historically marginalized groups, such as that perpetrated by former Googler James Damore. Prior work has shown that justification from legitimate authority figures increases discrimination against low status groups whereas justification from a non-legitimate authority does not (Brief, Dietz, Cohen, Pugh, & Vaslow, 2000). As such, the legitimation resulting from the election of a U.S. President who regularly articulates policy rationales justifying discrimination is likely a causal factor fueling the increase in U.S. hate crimes. While incidents of workplace aggression rarely sink to the level of hate crimes, the sense among high status group members that they have a legitimate grievance when they incur a loss relative to low status groups threatens to increase D&I norm violations in the form of workplace incivility, harassment and bullying of low status groups.

President Trump shows a pattern of inflaming such grievances at his numerous in-person rallies across the nation (Bort, 2018, November 5). By doing so, he increases the likelihood of workplace D&I norm violations which leaders must handle. A striking quality of these rallies is the high level of *enjoyment* evidenced by rally-goers as they applaud President Trump's hate-filled statements (Johnson & Li, 2018). The positive emotion associated with perpetrating aggression against low status groups is a central driver in my model explaining asymmetric D&I norm violations in the workplace (Figure 6.1).

Figure 6.1 depicts workplace intergroup aggression as a D&I norm violation, meaning that aggression against low status groups violates the norms of the organizational culture. As documented by Brief et al. (2000), validation by a legitimate leader increases such discriminatory behavior. In that study, when the President of a hypothetical client company gave a business justification for discriminating, students were only half as likely to include African American members on the client project team. In Figure 6.1, the effect of validation from a legitimate external leader is shown as a direct antecedent of D&I norm violations. As documented by Aquino and Douglas (2003) in their survey study of 308 employees in three organizations, the anger resulting from a perceived loss of relative status is a key trigger of interpersonal aggression, a subset of D&I norm-violating behaviors. Such perceived status losses might arise at a personal level when a high status group member loses a promotion to a member of a low status group. For example, Konrad, Ross, and Linnehan (2006) found in their experimental study that White students considered a promotion to be less fair when a Black man was promoted instead of an equivalent White man, and more fair when the White man received the promotion. Perceived status losses can also arise at a collective identity group level from seeing the members of low status groups such as women and racioethnic minorities increase their representation among senior leadership positions (a factor that seemed to trigger Damore's writing of his "manifesto"). Membership in a high status identity group is depicted as a moderator of the link between anger and violating a D&I norm due to the impact of unmet expectations of entitlement (O'Brien & Major, 2005). As such, the model indicates asymmetry in that high status groups are particularly likely to engage in D&I norm violations as a result of status losses relative to other identity groups.

The model leverages self-determination theory (Ryan & Deci, 2000) to explain the positive emotions driving and reinforcing acts of D&I norm violations. Violating a D&I norm in the workplace enhances feelings of self-determination because it demonstrates the inability of organizational leaders to control perpetrators against their will. Violating D&I norms also engenders the anticipation of social sanctioning. Anticipated social

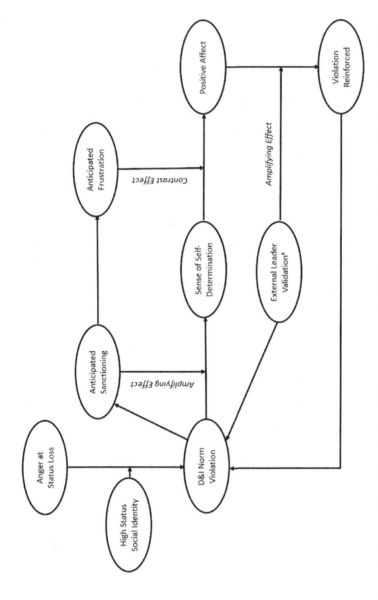

Note: All arrows indicate positive effects. [a]The model assumes that such validation occurs from leaders outside the work organization.

Figure 6.1. Model of organizational D&I norm violations.

sanctioning amplifies or strengthens the link between violating a norm and feeling self-determined because violating a norm in the face of greater sanctioning indicates having greater power to overcome external attempts at control.

Subsequently, the model indicates that a sense of self-determination leads to feelings of positive affect. Here, the anticipated frustration linked to social sanctioning amplifies this link due to the positive contrast between expecting a negative emotion and instead experiencing a positive one (i.e., rather than feeling frustrated, the perpetrator feels enjoyment). As such, the model indicates that more egregious violations involving stronger social sanctions ironically generate the most positive enjoyment outcomes for the perpetrator, due to their signaling of self-determined independent action. This amplified enjoyment might explain why D&I norm-violating acts are often accompanied by claims that these acts are disallowed (regardless of whether such claims are factual). As Damore stated about Google, "Google's left bias has created a politically correct monoculture that maintains its hold by shaming dissenters into silence" (Damore, 2017, p. 3).

The final step in the model shows how validation by a legitimate external leader amplifies the reinforcing effect of the intrinsic enjoyment of violating D&I norms. Individuals desire to repeat actions that are enjoyable and therefore intrinsically motivating. Validation of D&I norm violations by a legitimate external leader strengthens this reinforcing effect by articulating a justifying logic which ameliorates any sense of guilt or shame associated with inflicting hurt on vulnerable targets (Brief et al., 2000). In this way, irresponsible political leadership generates and perpetuates workplace D&I norm violations in a dynamic, self-sustaining cycle.

DISCUSSION AND CONCLUSIONS

While both symmetric and asymmetric approaches to D&I add value to the field, there is a need for theory articulating the distinctly different organizational processes and outcomes associated with membership in high versus low status identity groups. Asymmetric dynamics generate some of the most challenging incidents of D&I norm violations in organizations, and theory development is needed to provide leaders with solutions to these difficult problems. The need is particularly urgent when elected political leaders incite and inflame intergroup tensions by promulgating hateful rhetoric in order to build and maintain a power base. While the heatedness of political rhetoric varies over time, sadly, the voices of hate are continuously present in the environment (Southern Poverty Law Center, 2019), and organizational leaders must be prepared to deal with the D&I norm violations that they incite.

The impact on workplaces is broad and profound, as indicated by the asymmetric model of D&I norm violations developed in this paper. First, the anger inflamed by irresponsible politicians, such as President Trump (Corrington & Hebl, 2018; Konrad, 2018) fuels D&I norm violations that must be managed by organizational leaders. Second, by reinforcing violations of organizational values, irresponsible political leaders weaken norms of workplace civility. Third, irresponsible political leaders support the development of countercultural subgroups in organizations whose members validate each other's D&I norm-violating behavior.

This chapter's model of D&I norm violations also indicates several factors organizational leaders can attend to and manage to prevent and/ or mitigate the impact of these troubling incidents. First, organizational leaders must engage in problem-solving to reduce angry responses to the organizational advancement of historically marginalized groups. Such actions include providing accounts articulating the qualifications of individuals who are hired and promoted, explaining the business rationale for D&I activities, and showing openness to feedback on D&I activities as well as a willingness to make improvements to maximize fairness and equity. Second, leaders must strengthen workplace D&I norms by articulating expectations clearly and often and by holding organizational members accountable for norm violations that occur (i.e., D&I norm violations must be clearly and consistently sanctioned to avoid the contrast effect in Figure 6.1). Third, leaders must attend to the needs of the individual members of countercultural subgroups, ensuring that they receive equitable opportunities for self-determination and development. Providing appropriate outlets for fulfilling self-determination needs is likely to reduce counternormative aggression (Aquino & Douglas, 2003).

NOTES

1. Thank you, Derek Avery, for this fabulous metaphor.
2. This finding can also be explained as reflecting male subordinates' sensitivity to the relative status loss implied by being supervised by a member of the low-status gender category and resulting unwillingness to cooperate and perform well for a female supervisor.

REFERENCES

Abraham, M. (2017). Pay formalization revisited: Considering the effects of manager gender and discretion on closing the gender wage gap. *Academy of Management Journal, 60*(1), 29–54.

Aguinis, H., Beaty, J. C., Boik, R. J., & Pierce, C. A. (2005). Effect size and power in assessing moderating effects of categorical variables using multiple regression: a 30-year review. *Journal of Applied Psychology, 90*(1), 94–107.

Andersson, L. M., & Pearson, C. M. (1999). Tit for tat? The spiraling effect of incivility in the workplace. *Academy of Management Review, 24*(3), 452–471.

Aquino, K., & Douglas, S. (2003). Identity threat and antisocial behavior in organizations: The moderating effects of individual differences, aggressive modeling, and hierarchical status. *Organizational Behavior & Human Decision Processes, 90*(1), 195–208.

Baron, R. A., & Neuman, J. H. (1996). Workplace violence and workplace aggression: Evidence on their relative frequency and potential causes. *Aggressive Behavior, 22*(3), 161–173.

Berdahl, J. L. (2007). The sexual harassment of uppity women. *Journal of Applied Psychology, 92*, 425–437.

Bettencourt, B. A., Dorr, N., Charlton, K., & Hume, D. L. (2001). Status differences and in-group bias: A meta-analytic examination of the effects of status stability, status legitimacy, and group permeability. *Psychological Bulletin, 127*(4), 520–542.

Bort, R. (2018, November 5). Trump's closing message: Racism, violence and plenty of lies. Retrieved from https://bit.ly/2AlUhgY

Brief, A. P., Dietz, J., Cohen, R. R., Pugh, S. D., & Vaslow, J. B. (2000). Just doing business: Modern racism and obedience to authority as explanations for employment discrimination. *Organizational Behavior & Human Decision Processes, 81*(1), 72–97.

Byrne, D. (1971). *The attraction paradigm*. New York, NY: Academic Press.

Chatman, J. A., & O'Reilly, C. A. I. (2004). Asymmetric reactions to work group sex diversity among men and women. *Academy of Management Journal, 47*(2), 193–208.

Chattopadhyay, P. (1999). Beyond direct and symmetrical effects: The influence of demographic dissimilarity on organizational citizenship behaviors. *Academy of Management Journal, 42*(3), 273–287.

Chattopadhyay, P. (2003). Can dissimilarity lead to positive outcomes? The influence of open versus closed minds. *Journal of Organizational Behavior, 24*(3), 295–312.

Chattopadhyay, P., George, E., & Lawrence, S. A. (2004). Why does dissimilarity matter? Exploring self-categorization, self-enhancement, and uncertainty reduction. *Journal of Applied Psychology, 89*(5), 892–900.

Corrington, A., & Hebl, M. R. (2018). America clearly is not ready for a female president: Why? *Equality, Diversity & Inclusion: An International Journal, 37*(1), 31–43.

Cox, T., Jr. (2001). *Creating the multicultural organization: A strategy for capturing the power of diversity*. San Francisco, CA: Jossey-Bass.

Cox, T., Jr., & Blake, S. (1991). Managing cultural diversity: Implications for organizational competitiveness. *Academy of Management Executive, 5*(3), 45–56.

Damore, J. (2017, July). Google's ideological echo chamber. Retrieved from https://bit.ly/2wCkHqk

Duffy, M. K., Ganster, D. C., & Pagon, M. (2002). Social undermining in the workplace. *Academy of Management Journal, 45*(2), 331–351.

Dwertmann, D. J. G., Nishii, L. H., & van Knippenberg, D. (2016). Disentangling the fairness & discrimination and synergy perspectives on diversity climate: Moving the field forward. *Journal of Management, 42*(5), 1136–1168.

Ferdman, B. M. (2018). In Trump's shadow: Questioning and testing the boundaries of inclusion. *Equality, Diversity & Inclusion: An International Journal, 37*(1), 96–107.

Gallup. (2018). Trump Job Approval (Weekly). Retrieved from https://news.gallup.com/poll/203207/trump-job-approval-weekly.aspx

Geddes, D., & Konrad, A. M. (2003). Demographic differences and reactions to performance feedback. *Human Relations, 56*(12), 1485–1514.

Graham, K. A., Dust, S. B., & Ziegert, J. C. (2018). Supervisor-employee power distance incompatibility, gender similarity, and relationship conflict: A test of interpersonal interaction theory. *Journal of Applied Psychology, 103*(3), 334–346.

Greenhaus, J. H., Parasuraman, S., & Wormley, W. M. (1990). Effects of race on organizational experiences, job performance evaluations, and career outcomes. *Academy of Management Journal, 33*(1), 64–86.

Hajro, A., Gibson, C. B., & Pudelko, M. (2017). Knowledge exchange processes in multicultural teams: Linking organizational diversity climates to teams' effectiveness. *Academy of Management Journal, 60*(1), 345–372.

Harrison, D. A., & Klein, K. J. (2007). What's the difference? Diversity construct as separation, variety, or disparity in organizations. *Academy of Management Review, 32*, 1199–1228.

Hekman, D. R., Johnson, S. K., Foo, M.-D., & Yang, W. (2017). Does diversity-valuing behavior result in diminished performance ratings for non-White and female leaders? *Academy of Management Journal, 60*(2), 771–797.

Johnson, J., & Li, A. (2018, June 22). Chants, cheers, boos and the man at the center of it all. Retrieved from https://wapo.st/2IEZAim

Kabat-Farr, D., & Cortina, L. M. (2014). Sex-based harassment in employment: New insights into gender and context. *Law & Human Behavior, 38*(1), 58–72.

Konrad, A. M. (2018). Denial of racism and the Trump presidency. *Equality, Diversity & Inclusion: An International Journal, 37*(1), 14–30.

Konrad, A. M., Radcliffe, V., & Shin, D. (2016). Participation in helping networks as social capital mobilization: Impact on influence for domestic men, domestic women, and international MBA students. *Academy of Management Learning & Education, 15*(1), 60–78.

Konrad, A. M., Ritchie, J. E., Jr., Lieb, P., & Corrigall, E. A. (2000). Sex differences and similarities in job attribute preferences: A meta-analysis. *Psychological Bulletin, 126*(4), 593–641.

Konrad, A. M., Ross, G., & Linnehan, F. (2006). Is promoting an African American unfair? The triple interaction of participant ethnicity, target ethnicity, and ethnic identity. *Journal of Applied Social Psychology, 36*(5), 1215–1233.

Konrad, A. M., Seidel, M.-D., Lo, E., Bhardwaj, A., & Qureshi, I. (2017). Variety, dissimilarity, and status centrality in MBA networks: Is the minority or the majority more likely to network across diversity? *Academy of Management Learning & Education, 16*(3), 349–372.

Lawrence, B. S. (1997). The black box of organizational demography. *Organization Science, 8*(1), 1–22.

Lewis, J. A., & Neville, H. A. (2015). Construction and initial validation of the gendered racial microaggressions scale for Black women. *Journal of Counseling Psychology, 62*(2), 289–302.

Lindsey, A. P., Avery, D. R., Dawson, J. F., & King, E. B. (2017). Investigating why and for whom management ethnic representativesness influences interpersonal mistreatment in the workplace. *Journal of Applied Psychology, 102*(11), 1545–1563.

Liu, H., & Pechenkina, E. (2016). Staying quiet or rocking the boat? An autoethnography of organisational visual White supremacy. *Equality, Diversity & Inclusion: An International Journal, 35*(3), 186–204.

Maume, D. J., Jr. (1999). Glass ceilings and glass escalators: Occupational segregation and race and sex differences in managerial promotions. *Work & Occupations, 26*(4), 483–509.

McKay, P. F., Avery, D. R., & Morris, M. A. (2008). Mean racial-ethnic differences in employee sales performance: The moderating role of diversity climate. *Personnel Psychology, 61*, 349–374.

Nishii, L. H. (2013). The benefits of climate for inclusion for gender-diverse groups. *Academy of Management Journal, 56*(6), 1754–1774.

Nishii, L. H., & Mayer, D. M. (2009). Do inclusive leaders help to reduce turnover in diverse groups? The moderating role of leader-member exchange in the diversity to turnover relationship. *Journal of Applied Psychology, 94*, 1412–1426.

O'Brien, L. T., & Major, B. (2005). System-justifying beliefs and psychological well-being: The roles of group status and identity. *Personality & Social Psychology Bulletin, 31*(12), 1718–1729.

Pearce, J. L., & Xu, Q. J. (2012). Rating performance or contesting status: Evidence against the homophily explanation for supervisor demographic skew in performance ratings. *Organization Science, 23*(2), 373–385.

Pugh, S. D., Dietz, J., Brief, A. P., & Wiley, J. W. (2008). Looking inside and out: The impact of employee and community demographic composition on organizational diversity climate. *Journal of Applied Psychology, 93*, 1422–1428.

Redden, M., & Davis, N. (2017, August 6, August 6). Google staffer's hostility to affirmative action sparks furious backlash. *The Guardian*. Retrieved from https://bit.ly/2wjE2gE

Ridgeway, C. L. (1991). The social construction of status value: Gender and other nominal characteristics. *Social Forces, 70*(2), 367–386.

Ridgeway, C. L., & Balkwell, J. W. (1997). Group processes and the diffusion of status-beliefs. *Social Psychology Quarterly, 60*, 14–31.

Ridgeway, C. L., & Correll, S. J. (2006). Consensus and the creation of status beliefs. *Social Forces, 85*(1), 431–453.

Ryan, R. M., & Deci, E. L. (2000). Self-determination theory and the facilitation of intrinsic motivation, social development, and well-being. *American Psychologist, 55*(1), 68–78.

Salin, D. (2003). Ways of explaining workplace bullying: A review of enabling, motivating and precipitating structures and processes in the work environment. *Human Relations, 56*(10), 1213–1232.

Schneider, J. (2018, December 11). Hate crimes increased by 17% in 2017, FBI report finds. *CNN Politics.* Retrieved from https://cnn.it/2DFJQbv

Shenoy-Packer, S. (2015). Immigrant professionals, microaggressions, and critical sensemaking in the U.S. workplace. *Management Communication Quarterly, 29*(2), 257–275.

Shore, L. M., Randel, A. E., Chung, B. G., Dean, M. A., Ehrhart, K. H., & Singh, G. (2011). Inclusion and diversity in work groups: A review and model for future research. *Journal of Management, 37*(4), 1262–1289.

Simons, T., Friedman, R. A., Liu, L. A., & McLean Parks, J. (2007). Racial differences in sensitivity to behavioral integrity: Attitudinal consequences, in-group effects, and "trickle-down" among Black and non-Black employees. *Journal of Applied Psychology, 92*(3), 650–665.

Southern Poverty Law Center. (2019, February 19). New hate map helps users explore landscape of hate. Retrieved from https://www.splcenter.org/fighting-hate/intelligence-report/2019/new-hate-map

Spoelma, T. M., & Ellis, A. P. J. (2017). Fuse or fracture? Threat as a moderator of the effects of diversity faultlines in teams. *Journal of Applied Psychology, 102*(9), 1344–1359.

Sue, D. W., Bucceri, J., Lin, A. I., Nadal, K. L., & Torino, G. C. (2009). Racial microaggressions and the Asian American experience. *Asian American Journal of Psychology, S*(1), 88–101.

Sue, D. W., Capodilupo, C. M., Torino, G. C., Bucceri, J. M., Holder, A. M. B., Nadal, K. L., & Esquilin, M. (2007). Racial microaggressions in everyday life: Implications for clinical practice. *American Psychologist, 62*(4), 271–286.

Tajfel, H., & Turner, J. C. (1986). The social identity of intergroup behavior. In S. Worchel & W. G. Austin (Eds.), *Psychology and intergroup relations* (pp. 7–24). Chicago, IL: Nelson-Hall.

Thomas, K. M. (Ed.). (2008). *Diversity resistance in organizations.* New York, NY: Erlbaum.

Twenge, J. M. (2010). A review of the empirical evidence on generational differences in work attitudes. *Journal of Business & Psychology, 25,* 201–210.

van Knippenberg, D., De Dreu, C. K. W., & Homan, A. C. (2004). Work group diversity and group performance: An integrative model and research agenda. *Journal of Applied Psychology, 89,* 1008–1022.

Waters, R. (2017, August 8, August 8). Google engineer sacked over controversial gender memo. *Financial Times.* Retrieved from https://on.ft.com/2ujGYbQ

Westphal, J. D., & Shani, G. (2016). Psyched-up to suck-up: Self-regulated cognition, interpersonal influence, and recommendations for board appointments in the corporate elite. *Academy of Management Journal, 59*(2), 479–509.

Zapata, C. P., Carton, A. M., & Liu, J. T. (2016). When justice promotes injustice: Why minority leaders experience bias when they adhere to interpersonal justice rules. *Academy of Management Journal, 59*(4), 1150–1173.

CHAPTER 7

PROGRESS IN AFFIRMATIVE ACTION

How Backlash Is Holding Us Back

Andrew Lam
Dalhousie University

Eddy Ng
Bucknell University

INTRODUCTION

In August of 2017, Google engineer James Damore posted a 10-page missive against the company's diversity policies arguing that affirmative action (AA) hiring policies had resulted in a culture of extreme and unfair gender imbalances in the tech giant's workforce. Yet at the time of his complaint, Google's workforce was 69% male, 2% African American, with only 20% of females holding technical jobs, far below the national average of 26%. Google quickly responded with promises of greater diversity, but perhaps more importantly, this incident reflects the increasing animosity towards affirmative action policies (AAPs) expressed in backlash incidents in many Western democracies.

Pushing Our Understanding of Diversity in Organizations, pp. 153–182

AAPs are formal policy efforts which help disadvantaged and under-represented minority groups—such as women and people of color—move past systemic and ingrained racial and gender inequalities (Bobo, 1998; Kinder & Sanders, 1996). While equity seeking approaches exist, AAPs are the most effective method of promoting socioeconomic mobility for minorities (Hinrichs, 2012). Yet, despite its efficacy, AAPs face staunch opposition, with the most common critique being AAPs extend preferential treatment to undeserving groups and undermines the fundamental value of meritocracy cherished in Western democratic societies (Bobo & Kluegel, 1993). This opposition is rooted, in part, to violations of fairness rather than prejudicial beliefs alone (Bobocel, Son-Hing, Davey, Stanley, & Zanna, 1998; Heilman, McCullough, & Gilbert, 1996), which coincides with the "color-blind" narrative and a steady decline of traditional measures of racial prejudice and discrimination by Whites (Bobo, 1998; Schuman et al., 1997). Nevertheless, many consider the issues experienced by minor-ity groups (e.g., unemployment) are simply problems of individual ability, motivation, and work ethic (Lewis, 2004; Perry, 2001) rather than a con-sequence of structural inequity.

Economic insecurity among dominant social groups, often White men, and color-blind narratives result in increased incidents of backlash. In the US, AAPs are viewed to promote "reverse discrimination," which penal-izes dominant groups resulting in institutionalized backlash. In 2014, the US Supreme Court upheld a voter-approved ban on considering race in admissions to Michigan's public universities (Barnes, 2014; Liptak, 2014), following other precedents set by previous high-profile AA cases (DeSilver, 2014). More recently, the Justice Department under the Trump adminis-tration has moved against academic institutions who support AAPs. Fears of public challenges, loss of electorate power, and political opposition frequently sway policy makers to pivot towards less effective programs (Bakan & Kobayashi, 2007). These concessions, avoid voter and public backlash, but weaken policy efficacy. Backlash expressions also negatively affect women and minority applicants hired under AAPs in the form of stigmatization (presumed incompetence) and negative appraisals of ability or performance (Leslie, Mayer, & Kravitz, 2014; Resendez, 2002), in turn influencing self-perceived competence. AAP hires who report self-doubt choose less challenging roles (Heilman & Alcott, 2001), limiting their advancement and growth opportunities. Backlash also affects relationships and wellbeing at work, as AA hires experience antagonism, in the form of negative peer reviews and sabotage (Leibbrandt, Wang, & Foo, 2017) by their non-AA peers (Burke, 1997).

Researchers devote significant attention to understanding AAPs and the negative reaction AA elicits to improve policy effectiveness and support. Scholars focus on policy characteristics as varying levels of policy prescriptiveness affects perceptions fairness violations in differing ways (Harrison et al., 2006; Faniko et al., 2017). Research also found managerial beliefs and organizational practices (e.g., human resource management) also impact support and opposition to AAPs (Hiemstra & Derous, 2017; Levi & Fried, 2008). Yet despite scholarly efforts, there is little effort in understanding backlash and its manifestations. Furthermore, backlash often receives less or no research attention compared to AAPs as the primary topic of investigation. We argue that these issues have hindered our understanding of AA backlash, which is critically important in the present climate of divisiveness. Our intention here is, therefore, to map backlash in literature through summarizing previous work on backlash towards AA—how, when, and why—to help build a foundation for future work for minimizing backlash at work.

We begin with a short introduction to backlash by exploring its histori-cal underpinnings. We then provide an overview of backlash expressions evidenced in literature across various fields, including sociology, psychol-ogy, political sciences, public administration, and management. Next, we describe conditions that increase the risk of backlash that occur in public policies, the workplace, and institutions. We follow with several strategies found in research to reduce backlash against AA and consider how these strategies can be applied. Finally, we close with some implications towards current approaches to managing diversity and recommendations for future research attempts.

BACKGROUND ON AFFIRMATIVE ACTION BACKLASH

One view conceptualizes AA backlash incidents as overt and covert forms of dynamic resistance against progressive policy, mandates, and initiatives that promote the hiring, acceptance and advancement of historically mar-ginalized minority groups, such as women, people of color, the differently abled, and indigenous population (Crosby, 1994; Kidder, Lankou, Chrobot-Mason, Mollica, & Friedman, 2004). Backlash events are cumulative often (re)producing inequality, moral panic, and social divisions, and usually privileging dominant (White-male) groups (Garland, 2008; Hughey, 2014). Backlash is not necessarily rightist ideology, as many backlash defenders take neutral ground insisting opposition is based on violations of fairness (Bakan & Kobayashi, 2007; Bobocel, Son-Hing, Davey, Stanley, & Zanna, 1998; Pierce, 2013). This is problematic to policy makers and equity pro-ponents, as values of fairness are ingrained in Western democracies and fundamental to the neoliberal market, making backlash less an issue of equity but individual rights. Contemporary political and social volatility allows such past grievances avenues to erupt, making AAPs implemented in public and private sectors through legislation and past legal precedence (see Miller, 2017) targets for attack, and placing the future of equity efforts uncertain.

Coinciding with the Civil Rights Movement in the United States, the 1960s saw racial tensions spur the conception of the equity policy term "affirmative action" by President John F. Kennedy in 1961, who called for the aggressive hiring of minorities in the federal government (Chrisman, 2013). President Lyndon B. Johnson followed suit with Executive Order 11246 in 1965, establishing the requirements for AA practices when procuring for federal contracts. This policy sought to end discrimination and create jobs for urban minorities, but more importantly, it shifted responsibility of responding to discrimination from individuals to businesses, unions, and the federal government (Crosby, 2004). By addressing historic exploitation through formal governmental policy, AAPs become a new publicly recognized distributive order whereby marginalization is a systemic issue, and by the end of the late-1990s, AAPs were accepted as the primary tool to remedy historical discrimination (Premdas, 2016).

The 1970s, however, saw the US economy fall into recession, where stable factory jobs were downsized or outsourced overseas (Cowie, 2010). Disenchanted and out of work White men, who viewed themselves as deserving citizens, felt unfairly treated by governmental policies, minority hiring practices, and continued demands by minorities for equal resources and opportunities (Hughey, 2014, p. 722). White men quickly claimed centrist positions and challenged the fairness and constitutionality of equity policies (Bakan & Kobayashi, 2007; Burke & Black, 1997; Taylor, 1995). A critical point surfaced in the case of *University of California v. Bakke*, 438 U.S. 265 (1978), a landmark case on equity policy backlash. Allan Bakke, a 35-year-old White male and former Vietnam war veteran, was declined admission to the University of California, Davis Medical School in 1973 and 1974. Under the university's AAP, minority students with weaker academic profiles were accepted. Bakke filed the lawsuit against the university after his application was declined a second time arguing that he was rejected based on race, and that his civil rights was violated (Benfell, 1977). Although the Supreme Court decided against the University of California, stating that the school had violated the equal protection clause, AAPs could continue in higher education and employment, and policies based solely on race or merit were deemed to be illegal (Bakan & Kobayashi, 2007, p. 152). This case set important precedence in how AA was viewed in two ways. First, Justice Lewis Powell's support of using race is a factor in school admissions programs made diversity and equity a formal government interest (Brodin, 2017). Second, *Bakke's* win cemented ideas of "reverse discrimination," where equity policies are publicly recognized to be inherently discriminatory to majority groups (Bakan & Kobyashi, 2007; Hughey, 2014).

These ideas reverberated into the 1980s with the Reagan administration, with neoliberalism and open political and social hostility against AAPs. Reagan's neoliberal attitudes towards small government spending, minimal federal regulation and taxation resonated with the still-struggling White male majority (Dobbin, 2009). AAPs were the natural target, as they took away jobs from hard-working White men and gave them to minority populations that did not fully embody American values of merit—ability and qualifications (Anderson, 2004; Pierce, 2013; Taylor & Liss, 1992). Reagan failed to fully dismantle AAPs; however federal equity policies were left largely unenforced, leaving responsibility to individual organizations and institutions (Agocs & Burr, 1996; Dobbin, 2009). Many continued to support AAPs to avoid discrimination lawsuits, but due to its unpopularity, organizations applied a much more passive policy (Beller, 1984; Crosby, 1994; Holloway, 1989; Taylor & Liss, 1984). Importantly, the federal government was no longer responsible for social issues, shifting the responsibility for equity back to the public and individuals (Pierce, 2013). The prevailing view was that minority struggles were a result of group dysfunction rather than historic structural inequality. These sentiments reflected the social antagonism towards minority groups at the time, with conservative leaders blaming feminists, liberals, socialists, and Marxists for the degradation of American values and oppression of deserving White men (Hughey 2014). Progressive policies were viewed as discriminatory and hand-outs given to entitled, self-victimized minorities, and unfairly took opportunities away from more deserving White males (Rhodes, 2010; Hughey, 2014). In an infamous television commercial for White congressman Jesse Helms, a White hand was shown crumpling a rejection letter while a narrator intoned, *"You wanted that job, you were qualified, but it had to go to a minority because of quotas"* (Clayton, 1992). The 1980s and 1990s thereby saw the rise of White males as victims of unjust policies (Savran, 1998).

Another noteworthy case was *Adarand Constructors, Inc. v. Federico Peña, Secretary of Transportation*, 515 U.S. 200 (1995). Adarand Constructors Inc., a White-owned company, had lost a guardrail contract to a Gonzales Construction, despite putting in a lower bid. However, since Gonzales Construction had been certified as a disadvantaged business, they were protected by the Federal AAPs at the time and was awarded the contract. Adarand Constructors, Inc. subsequently filed a suit against the Department of Transportation arguing that the AAP was unconstitutional. The federal district court ruled in favor of the Department of Transportation sparking severe and cascading political backlash. As a response, Senator Bob Dole (R-KS) introduced the Equal Opportunity Act (1995), outlawing all federal race- and gender-preference programs. In 1996, the University of California ended preferential policies in admissions and hiring (Pierce, 2012). The same year saw California ballot proposition 209, known as the California Civil Rights Initiative, prohibiting state institutions from considering minority factors as part of public employment, contracting and education passed (Hughey, 2014, p. 725). In this short span, African American employment dropped 5.5%, while Latino employment dropped 6.9% (Holmes, 1996). By the late 1990s, any gains from the initial inception of AAPs by the Johnson administration was largely reversed (Pierce, 2013).

The 2008 election of U.S. President Barack Obama saw conservative movements, like the Tea Party and Birthers, signal modern forms of explicit and aggressive backlash (Hughey, 2014). To many Americans, the election of an African American president meant that a quintessential racial "other" had taken control of a nation. Critically, however, conservative movements are not monolithically hostile towards governmental policies; rather opposition is focused on the perceived "handouts" to undeserving groups, marked by racial and ethnic stereotypes (see Williamson, Skocpol, & Coggin, 2011). Thus, while economic insecurity—due to globalization —is the explicit rationale, opposition to AAPs are heavily influenced by race and culture (Burghart & Zeskind, 2010). Such hard-line conservative movements consist of a small minority, but nevertheless reflect growing popularity of a color-blind and post-racial society (Gallagher, 2003). Notions of race, racism, and historic or systemic prejudices are dismissed as constructions of progressive identity politics, and are often mocked or ignored (Doane, 2017; Miller, 2017; Yancy & Davidson, 2014). These trends draw broad similarities to the culture wars seen during the civil rights era (see Eastland, 1997), but the current reincarnation sees debates concerning race and prejudice as a hostile zero-sum game where minority gains are made at the expense of White majorities (Norton & Sommers, 2011). In sum, with President Barack Obama's election as president, the perceived prominence of minorities in fields like popular culture, the workplace, and politics, and the loss of opportunities for White group members have made many Whites fearful of reverse discrimination and a White minority (see Craig & Richeson, 2017; Craig, Rucker, & Richeson, 2018). Following the election of President Donald Trump, and bolstered by an unapologetic right-wing Supreme Court, progressive policies become targets of an active and aggressive conservative base (Ng & Stamper, 2018). This makes backlash an increasingly lethal threat to AAPs, with far reaching consequences for various stakeholders.

THE EXPRESSIONS OF BACKLASH

As backlash is broadly described as any resistance against progressive policy (see Kidder et al., 2004), its expressions are equally as broad. Drawing from extant literature from various fields, this section describes some important expressions and consequences of backlash.

Policy Concession and Accommodation

Fear of backlash or continued backlash from the public can compel policy makers to pivot to avoid disapproval and to gain legitimacy though pragmatically passing versions of progressive policies that reflect the majority (Young, 2002). The repeated practice of concessions and accommodation to backlash is where AAPs lose their efficacy. Thus, political acquiescence is equally or more powerful than explicit and dynamic forms of backlash -- such as protest, where backlash defenders become confident and aggressive resulting in ineffective equity outcome. Bakan & Kobayashi (2007) explores trend in Canada through two important case studies: (1) the Abella Commission, and (2) the Ontario (provincial) government's attempt to implement AA legislation in the 1990s. The Abella Commission, (Abella, 1984), was tasked with crafting a Canadian equivalent of American AAP. The Commission resulted in the Canadian Employment Equity Act (1986) (Agocs & Burr, 1996), which avoided backlash seen in the US and were more palatable to conservatives by adopting the less controversial terminology of "employment equity." Yet, along with this change in terminology, the Act carried a narrow and ineffective scope: equity policies were not applied to educational institutions, only a small segment of the workforce was included, and employers were not sanctioned for failing to achieve representation goals. A decade later during the 1990s, the Ontario government repeated these concessions. To pass an equity policy, Premier Bob Rae watered down provisions and surrendered responsibility for goals to employers to accommodate "different kinds of workplaces and workforces" (Bakan & Kobayashi, 2007). A few years later, the policy was repealed, and equity was no longer a focus. Even in Canada, which is socially progressive, pragmatism and fear of backlash led, rather than avoided, to greater backlash.

Reproduction of Structural Inequality

Backlash can reproduce existing structural inequality through both the legal sphere and everyday discursive practices. Legal expressions of backlash set important precedence in determining subsequent cases with similar interests. In *University of California v. Bakke* (1978) race was importantly legitimized as a compelling interest in higher education and as a national value (see Ball, 2000). As such, diversity as a value and AAPs as a policy were both formally recognized by the state; however, it was also articulated that AAPs were not remedies for past societal discrimination, but rather as a means for economic interests with tenants in neoliberalism (Hode & Meisenbach, 2016). In this way, the definition of diversity was formally separated from its systemic and historical underpinnings, with violations only being recognized when individual or state economics are infringed. Legal backlash expressions can result in a formalized narrow scope of diversity, allowing prejudicial inequality to continue. Discursive practices of "racing for innocence" in the workplace are similar. Specifically, Pierce (2003) illustrated how White middle-class men use speech to disavow accountability and proclaim innocence for instances of prejudice in the workplace while simultaneously acting prejudicially (p. 54). Racing for innocence has tenants in neoliberalism where values and sociality are enshrined in the individual experience. Prejudicial instances are then narrowly viewed as unusual, isolated and personal incidents, not as broader expressions of systemic injustice. Subjects used the innocent speech to claim neutrality and color-blindness, insisting that racial inequality had improved or were nonexistent. Highlighted incidents of prejudice were blamed on minority inadequacy and AA were redundant policies unfairly costing deserving White men jobs. AA backlash expressed in the legal realm or in the workplace narrow the scope of understanding of diversity values and prejudicial expressions, allowing inequality to continue.

Organizational Attractiveness and Perceived Quality

Organizations and institutions that implement AAPs can also experience backlash. James, Brief, Dietz and Cohen (2001) found White prospective job recruits rate a potential employer whose AAP is framed as explicitly benefiting black and people of color as less attractive than organizations whose AAPs are framed more broadly. Thus, poorly framed AAPs can illicit backlash from prospective employees and damage employer image, making organizations that implement equity policies appear less attractive to some White candidates. Similarly, organizations with AAPs may convey that they hire underqualified (and undeserving) candidates, thereby hurting a company's perceived talent quality. Kimura (1997) infamously opposed gender-based AAPs in academia, arguing that it leads to a decline in the quality of female academics, reduced respect for the professoriate, poorer education for students, and a deterioration in the relationship between male and female colleagues. She also argued that preferential hiring policies are fundamentally (and morally) flawed, as they erroneously deny native biological differences between male and female employees. Although unpopular, Kimura's (1997) comments reflects the opinions of many backlash defenders who argue AAPs will negatively impact perceived organizational quality.

Negative Stereotyping

In addition to policy concessions and portraying organizations as having poor talent quality, backlash can evoke negative stereotypes that affect women and minorities' hiring and advancement. Negative stereotypes of women and minorities are found to influence human resource decisions (Greengard, 2003). Stereotypes derived from social gender roles ascribe communal traits (such as people-oriented, warm, and kind) to women (Williams & Best, 1990). Men on the other hand are stereotyped as more agentic (i.e., more achievement-oriented, competent, and confident). Research found gender stereotyping impacts career, as those who exhibit nonconforming traits, or pursue careers that do not fit gender roles to experience backlash (Phelan & Rudman, 2010; Rudman & Glick, 2001).

Oppenheimer and Wiesner (1990) report that when AAP is present, gender stereotyping is suppressed; employers favored male candidates for nursing jobs (stereotypically communal) and female candidates for police jobs (stereotypically agentic) granted that candidates were equally qualified. However, they found that female recruiters, under AAP, selected a female for both jobs. Oppenheimer and Wiesner (1990) interpreted this to suggest that traditionally female jobs might evoke greater gender stereotypes than male jobs. Continuing this research thread, Ng and Wiesner (2007) found gender stereotypes to play a role. When AAP is present, women are again more likely to be hired than men; however, when AAPs were stronger (or more coercive), women experience backlash and were hired less often. This follows Coate and Glenn (1993) who found that although AAPs can eliminate stereotypes, it is equally possible that stereotypes may persist or strengthen, as employers can view AAP hires as unequally productive. Furthermore, workers who are favored undercut incentives to acquire new or necessary skills. Gender-role prejudices are found to be most harmful to women seeking leadership positions (Eagly & 2002), as male managers describe female managers more negatively than male managers (Heilman, Block, & Martell, 1995). A more recent study by Faniko et al. (2017) found similar results. Women who benefited from a strong AAPs were perceived as more communal than agentic, while those who benefited from weaker AAPs were perceived as more agentic than communal. Taken together, this suggests that backlash is expressed by emphasizing gender-stereotypical or counter stereotypical traits which negate the positive outcomes expected of AAPs.

Gendered stereotyping and backlash also extend beyond women and into the LGBTQ community. LGBTQs commonly experience invisibility, erasure, and silence, even in organizations with "gay friendly" policies (Hill, 2009). In instances of backlash, supporters would argue LGBTQ minorities are bearable if they don't flaunt their sexuality (Kumashiro, 2002). Like women and racial minorities, LGBTQs are resented due to the attention and perceived advantages they receive. Furthermore, due to a lack of social sanctions against homophobia, backlash incidents against LGBTQs are often much more explicit than against females or racial minorities, evidenced by antigay shareholder activism at stockholder meetings or refusal to partake in teams with LGBTQs (Hill, 2009, p. 39).

Perceived (Self) Incompetence

Heilman, Block, and Lucas (1992) conducted two studies to investigate whether the stigma of incompetence is associated with those who were hired under AAPs. In the first study, they found female AA hires were perceived as incompetent regardless of job type; stereotyping in addition to perceptions of incompetence increased for females hired for male "stereotyped" jobs. They interpreted these findings to suggest subjects believed qualifications played less of a role in hiring decisions under AAP. Furthermore, AAP hires were thought to be more passive and communal than regular hires, regardless of the gender of the candidate. In their second study, the authors found the stigma of incompetence affected no only White women, but black men and women as well. Career progression was found to be less likely for AAP hires. Thus, the stigma of incompetence can result in prejudice and serious career consequences for women and minorities. Krook (2015) argues that the increased presence of women in politics and in government arising from AAPs undercuts the ability of women to participate as equals and to exercise authority. Not surprisingly, she notes that AAPs do not adequately attain equality (to achieve a critical mass) especially in a male dominated environment. Taken together, the stigma of incompetence can result in prejudice and serious career consequences for women and minorities.

This stigma, however, can also impact self-perception and self-ascribed capacity. Islam and Zilenovsky (2011) tested whether AAPs would negatively affect women's self-expectations of leadership. Their study follows previous work by Heilman and Alcott (2001) who found self-perceptions to negatively affect self-efficacy, capacity, and achievement motivation. Swann, Johnson and Bosson (2009) similarly report that self-ascriptions can result in women underestimating their own capacity. Islam and Zilenosvsky (2011) found partial support for these studies. Specifically, women's desire but not self-ascribed capacity to lead is reduced when they believe that AAPs were a factor. These results were moderated by justice perceptions, or how fair they thought the equity policies were. Specifically, those who believed AA was fair and believed that they were hired under such policies had higher self-ascribed leadership capacity and motivation to achieve, compared to hires who viewed AAPs to be unfair. In this way, backlash can influence minority perceptions of ability, as well as impact their motivation for leadership achievement.

Peer Avoidance and Sabotage

Finally, backlash also negatively impacts workplace relationships. Faniko et al. (2017) found that women hired under strong AAPs are perceived as threatening to men. The researchers add that members of dominant groups (men) strategically apply stereotyping to AA beneficiaries in attempts to bolster their social standing within the organization. This shows that high-status in-groups essentialize lower-status out-groups when under threat (Morton et al., 2009). Of note, weaker policies evoke lower perceptions of threat. Furthermore, female leaders who succeeded though conventional means, and therefore exhibit agentic traits, were critical and attempt to distance themselves from other female colleagues who were unable to overcome stereotypes, especially those hired under equity policies. These results replicate previous research that find gender quotas fuel conflict among female coworkers, as those hired under AAPs are regarded as less legitimate, qualified, and competent (Whelan & Woods, 2012). Interpersonal workplace aggression can also take the form of sabotage during peer reviews. Leibbrandt, Wang, and Foo (2017) explored the impact strong AAP has on sabotage and peer (performance) review in the workplace and found that in instances where peer review is available, women hired under gender quotas become targets of sabotage by other women. Interestingly, women tend to focus on sabotaging other women hired under gender quotas whereas men sabotage indiscriminately. Therefore, backlash towards AAPs can create environments of passive or aggressive hostility among peers in the workplace.

WHY BACKLASH OCCURS?

As we show in this section, a multitude of factors contribute to instances of backlash against AAPs. Not only are there structural conditions that can increase the likelihood of opposition, but psychological and ethical concerns also motivate individuals to engage in or support backlash.

Organizational Justice Violations

A recurring theme in literature points to fairness violations as a primary rationale of backlash defenders. Decisions such as hiring, promotions, or acceptance into universities are expected to be based on merit, rather than secondary characteristics of ethnicity or gender (Steele, 1990). Thus, when AAPs are applied in these decisions, they are often viewed as a violation of organizational justice, or the principles of fair and equal treatment (Crosby, Iyer, Clayton, & Downing, 2003; Hideg & Ferris, 2017; Liptak, 2014; Nacoste, 1990). Organizational justice has three components: procedural, distributive, and interactional justice (Cropanzano, Slaughter, & Bachiochi, 2005). Procedural justice focuses on the consistency of procedures associated with human resource decisions. Equity policies that advantages minority characteristics, but disadvantages others in human resource decisions violate procedural justice norms (Bobocel, Hing, Davey, Stanley, & Zanna, 1998). Distributive justice refers to the fairness of the distribution of resources or outcomes (Aberson, 2007; Adams, 1965), and occurs when individuals perceive opportunities are not allocated to the most meritorious candidate (Nacoste, 1987). Individuals with stronger merit beliefs have little support for AAPs. Interactional justice violations occur when individuals are perceived to be treated without respect or sensitivity and are not given explanations for decisions (Colquitt, 2001). AAPs are found to be insensitive to more meritorious individuals when human resource explanations are inadequate (Cropanzano, Slaughter, & Bachiochi, 2005; Robinson, Seydel, & Douglas, 1998). Heilman, McCullough and Gilbert (1996) also noted that distributive justice violations can have an additive effect on procedural justice violations. Specifically, the belief of not receiving a deserving reward may add to perceptions of biased human resource procedures, resulting in greater backlash. In general, greater organizational justice violations result in more instances of backlash.

Policy Type and Prescriptiveness

AAPs can be placed along a continuum of policy prescriptiveness (strength) where demographic characteristics are weighted against merit (Harrison, Mayer, Leslie, Kravitz, & Lev-Arey, 2006; Pious, 1996). As policy prescriptiveness increases, race and gender characteristics are prioritized over merit and the power of decision makers. We describe four forms of prescriptiveness. The weakest AAPs come in for of *opportunity enhancement*. These policies offer minority groups small benefits in the form of training to improve qualifications, but only merit is considered in selection decisions (Faniko, Burckhardt, Sarrasin, Lorenzi-Cioldi, & Sorenson, 2017;

Pous, 1996). Second, *equal opportunity* policies require decision makers to limit negative evolutions of minority group candidates. However, minority group candidates must be of comparable in qualifications to be selected. Third, *tiebreak* policies, also called weak preferential treatment, permit decision makers to select minority group candidates in instances where all other qualifications are equivalent. In these instances, minority group members have a small positive weight. The most prescriptive policy, *strong preferential treatment* policies, prioritize minority group membership even among candidates with inferior qualifications over majority group members. Quota policies fall under this level of prescriptiveness, where a minimum percentage of positions are allocated for underrepresented groups (Faniko et al., 2017).

Since merit is emphasized over demographic characteristics and group membership, increases in policy strength or prescriptiveness results in greater opposition due to violation of organizational justice beliefs (Colquitt, Conlon, Wesson, Porter, & Ng, 2001; Harrison et al., 2006; Gilliland, 1993; Kravitz, 1995). Furthermore, stigmatization of beneficiaries increases as prescription increases (Heilman et al., 1992). Evans (2003) found African American applicants were rated lower in comparison to White applicants under strong prescriptive policies. Furthermore, African-American successes were attributed less to individual factors as they were viewed to have low achievement orientation. Gender-based equity policies also suffer the same consequences. Women's inclination to apply for leadership roles is reduced, when they are stigmatized with lower leadership ratings (Crosby, Sabattini, & Aizawa, 2013; Leslie et al., 2014). Even weak AAPs are viewed negatively (Hideg & Ferris, 2017), as AAP applicants are treated differently under merit-based selection given qualifications between minority group members are the same as majority group members.

Individual and Psychological Determinants of Backlash

Individual beliefs and attitudes such as self-interest, prejudice, stratification beliefs, and conservatism increase the likelihood of backlash towards AAPs. Self-interest is found to strongly predict reactions to AA. Individuals will support equity policies that enhance oneself and oppose policies that hurt them (Harrison et al., 2006; Lehman & Crano, 2002; Levi & Fried, 2008). Collective self-interest finds that when dominant groups believe minority gains would take away from dominant groups, they are significantly more opposed to AAPs (Bobo, 1998). Lowery, Unzueta, Knowles, and Goff (2006) find policy support is related to how Whites affect fellow ingroup members, but not for minorities. They also find that when focused on losses for Whites, White identity is negatively related to AA support.

However, others find AAPs which do not harm dominant groups can still illicit backlash due to perceived threats to their dominant group positions. Son et al. (2002) suggest that minority groups can still be hindered by malice-free attempts to maintain dominant group privilege. Additionally, Harrison et al. (2006) note self-interest can minimize potentially negative outcomes; the potential positive outcomes minority groups may attain from AA can reduce expectant backlash in the form of stigmatization and stereotyping.

Greater levels of prejudicial beliefs also evoke greater opposition against AAPs (Harrison et al., 2006; James et al., 2001). For example, racism is found to be a strong predictor of negative attitudes towards AAPs (Bobo and Kluegel, 1993; Dovidio and Gaertner, 1996; Sears, Van Laar, Carrillo, & Kosterman, 1997). Old-fashioned racism, based on assumptions of minority inferiority, has become less socially acceptable giving way to modern racism. However, modern racism denies that opposition is based on discrimination or inequality, but on claims of minority's inability, lack of competence, laziness (Henry & Sears, 2002) or justice violations (Dovidio & Gaertner, 2000). More recent studies find racial prejudice to be related to perceptions of AAPs and satisfaction with promotion opportunities (James, Brief, Dietz, & Cohen, 2001). This relationship was negligible among those who were not racially prejudiced. Similarly, sexism has shifted old-fashioned sexism—beliefs in natural gender roles—towards new sexism that denies discrimination against women (Swim, Aikin, Hall, & Hunter, 1995, p. 199). Interestingly, gender-based equity policies are equally opposed by individuals holding sexist beliefs, even if gender is not explicitly outlined, since individuals assume the policy will benefit women (Kravitz et al., 2000). Prejudice, nevertheless, continues to be a critical factor in predicting backlash support or opposition.

Stratification beliefs are found to greatly impact support for AAPs. Those who do not believe discrimination exists do not support AA (Jacobson, 1985; Kravitz & Klineberg, 2000). Stratification can be represented along a continuum ranging from individualism to egalitarianism (Rasinski, 1987; Taylor, 1991). Those high in individualism believe success and failure are based on individual characteristics (Benokraitis & Feagin, 1995; Bobo & Kluegel, 1993; Tuch & Hughes, 1996). Equity policies, which focus on group equality, contradict individual values of meritocracy, hard-work, and individual achievement (Crosby, 1994; Ozawa, Crosby, & Crosby, 1996). Inequalities faced by groups are only recognized if individual rights are violated (Kemmelmeier, 2003). At the same time, meritocracy is used to deny inequality, as achievements and failures are explained as deserving merit rather than by other explanations, such as unearned privilege (Kane & Whipkey, 2009; Knowles & Lowery, 2012). For some societies that widely accept individualism and are rarely exposed to alternate belief systems, the doctrine of individualism has prevented equity policies from receiving widespread support (Giampetro & Kubasek, 1988; Augoustinos, Tuffin, & Every, 2005). The literature largely views values of individualism to have a propensity to provide support for backlash.

Stratification beliefs are also reflected in political orientation. Egalitarianism is consistent with political liberalism, whereas individualism is traditionally a conservative belief (Baunach, 2002). Liberals believe governments should take active roles in assisting those with structural disadvantages. Conservatives may agree discrimination should be eliminated but believe in limited government interference, and thus are more likely to oppose equity policies (Abramowitz, 1994). This conflict can also be observed demographically. Conservatives generally appeal to White majority groups, particularly men, while ethnic minorities and women appeal to more liberal platforms (Jones, 2005). Conflict in political values and the issue of equity policies simply serve as a new conduit for prejudicial and dominance-related motives (Federico & Sidanius, 2002).

Demographic Variables: Gender, Race, and Education

Individual demographic characteristics such as gender, race, and education are also related to backlash support. According to self-interest, groups which benefit from AAPs are most likely to support equity policies. As such, women are more likely to support AAPs more than men, even for race-based policies (Aberson & Haag, 2003; Kravitz & Platania, 1993; Kravits & Klineberg, 2000), while, men generally oppose AA (Harrison et al., 2006). Personal experiences of discrimination increase women's support (Mor Borak, Cherin, & Berkman, 1998), while men are found to be more conservative and likely to be threatened by societal changes (Smith & Selzer, 1992).

Whites oppose AAPs more frequently than racial minority groups (Fine, 1992; Fletcher & Chalmers, 1991; Kinder & Sanders, 1990; Kravitz & Platania, 1993; Parker et al., 1997). Some further argue that race is a stronger predictor of policy support than gender, even for gender-based policies (Bell et al., 1997; Bobo, 1998). Baunach (2002) suggests this is because racism contains elements of racial hatred absent in sexism. Whites are more likely to see organizations without equity policies as fairer and more inclusive than other groups (Borak et al., 1998) and equity policies as unfair and detrimental to both Whites and minority groups (Oh, Choi, Neville, Anderson, & Landrum-Brown, 2010). Crosby et al. (2003) note that Whites may be forced to acknowledge their racist beliefs or how they benefited from racially stratified societies (i.e., White privilege). Asian-Americans also generally support equity policies but hold views that are closer to Whites than blacks and Latinos (Sax & Arredondo, 1999). This may be because Asian-Americans are considered as model minorities since they are typically not the direct beneficiaries (Oh et al., 2010). Asian-Americans are also more likely to attribute their success to hard work and are less likely acknowledge social inequality (Inkelas, 2003).

Multiracial individuals have a complex ethnic and racial identity, which can change according to social context. Identity is dependent on self-perceived similarity to group architypes (Lakoff, 1987), and they are more likely to engage when encountering other members of the same group (Smith & Zarate, 1990). The extent to which multiracial individuals who are a part of both minority and dominant groups depends on the degree they can self-categorize (Good, Chavez, & Sanchez, 2010). This is dependent on internal factors—such as cognitive self-identification with dominant or minority groups, or external factors—such as social experiences with dominant or minority groups (Good, Chavez, & Sanchez, 2010; Sanchez & Bonam, 2009; Wenzel, 2000). For multiracial individuals, those who internally self-identify and experience being a White majority while having less self-perceived similarities with other minorities are more likely to oppose AAPs.

In general, education is associated with greater liberal and egalitarian views (Case, Greeley, & Fuchs, 1989) and a reduction in prejudice (McClosky & Zaller, 1984; Sniderman et al., 1991), thus resulting in support for AAPs. Recent research, however, finds individuals with higher education may believe equity policies challenge meritocracy, and thus oppose AAPs. More educated individuals have a better understanding of political ramifications, allowing them to make informed choices on policies affecting personal group interest (Federico & Sidanius, 2002). First, these individuals can cohesively connect and integrate complex theories and beliefs, such as conservativism or group hierarchy (Federico & Sidanius, 2002; Lavine, Thomsen, & Gonzales, 1997; Zaller, 1992). Second, more educated individuals can better articulate complex and persuasive defenses in opposition to AAPs (Jackman & Muha, 1984). Thus, it is not surprising to find better educated, White group members to oppose AAPs (Federico & Sidanius, 2002).

Organizational Support and Human Resource Management

Managerial beliefs and organizational practices also impact attitudes toward AAPs (Hiemstra & Derous, 2017; Kalev, Dobbin, & Kelly, 2006). As organizational decision makers, managers who oppose AAPs do what is minimally required, reducing equity policy effectiveness (Shen, Chanda, D'Netto, & Monga, 2009). In contrast, organizations that support AAPs are more likely to take steps to ensure AAPs are communicated and perceived as fair (Harrison et al., 2006). These practices, in turn, influences support for AAPs among organizational members. Marylee (1995) found dominant group members whose employers reinforce equity policies are less prejudiced and are more supportive of race-based interventions. They are also more likely to acknowledge discrimination and disadvantages minorities face are attributed to systemic barriers rather than personal or merit-based reasons. Backlash among organizational members are most likely occur in organizations where decision makers are personally opposed to or do not convey or promote support for equity.

The type of human resource management practices also impacts support of AA. Levi and Fried (2008) explored White and African American differences in attitudes towards AAP hiring, promotion, training, and layoffs. They found AAPs when applied to layoff and promotion decisions elicited the greatest opposition, while hiring and training elicited lesser resistance. These trends are explained in various ways. First, there are greater procedural violations occurring in layoffs and promotions, than there are in hiring or training since these activities are more to follow clear rules and have well-defined outcomes. AAPs applied to layoffs elicit the greatest opposition, as they are traditionally subject to strict guidelines of seniority and merit. Second, layoffs represent a zero-sum situation, where when one individual is laid off, another is retained. Similarly, those that are passed in promotions would blame the failure solely on equity policies, especially among organizations with limited promotional opportunities. Failure in hiring or training are diffused among a greater number of individuals. Those who were not hired see opportunities in other employers and those who were not included in training may see a future opportunity.

MINIMIZING BACKLASH

The threat of backlash is greatest in instances of organizational justice violations. AAPs are perceived as unfair by dominant group members who are not afforded the same benefits. More prescriptiveness policies which emphasize group characteristics saw the greatest backlash. Here we review avenues to help minimize organizational justice violations and promote buy-in to ensure equity efforts.

Clarity in Framing

Attitudes towards AAPs are affected by implicit associations and assumptions of tacit policy characteristics and can be of equal or greater importance than the actual policy framework (Eberhardt & Fiske, 1994). Many respondents often believe AAPs are highly prescriptive where minority characteristics are emphasized over merit (Kravitz & Platania, 1993; Kravitz, et al., 2008). When policies are presented generically with little detail, they tend to be interpreted through the personal biases individuals hold (Arriola & Cole, 2001; Golden, Hinkle, & Crosby, 2001). For instance, individuals who subscribe to stratification ideologies believe in individualism, hold conservative values, have lower egalitarian beliefs, and were more likely to believe minorities deserved economic difficulties (Kluegal & Smith, 1986; Smith & Kluegel, 1984). These beliefs can further be shaped by the views and opinions of respected individuals (Bell, Harrison, & McLaughlin, 2000). When AAPs are unclear or poorly explained, individuals are likely to interpret them through their own knowledge and biases, resulting in greater opposition and resistance (McGowan & Ng, 2016).

Policy framing is also linked with beliefs. Policy descriptions justified as giving advantages to minorities, rather than reducing opportunities of dominant groups receive greater support (Gamliel, 2007). Whites rated organizations with AAPs benefitting AfricanAmericans less attractive than when AAPs targeted minorities generally (James, Dietz, Brief, & Cohen, 2001). The competency of minority members was judged more negatively under policies which are labelled "affirmative action" rather than "diversity" (Awad, 2013). When favorable outcomes are presented prior to procedural information, individuals rate the procedures and outcomes of quota and less prescriptive procedures equally as fair (Van den Bos, Wilke, Lind, Vermunt, 1998). Procedural and distributive justice concerns are, therefore, minimized when outcome information is also presented. Friedrich, Lucas and Hodell (2005) also found that including more outcome information, like organizational frequencies of minority and dominant groups being selected, increased policy support. Additionally, distributive justice concerns are minimized when information about candidates of equal merit are made explicit (Bobocel et al., 1998), although it is unclear such effects persist over time (Aberson, 2007). More generally, to limit opposition, procedures must explicitly communicate fairness and include positive equity arguments that promote change (Aberson, 2003; Kravitz & Platania, 1993; Tougas & Veilleux, 1989). These justifications can evoke positive beliefs since they convey concerns for individual wellbeing and whether decision makers could and should act differently (Harrison et al., 2006). Interestingly, Aberson (2016) found that justification and positive framing are effective only in tiebreaker and recruitment policies, suggesting the strength of policies matter.

Policy makers should also account for message salience, as literature finds justifications to be more effective when processed centrally. White, Charles, and Nelson (2008) found higher levels of AAP support when information is presented clearly, explicitly, and processed centrally. This is based on Petty and Cacioppo's elaboration likelihood model (ELM), where messages are processed either through the central or peripheral routes. The central route is a deep, careful and semantic evaluation of arguments; the peripheral route is a cursory evaluation of associated physical cues. Information processed centrally applies the greatest cognitive effort and exhibit the greatest attitude change over time (Aizen, Brown, & Rosenthal, 1996). Conversely, information processed peripherally exhibit little change in attitude and simple fleeting inferences. Interestingly, positive information expressing the benefits of AAPs and support both beneficiaries and nonbeneficiaries result in greater support compared to negative or threatening information.

Promoting Dialectical Thought Through Training and Education

Organizational attempts at promoting dialectical thinking to minimize negative evaluations of AA and threats of backlash appear helpful. Dialectical thinking is a cognitive style where concepts, events, and objects are inherently related (Peng & Nisbett, 1999; Srivstava et al., 2010). High dialectical thinking is shown to support equity policies (Hideg & Ferris, 2017). High dialectical thinkers take a holistic view and are more likely to discount inconsistencies (Hideg & Ferris, 2017; Ji et al., 2001), while low dialectical thinkers expect consistency in events and believe in absolutes, such as good and bad. Low dialectical thinkers are, therefore, uncomfortable with inconsistencies and seek to resolve them by opposing equity policies and upholding organizational justice (Hideg & Ferris, 2017). High dialectical thinking is supportive of equity policies, as individual and inconsistent violations of fairness or merit, is fair on a broader scale. This may contribute to feelings of (White) guilt, or more specifically, perceiving relative deprivation of others. High dialectic thinkers can connect an acknowledgement and feelings of guilt for collective wrongs against minorities with an awareness of advantages and gratitude for being White (Steele, 1990; Swim & Miller, 1999).

Experiences with (racial) diversity, personal experiences of discrimination, and perceptions of discrimination promote dialectical thought and strongly impact stratification beliefs (Gurin, Nagda, & Lopez, 2004; Harrison et al., 2006). Students with diverse educational experiences report greater political engagement, democratic or liberal beliefs, and perspective taking (Gurin, Nagda, & Lopez, 2004). Employees with experiences with diversity also report increased support for equity policies (Aberson & Haag, 2003). Aberson (2007) found positive diversity experiences promotes compatibility between minority and majority groups. Those who believe discrimination exists are more likely to support AAPs (Harrison et al.,

2006). Whites who experienced or perceive discrimination also increase their support for AAPs. Minorities experiencing discrimination are more likely to support AAPs, regardless of ideology and express stronger intentions to apply to organizations with AAPs (Slaughter, Bachiochi, & Sinar, 2002; Yiztak et al., 2001).

Training and educational programs can enhance and create diversity experiences, perceptions of discrimination, and dialectical thought. While such programs promote awareness and help identify personal sources of resistance, caution is required as they may result in greater backlash (Hill, 2009). Mobley and Payne (1992) offer several important factors to consider when implementing training. First, they suggest involving employees to identify issues and general attitudes, to ensure employees feel involved and vested in the process. During training, acknowledge resistance instead of minimizing or ignoring it, to avoid further threats of backlash. Allow participants to engage (have a voice) and direct their own discoveries. Sameness with others should also be valued as it plays a role in identity development and building cohesion. Specifically, they caution against devaluing sameness in efforts to value diversity in the workplace. Lastly, political correctness should not be involved, as this increases cynicism, distrust between groups, and increases the threat of backlash. Hill (2009) emphasizes the importance of inclusion, where all groups can interact in a free, open and honest space.

CONCLUSION

In response to increasing backlash incidents towards affirmative action policies, this chapter draws from extant literature from various fields to bring forth a clearer understanding of backlash and its manifestations in the workplace. Backlash, broadly defined as overt and covert forms of dynamic resistance against equity policies, have serious repercussions. Policy makers practicing concession and accommodation in fear of backlash often apply ineffective AAPs, eliciting more antagonism from both opposition and dissatisfied supporters. Backlash in the legal realm or workplaces that often view values of diversity through a neoliberal aperture continues the reproduction of inequality and power. Organizational attractiveness and low perceived institutional quality can occur, as can negative stereotyping and stigmas of incompetency from (non)beneficiaries. This affects motivations to succeed and increases possibility of peer sabotage.

Literature reports many conditions that support backlash incidents and beliefs. Organizational justice violations are a recurring theme, where AAPs violate values of meritocracy and fairness. As such, increasing prescriptiveness (strength) of policies, where demographic traits are weighted more than merit increase the likely hood of backlash. Yet, individual values and psychological determinants, like high self-interest and prejudicial beliefs and low stratification beliefs, can also increase backlash. It follows that demographic variables, like gender and race, would also predict instances of backlash. Education generally decreases backlash support yet can interact with prejudicial beliefs to produce staunch and coercive expressions of backlash. Low organizational or managerial support, as well as in workplace layoff or promotions can escalate backlash. Reducing backlash is challenging due to the breadth of expressions and conditions, however, clear framing, policy descriptions, and training to promote dialectical thought are found in research to minimize backlash events.

In conclusion, our review reveals literature to have a good grasp on many of the expressions and conditions of AA backlash. Yet, there is still tremendous opportunity for substantive contributions. Notably, there is a need for work on identifying how backlash incidents affect a broader range of minorities, like LGBTQs or other marginalized groups. More pressing is the need for literature to explore backlash in policy, especially in environments where values of diversity and equity are increasingly being questioned. Specifically, strategies in which social equity can be effectively promoted in legislation and avenues, where AAPs are implemented in education and workplaces without aggravating tensions. AAPs have helped close gaps in minority representation in education and the workforce, but such policies face precarity as environments become increasingly and routinely hostile. As backlash threat increases, efforts in literature must do the same.

REFERENCES

Abella, R. S. (1984). *Report of the Commission on Equality in Employment* (Vol. 1). Supply and Services Canada.

Aberson, C. L. (2007). Diversity, merit, fairness, and discrimination beliefs as predictors of support for affirmative-action policy actions. *Journal of Applied Social Psychology, 37*(10), 2451–2474.

Aberson, C. L. (2016). Policy type and justification influences on support for affirmative action policies. *Journal of Personnel Psychology, 15*(2), 90–93.

Aberson, C. L., & Haag, S. C. (2003). Beliefs about affirmative action and diversity and their relationship to support for hiring policies. *Analyses of Social Issues and Public Policy, 3*(1), 121–138.

Abramowitz, A. I. (1994). Issue evolution reconsidered: Racial attitudes and partisanship in the US electorate. *American Journal of Political Science*, 1–24.

Adams, J. S. (1965). Inequity in social exchange. In *Advances in experimental social psychology* (Vol. 2, pp. 267–299). Academic Press.

Agocs, C., & Burr, C. (1996). Employment equity, affirmative action and managing diversity: Assessing the differences. *International Journal of Manpower, 17*(4), 30–45.

Ajzen, I., Brown, T. C., & Rosenthal, L. H. (1996). Information bias in contingent valuation: effects of personal relevance, quality of information, and motivational orientation. *Journal of environmental economics and management*, *30*(1), 43–57.

Anderson, T. H. (2004). *The pursuit of fairness: A history of affirmative action*. Oxford University Press.

Arriola, K. R. J., & Cole, E. R. (2001). Framing the affirmative-action debate: Attitudes toward out-group members and white identity. *Journal of Applied Social Psychology*.

Augoustinos, M., Tuffin, K., & Every, D. (2005). New racism, meritocracy and individualism: constraining affirmative action in education. *Discourse & Society*, *16*(3), 315–340.

Awad, G. H. (2013). Does policy name matter? The effect of framing on the evolutions of African American applicants. *Journal of Applied Social Psychology*, *43*(S2), E379–E387.

Bakan, A. B. & Kobayashi, A. (2007). Affirmative action and employment equity: Policy, ideology, and backlash in Canadian context. *Studies in Political Economy*, *79*(1), 145–166.

Ball, H. (2000). *The Bakke case: Race, education, & affirmative action. Landmark law cases and American society*. Kansas, University Press of Kansas.

Barnes, R. (2014). Supreme court upholds Michigan's ban on racial preferences in university admissions. *The Washington Post*.

Baunach, D. M. (2002). Progress, opportunity, and backlash: Explaining attitudes toward gender-based affirmative action. *Sociological Focus*, *35*(4), 345–362.

Bell, M. P., Harrison, D. A., & McLaughlin, M. E. (1997). Asian American attitudes toward affirmative action in employment: Implications for the model minority myth. *The Journal of Applied Behavioral Science*, *33*(3), 356–377.

Bell, M. P., Harrison, D., A., & McLaughlin, M. E. (2000). Forming, changing, and acting on attitude toward affirmative action programs in employment: A theory-driven approach. *Journal of Applied Psychology*, *85*(5), 784–798.

Beller, A. (1984). Trends in occupational segregation by sex and race. *Sex Segregation in the Workplace: Trends, Explanations, Remedies*, 11–16.

Benfell, C. (1977). Should the Constitution really be color blind. *Barrister*, *4*, 11.

Benokraitis, N. V., & Feagin, J. R. (1995). *Modern sexism: Blatant, subtle, and covert discrimination*. Pearson College Division.

Bobo, L. (1998). Race, interests, and beliefs about affirmative action: Unanswered questions and new directions. *American Behavioral Scientist*, *41*(7), 985–1003.

Bobo, L., & Kluegel, J. R. (1993). Opposition to race-targeting: Self-interest, stratification ideology, or racial attitudes? *American Sociological Review*, 443–464.

Bobocel, D. R., Son-Hing, L. S., Davey, L. M., Stanley, D. J., & Zanna, M. P. (1998). Justice-based opposition to social policies: Is it genuine? *Journal of Personality and Social Psychology*, *75*(3), 653–669.

Brodin, M. S. (2017). From dog-whistle to megaphone: The Trump regime's cynical assault on affirmative action. *National Lawyers Guild Review*, *74*, 65.

Burke, R. J., & Black, S. (1997). Save the males: Backlash in organizations. In *Women in Corporate Management* (pp. 61-70). Springer, Dordrecht.

Burghart, D., & Zeskind, L. (2010, Fall). Tea Party Nationalism. *Institute for Research & Education on Human Right*.

Canadian Employment Equity Act 1986 (S.C.) c. 44 (Can.). Retrieved from https://laws-lois.justice.gc.ca/eng/acts/e-5.401/FullText.html

Case, C. E., Greeley, A. M., & Fuchs, S. (1989). Social determinants of racial prejudice. *Sociological Perspectives*, 32(4), 469-483.

Chrisman, R. (2013). Affirmative action: Extend it. *The Black Scholar*, 43(3), 71-73.

Clayton, S. D., & Crosby, F. J. (1992). *Justice, gender, and affirmative action*. University of Michigan Press.

Coate, S., & Loury, G. C. (1993). Will affirmative-action policies eliminate negative stereotypes? *The American Economic Review*, 1220-1240.

Colquitt, J. A. (2001). On the dimensionality of organizational justice: A construct validation of a measure. *Journal of Applied Psychology*, 86(3), 386-400.

Colquitt, J. A., Conlon, D. E., Wesson, M. J., Porter, C. O. L. H., & Ng, K. Y. (2001). Justice at the millennium: A meta-analytic review of 25 years of organizational justice research.

Cowie, J. (2010). *Stayin'alive: the 1970s and the last days of the working class*. The New Press.

Craig, M. A., & Richeson, J. A. (2017). Information about the US racial demographic shift triggers concerns about anti-white discrimination among the prospective white "minority". *PloS one*, 12(9).

Craig, M. A., Rucker, J. M., & Richeson, J. A. (2018). Racial and political dynamics of an approaching "majority-minority" United States. *The ANNALS of the American Academy of Political and Social Science*, 677(1), 204-214.

Crosby, F. J., Sabattini, L., & Aizawa, M. (2013). Affirmative action and gender equality. *The SAGE handbook of gender and psychology*, 484-499.

Cropanzano, R., Slaughter, J. E., & Bachiochi, P. D. (2005). Organizational Justice and Black Applicants' Reactions to Affirmative Action. *Journal of Applied Psychology*, 90(6), 1168-1184.

Crosby, F. J. (1994). Understanding affirmative action. *Basic and Applied Social Psychology*, 15(1&2), 13-41.

Crosby, F. J. (2004). *Affirmative action is dead: Long live affirmative action*. Yale University Press.

Crosby, F. J., & Iyer, A, Clayton, S., & Downing, R. A. (2003). Affirmative Action: Psychological Data and the Policy Debates. *American Psychologist*, 58(2), 93-115.

DeMatteo, J. S., Dobbins, G. H., Myers, S. D., & Facteau, C. L. (1996). Evaluations of leadership in preferential and merit-based leader selection situations. *The Leadership Quarterly*, 7(1), 41-62.

DeSilver, D. (2014, April 22). Supreme Court says states can ban affirmative action; 8 already have. *Pew Research Center.*

Doane, A. (2017). Beyond color-blindness:(Re) theorizing racial ideology. *Sociological Perspectives*, 60(5), 975-991.

Dobbin, F. (2009). *Inventing equal opportunity*. Princeton University Press.

Dovidio, J. F., & Gaertner, S. L. (1996). Affirmative action, unintentional racial biases, and intergroup relations. *Journal of Social Issues*, 52(4), 51-75.

Dovidio, J. F., & Gaertner, S. L. (2000). Aversive racism and selection decisions: 1989 and 1999. *Psychological Science*, 11(4), 315-319.

Eagly, A. H., & Karau, S. J. (2002). Role congruity theory of prejudice toward female leaders. *Psychological Review, 109*(3), 573–598.

Eastland, T. (1997). *Ending affirmative action: The case for colorblind justice.* Basic Books.

Eberhardt, J. L., & Fiske, S. T. (1994). Affirmative action in theory and practice: Issues of power, ambiguity, and gender versus race. *Basic and Applied Social Psychology, 15*(1–2), 201–220.

Equal Opportunity Act 1995 (s.) 1085 (US.). Retrieved from https://www.govtrack.us/congress/bills/104/s1085

Evans, D. C (2003). A comparison of the other-directed stigmatization produced by legal and illegal forms of affirmative action. *Journal of Applied Psychology, 88*(1), 121–130.

Faniko, K., Burckhardt, T., Sarrasin, O., Lorenzi-Cioldi, F., Sorenson, S. O., Iacoviello, V., & Mayor, E. (2017). Quota women are threatening to men: Unveiling the (counter)stereotypization of beneficiaries of affirmative action policies. *Swiss Journal of Psychology, 76*(3), 107–116.

Federico, C. M., & Sidanius, J. (2002). Racism, ideology, and affirmative action revisited: The antecedents and consequences of "principled objections" to affirmative action. *Journal of Personality and Social Psychology, 82*(4), 488–502.

Fine, T. S. (1992). The impact of issue framing on public opinion: Toward affirmative action programs. *The Social Science Journal, 29*(3), 323–334.

Flelcher, J. F., & Chalmers, M. C. (1991). Attitudes of Canadians toward affirmative action: Opposition, value pluralism, and nonattitudes. *Political Behavior, 13*(1), 67–95.

Friedrich, J., Lucas, G., & Hodell, E. (2005). Proportional reasoning, framing effects, and affirmative action: Is siex of one really half a dozen of another in university admissions? *Organizational Behavior and Human Decision Processes, 98*(2), 195–215.

Garland, D. (2008). On the concept of moral panic. *Crime, Media, Culture, 4*(1), 9–30.

Gallagher, C. A. (2003). Color-blind privilege: The social and political functions of erasing the color line in post race America. *Race, Gender & Class*, 22–37.

Greengard, S. (2003). Gimme attitude. *Workforce*, 56–80. Retrieved from https://www.workforce.com/news/gimme-attitude

Golden, H., Hinkle, S., & Crosby, F. (2006). Reactions to affirmative action, substance and semantics. *Journal of Applied Social Psychology, 31*(1), 73–88.

Gamliel, E. (2007). To accept or to reject: The effects of framing on attitudes toward affirmative action. *Journal of Applied Social Psychology, 37*(4), 683–702.

Giampetro, A., & Kubasek, N. (1988). Individualism in America and its implications for affirmative action. *Journal of Contemporary Law, 14*, 165.

Gilliland, S. W. (1993). The perceived fairness of selection systems: An organizational justice perspective. *Academy of management review, 18*(4), 694–734.

Good, J. J., Chavez, G. F. & Sanchez, D. T. (2010). Sources of self-categorization as minority for mixed-race individuals: Implications for affirmative action entitlement. *Cultural Diversity and Ethnic Minority Psychology, 16*(4), 453–460.

Gurin, P., Nagda, B. R. A., & Lopez, G. E. (2004). The benefits of diversity in education for democratic citizenship. *Journal of Social Issues, 60*(1), 17–34.

Harrison, D. A., Kravitz, D. A., Mayer, D. M., Leslie, L. M., & Lev-Arey, D. (2006). Understanding attitudes toward affirmative action programs in employment: Summary and meta-analysis of 35 years of research. *Journal of Applied Psychology*, *91*(5), 1013–1036.

Heilman, M. E., & Alcott, V. B. (2001). What I think you think of me. Women's reactions to being viewed as beneficiaries of preferential selection. *Journal of Applied Psychology*, *86*(4), 574–582.

Heilman, M. E., Battle, W. S., Keller, C. E., & Lee, R. A. (1998). Type of affirmative action policy: A determinant of reactions to sex-based preferential selection? *Journal of Applied Psychology*, *83*(2), 190.

Heilman, M. E., Block, C. J., & Lucas, J. A. (1992). Presumed incompetent? Stigmatization and affirmative action efforts, 77(4), 536–544.

Heilman, M. E., Block, C. J., & Martell, R. F. (1995). Sex stereotypes: Do they influence perceptions of managers? *Journal of Social Behavior and Personality*, *10*(4), 237–252.

Heilman, M. E., McCullough, W. F., & Gilbert, D. (1996). The other side of affirmative action: Reactions of nonbeneficiaries to sex-based preferential selection. *Journal of Applied Psychology*, *81*(4), 346.

Henry, P. J., & Sears, D. O. (2002). The symbolic racism 2000 scale. *Political Psychology*, *23*(2), 253–283.

Hiemstra, A. M. F., Derous, E., & Born, M. P. (2017). Psychological predictors of cultural diversity support at work. *Cultural Diversity and Ethnic Minority Psychology*, *23*(3), 312–322.

Hideg, I., & Ferris, D. L. (2017). Dialectical thinking and the fairness-based perspectives of affirmative action. *Journal of Applied Psychology*, *102*(5), 782–801.

Hill, R. J. (2009). incorporating queers: Blowback, backlash, and other forms of resistance to workplace diversity initiatives that support sexual minorities. *Advances In Developing Human Resources*, *11*(1), 37–53.

Hinrichs, P. (2012). The effects of affirmative action bans on college enrollment, educational attainment, and the demographic composition of universities. *Review of Economics and Statistics*, *94*(3), 712–722.

Hode, M. G., & Meisenbach, R. J. (2016). Reproducing whiteness through diversity: A critical discourse analysis of the pro-affirmative action amicus briefs in the fisher case. *Journal of Diversity in Higher Education*, *10*(2), 162–180.

Holloway, F. A. (1989). What is affirmative action? In *Affirmative action in perspective* (pp. 9–19). New York, NY: Springer.

Holmes, S. A. (1996). For Hispanic poor, no silver lining. *New York Times*, p. E5.

Hughey, M. W. (2014). White backlash in the 'post-racial' United States. *Ethnic and Racial Studies*, *37*(5), 721–730.

Inkelas, K. K. (2003). Caught in the middle: Understanding Asian Pacific American perspectives on affirmative action through Blumer's group position theory. *Journal of College Student Development*, *44*(5), 625–643.

Islam, G., & Zilenovsky, S. E. S. (2011). Affirmative action and leadership attitudes in Brazilian women managers: The moderating influence of justice perceptions. *Journal of Personnel Psychology*, *10*(3), 139–143.

Jackman, M. R., & Muha, M. J. (1984). Education and intergroup attitudes: Moral enlightenment, superficial democratic commitment, or ideological refinement? *American Sociological Review*, 751–769.

Jacobson, C. K. (1985). Resistance to affirmative action: Self-interest or racism? *Journal of Conflict Resolution, 29*(2), 306–329.

James, E. H., Brief, A. P., Dietz, J., & Cohen, R. R. (2001). Prejudice matters: Understanding the reactions of whites to affirmative action programs targeted to benefit Blacks. *Journal of Applied Psychology, 86*(6), 1120–1128.

Ji, L. J., Nisbett, R. E., & Su, Y. (2001). Culture, change, and prediction. *Psychological science, 12*(6), 450–456.

Jones, J. M. (2005, August, 23). Race, ideology, and support for affirmative action. *Gallup Website*. Retrieved from https://news.gallup.com/poll/18091/race-ideology-support-affirmative-action.aspx

Kalev, A., Dobbin, F., & Kelly, E. (2006). Best practices or best guesses? Assessing the efficacy of corporate affirmative action and diversity policies. *American Sociological Review, 71*, 589–617.

Kane, E. W., & Whipkey, K. J. (2009). Predictors of public support for gender-related affirmative action: Interests, gender attitudes, and stratification beliefs. *Public Opinion Quarterly, 73*(2), 233–254.

Kemmelmeier, M. (2003). Individualism and attitudes toward affirmative action: Evidence from priming experiments. *Basic and Applied Social Psychology, 25*(2), 111–119.

Kidder, D. L., Lankau, M. J., Chrobot-Mason, D., Mollica, K. A., & Friedman, R. A. (2004). Backlash toward diversity initiatives: Examining the impact of diversity program justification, personal and group outcomes. *International Journal of Conflict Management, 15*(1), 77–102.

Kimura, D. (1997). Affirmative action policies are demeaning to women in academia. *Canadian Psychology, 38*(4), 238–242.

Kinder, D. R., & Sanders, L. M. (1996). *Divided by color: Racial politics and democratic ideals*. University of Chicago Press.

Kluegel, J. R., & Smith, E. R. (1986). *Beliefs about inequality: Americans' views of what is and what ought to be*. Hawthorne, NY: Aldine de Gruyter.

Knowles, E. D., & Lowery, B. S. (2012). Meritocracy, self-concerns, and whites' denial of racial inequity. *Self and Identity, 11*(2), 202–222.

Kravitz, D. A. (1995). Attitudes toward affirmative action plans directed at blacks: Effects of plan and individual differences. *Journal of Applied Social Psychology, 25*(24), 2192–2220.

Kravitz, D. A., Bludau, T. M., & Klineberg, S. L. (2008). The impact of anticipated consequences, respondent group, and strength of affirmative action plan on affirmative action attitudes. *Group & Organizational Management, 33*(4), 361–391.

Kravitz, D. A., & Klineberg, S. L. (2000). Reactions to two versions of affirmative action among Whites, Blacks, and Hispanics. *American Psychological Association, 85*(4), 597–611.

Kravitz, D. A., & Platania, J. (1993). Attitudes and beliefs about affirmative action: Effects of target and of respondent sex and ethnicity, *Journal of Applied Psychology, 78*(6), 928–938.

Krook, M. L. (2015). Empowerment versus backlash: Gender quotas and critical mass theory. *Politics, Groups, and Identities, 3*(1), 184–188.

Kumashiro, K. (2002). *Troubling education:" Queer" activism and anti-Oppressive pedagogy*. Routledge.

Lavine, H., Thomsen, C. J., & Gonzales, M. H. (1997). A shared consequences model of the development of inter-attitudinal consistency: The influence of values, attitude-relevant thought, and expertise. *Journal of Personality and Social Psychology, 72*, 735–749.

Lehman, B. J., & Crano, W. D. (2002). The pervasive effects of vested interest on attitude–criterion consistency in political judgment. *Journal of Experimental Social Psychology, 38*(2), 101–112.

Leibbrandt, A., Wang, L. C., & Foo, C. (2017). Gender quotas, competitions, and peer review: Experimental evidence on the backlash against women. *Management Science*, Advance online publication. https://doi.org/10.1287/mnsc.2017.2772

Leslie, L. M., Mayer, D. M., & Kravitz, D. A. (2014). The stigma of affirmative action: a stereotyping-based theory and meta-analytic test of the consequences for performance. *Academy of Management Journal, 57*(4), 964–989.

Levi, A. S., & Fried, Y. (2008). Differences between African Americans and Whites in Reactions to affirmative action programs in hiring, promotion, training, and layoffs. *Journal of Applied Psychology, 93*(5), 1118–1129.

Lewis, A. E. (2004). What group?" Studying Whites and Whiteness in the era of "color-blindness. *Sociological Theory, 22*(4), 623–646.

Liptak, A. (2014). Court backs Michigan on affirmative action. *New York Times, 22*.

Lowery, B. S., Unzueta, M. M., Knowles, E. D., & Goff, P. A. (2006). Concern for the in-group and opposition to affirmative action. *Journal of Personality and Social Psychology, 90*(6), 961–974.

McClosky, H., & Zaller, J. (1984). *The American ethos: Public attitudes toward democracy and capitalism*. Cambridge, MA: Harvard University Press.

McFarland, S. G. (1989). Religious orientations and the targets of discrimination. *Journal for the Scientific Study of Religion, 28*, 324–336.

McGowan, R. A., & Ng, E. S. (2016). Employment equity in Canada: Making sense of employee discourses of misunderstanding, resistance, and support. *Canadian Public Administration, 59*(2), 310–329.

Miller, C. (2017). The persistent effect of temporary affirmative action. *American Economic Journal: Applied Economics, 9*(3), 152–190.

Mobley, M & Payne, T. (1992). Backlash! The challenge to diversity training. *Training & Development, 46*(12), 45–52.

Mor Barak, M. E., Cherin, D. A., & Berkman, S. (1998). Organizational and personal dimensions in diversity climate: ethnic and gender differences in employee perceptions. *Journal of Applied Behavioural Science, 34*(1), 82–104.

Morton, T. A., Hornsey, M. J., & Postmes, T. (2009). Shifting ground: The variable use of essentialism in contexts of inclusion and exclusion. *British Journal of Social Psychology, 48*, 35–59.

Nacoste, R. W. (1987). But do they care about fairness? the dynamics of preferential treatment and minority interest. *Basic and Applied Social Psychology, 8*(3), 177–191.

Nacoste, R. B. (1990). Sources of stigma: Analyzing the psychology of affirmative action. *Law & Policy*, *12*(2), 175–195.

Norton, M. I., & Sommers, S. R. (2011). Whites see racism as a zero-sum game that they are now losing. *Perspectives on Psychological Science*, *6*(3), 215–218.

Ng, E. S., & Stamper, C. L. (2018). A Trump presidency and the prospect for equality and diversity. *Equality, Diversity and Inclusion: An International Journal*, *37*(1), 2–13.

Ng. E. S., & Wiesner, W. H. (2007). Are men always picked over women? The effects of employment equity directives on selection decisions. *Journal of Business Ethics*, 76, 177–187.

Oh, E., Choi, C. C., Neville, H. A., Anderson, C. J., & Landrum-Brown, J. (2010). Beliefs about affirmative action: A test of the group self-interest and racism beliefs models. *Journal of Diversity in Higher Education*, *3*(3), 163–176.

Oppenheimer, R. J., & Wiesner, W. H. (1990) *Sex discrimination: Who is hired and do employment equity statements make a difference?* Proceedings of the 11th Annual Conference of the Administrative Sciences Association of Canada, Personnel and Human Resources Division.

Ozawa, K., Crosby, M., & Crosby, F. (1996). Individualism and resistance to affirmative action: A comparison of Japanese and American Samples. *Journal of Applied Social Psychology*, *26*(13), 1138–1152.

Parker, C. P., Baltes, B. B., & Christiansen, N. D. (1997). Support for affirmative action, justice perceptions, and work attitudes: A study of gender and racial-ethnic group differences. *Journal of Applied Psychology*, *82*(3), 376.

Peng, K., & Nisbett, R. E. (1999). Culture, dialectics, and reasoning about contradiction. *American psychologist*, *54*(9), 741.

Perry, P. (2001). White means never having to say you're ethnic: White youth and the construction of "cultureless" identities. *Journal of Contemporary Ethnography*, *30*(1), 56–91.

Phelan, J. E., & Rudman, L. A. (2010). Prejudice toward female leaders: Backlash effects and women's impression management dilemma. *Social and Personality Pscyhology Compass*, *4*(10), 807–820.

Pierce, J. L. (2003). "Racing for Innocence": Whiteness, corporate culture, and the backlash against affirmative action. *Qualitative Sociology*, *26*(1), 53–69.

Pierce, J. (2012). *Racing for innocence: Whiteness, gender, and the backlash against affirmative action*. Stanford University Press.

Pierce, J. L. (2013). White racism, social class, and the backlash against affirmative action, *Sociology Compass*, *7*(11), 914–926.

Pious, S. (1996). Ten myths about affirmative action. *Journal of Social Issues*, *52*(4), 25–31.

Premdas, R. (2016). Social justice and affirmative action. *Ethnic and Racial Studies*, *39*(3), 449–462.

Rasinski, K. A. (1987). What's fair is fair—Or is it? Value differences underlying public views about social justice. *Journal of personality and social Psychology*, *53*(1), 201.

Resendez, M. G. (2002). The stigmatizing effects of affirmative action: An examination of moderating variables. *Journal of Applied Social Psychology*, *32*(1), 185–206.

Rhodes, J. (2010). White backlash, 'unfairness' and justifications of British National Party (BNP) support. *Ethnicities*, *10*(1), 77–99.

Robinson, R. K., Seydel, J., & Douglas, C. (1998). Affirmative action: The facts, the myths, and the future. *Employee Responsibilities and Rights Journal*, *11*(2), 99–115.

Rudman, L. A., & Glick, P. (2001). Prescriptive gender stereotypes and backlash toward agentic women. *Journal of Social Issues*, *57*(4), 743–762.

Sanchez, D. T., & Bonam, C. M. (2009). To disclose or not to disclose biracial identity: The effect of biracial disclosure on perceiver evaluations and target responses. *Journal of Social Issues*, *65*(1), 129–149.

Savran, D. (1998). *Taking it like a man: White masculinity, masochism, and contemporary.* Princeton University Press.

Sax, L. J., & Arredondo, M. (1999). Student attitudes toward affirmative action in college admissions. *Research in Higher Education*, *40*(4), 439–459.

Schuman, H., Steeh, C., Bobo, L., & Krysan, M. (1997). *Racial attitudes in America: Trends and interpretations.* Harvard University Press.

Sears, D. O., Van Laar, C., Carrillo, M., & Kosterman, R. (1997). Is it really racism? The origins of White Americans' opposition to race-targeted policies. *The Public Opinion Quarterly*, *61*(1), 16–53.

Shen, J., Chanda, A., D'Netto, B., & Monga, M. (2009). Managing diversity through human resource management: An international perspective and conceptual framework. *International Journal of Human Resource Management*, *20*, 235–251.

Slaughter, J. E., Sinar, E. F., & Bachiochi, P. D. (2002). Black applicants' reactions to affirmative action plans: Effects of plan content and previous experience with discrimination. *Journal of Applied Psychology*, *87*(2), 333.

Smith, E. R., & Zarate, M. A. (1990). Exemplar and prototype use in social categorization. *Social cognition*, *8*(3), 243–262.

Sniderman, P. M., Piazza, T., Tetlock, P. E., & Kendrick, A. (1991). The new racism. *American Journal of Political Science*, *35*(2), 423–447.

Son-Hing, L. S., Bobocel., D. R., & Zanna, M. P. (2002). Meritocracy and opposition to affirmative action: Making concessions in the face of discrimination. *Journal of Personality and Social Psychology*, *83*(3), 493–509.

Steele, S. (1990). *The content of our character* (Vol. 38). New York, NY: St. Martin's Press.

Swann Jr., W. B., Johnson, R. E., & Bosson J. K. (2009). Identity negotiation at work. *Research in Organizational Behavior*, *29*, 81–109.

Swim, J. K., Aikin, K. J., Hall, W. S., & Hunter, B. A. (1995). Sexism and racism: Old-fashioned and modern prejudices. *Journal of Personality and Social Psychology*, *68*(2), 199.

Swim, J. K., & Miller, D. L. (1999). White Guilt: Its Antecedents and Consequences for Attitudes Toward Affirmative Action. *Society for Personality and Social Psychology*, *25*(4), 500–514.

Taylor, B. R. (1991). *Affirmative action at work: Law, Politics, and Ethics.* Pittsburgh, PA, University of Pittsburgh Press.

Taylor, M. C. (1995). White backlash to workplace affirmative action: Peril or myth? *Social Forces*, *73*(4), 1385–1414.

Taylor, W. L., & Liss, S. M. (1992). Affirmative action in the 1990s: Staying the course. *The Annals of the American Academy of Political and Social Science*, *523*(1), 30–37.

Tougas, F., & Veilleux, F. (1989). Who likes affirmative action: Attitudinal processes among men and women. In *Affirmative action in perspective* (pp. 111–124). New York, NY: Springer.

Tuch, S. A., & Hughes, M. (1996). Whites' racial policy attitudes. *Social Science Quarterly*, 723–745.

University of California Regents v. Bakke, 438 U.S. 265, 98 S. Ct. 2733, 57 L. Ed. 2d 750 (1978)

Van den Bos, K., Wilke, H. A. M., Lind, E. A., & Vermunt R. (1998). Evaluating outcomes by means of the fair process effect: Evidence for different processes in fairness and satisfaction judgement. *Journal of Personality and Social Psychology*, *74*(6), 1493–1503.

Virtanen, S. V., & Huddy, L. (1998). Old-fashioned racism and new forms of racial prejudice. *The Journal of Politics*, *60*(2), 311–332.

Wakabayashi, D. (2017, Aug. 8). Contentious memo strikes nerve inside Google and out. *The New York Times*. Retrieved from https://www.nytimes.com/2017/08/08/technology/google-engineer-fired-gender-memo.html

Wenzel, M. (2000). Justice and identity: The significance of inclusion for perceptions of entitlement and the justice motive. *Personality and social psychology bulletin*, *26*(2), 157–176.

Whelan, J., & Wood, R. (2012, May). Targets and quotas for women in leadership: A global review of policy, practice and psychological research, gender equality project, centre for ethical leadership. Retrieved from https://sage-pilot.uq.edu.au/files/121/targets_and_quotas_report_2012.pdf

White, F. A., Charles, M. A., & Nelson, J. K. (2008). The role of persuasive arguments in changing affirmative action attitudes and expressed behavior in higher education. *Journal of Applied Psychology*, *93*(6), 1271.

Williams, J. E., & Best, D. L. (1990). *Measuring sex stereotypes: A multination study* (Revised ed.). SAGE.

Williams, M. J., & Tiedens, L. Z. (2016). The subtle suspension of backlash: A meta-analysis of penalties for women's implicit and explicit dominance behavior. *Psychological Bulletin*, *142*(2), 165-197.

Williamson, V., Skocpol, T., & Coggin, J. (2011). The Tea Party and the remaking of Republican conservatism. *Perspectives on Politics*, *9*(1), 25–43.

Yancy, G., & del Guadalupe Davidson, M. (Eds.). (2014). *Exploring race in predominantly white classrooms: Scholars of color reflect*. Routledge.

Young, I. M. (2002). *Inclusion and democracy*. Oxford University press on demand.

Young, M. D. (2005). Shifting away from women's issues in educational leadership in the US: Evidence of a backlash? *International Studies in Educational Administration*, *33*(2), 31–42.

CHAPTER 8

MANAGING DIVERSITY AND INCLUSION THROUGH MANAGERIAL INTERPERSONAL SKILLS (MIPS)

Shaun Pichler
California State University

There is no doubt that we are living and working in a more diverse environment today than ever before. The labor force of the United States and other industrialized countries is increasingly diverse in terms of race and ethnicity, gender, and age, among other dimensions (e.g., Berger, Essers, & Himi, 2017; Roberson, 2012; Truxillo, Fraccaroli, Yaldiz, & Zaniboni, 2017). A variety of macro-level trends from globalization to technological advancement and global labor force migration are related to the increasing multiculturalism of the modern workplace (Kossek & Pichler, 2007). While human resources are perhaps an organization's most important asset (Barney & Wright, 1998), there is conflicting evidence as to the benefits of diversity in human resources (Kochan et al., 2003). The academic and business presses are replete with suggestions as to how to manage diversity and inclusion. These often focus on certain policies (e.g., nondiscrimination policies, Pichler, Beenen, Livingston, & Riggio, 2018), practices (e.g., diversity training, King, Dawson, Kravitz, & Gulick, 2012), change initiatives (Stevens, Plaut, & Sanchez-Burks, 2008), or the role of top executive

Pushing Our Understanding of Diversity in Organizations, pp. 183–213
Copyright © 2020 by Information Age Publishing
183

support (Ng, 2008; Pichler, Ruggs, & Trau, 2017) as means by which to manage diversity and inclusion.

There is plenty of criticism as to the effectiveness of these interventions (e.g., Bregman, 2012). There are a number of reasons as to why diversity initiatives are sometimes ineffective or might be perceived as ineffective. A key issue here is that many organizations adopt diversity initiatives in an attempt to reduce the risk of discrimination lawsuits instead of thinking strategically about which initiative(s) might be best suited to their needs (Kulik & Roberson, 2008). Diversity training is perhaps the most common type of diversity initiative (Esen, 2005). Some studies have shown that diversity training and other initiatives can lead to backlash among majority group members (e.g., Kaplan, 2006; Kidder, Lankau, Chrobot-Mason, Mollica, & Friedman, 2004), or to results in directions opposite than expected (i.e., more differential treatment among training vs. control group; Sanchez & Medkik, 2004). What seems important for diversity initiatives to be effective is that a needs assessment is conducted; the initiative(s) chosen match the needs assessment; that the rationale for the initiative(s) are explained carefully to employees; and proper appropriate evaluation metrics are chosen (Kidder et al., 2004; Kulik & Roberson, 2008)

Moreover, the literature is relatively silent on the role that front-line supervisors and managers play in managing diversity and inclusion. For instance, a Google Scholar search using terms such as "managers" or "supervisors" with "diversity and inclusion" or "diversity management" returns few results about line managers. This is surprising since managers are responsible for the implementation of diversity-related policies and practices. For instance, research has shown that managers have extensive decision control as to how work-family benefits are utilized (Kossek, Ollier-Malaterre, Lee, Pichler, & Hall, 2016). Managers are responsible for a range of employment decisions, such as selection, compensation, and promotion decisions, all of which have been shown to be affected by managers' biases (e.g., Pichler, Varma, & Bruce, 2010; Purkiss, Perrewé, Gillespie, Mayes, & 2006). Much of the diversity literature has focused on conflict between individuals in workgroups (e.g., Jehn, Northcraft, & Neale, 1999)—and the responsibility for managing this conflict falls on line managers. Thus, it seems that frontline supervisors and managers are centrally important to managing diversity and inclusion in organizations. This being the case, the next logical question becomes: How can organizations help ensure that managers have skills needed to manage diversity effectively?

The overarching thesis of the current chapter is that managerial interpersonal skills (MIPS) are essential not only to the effective management of people in general, but to managing diversity and inclusion. Interpersonal skills help managers understand differences between people; motivate others who are different from them; provide support to individuals based on their unique needs; and manage conflict in workgroups (Pichler, Beenen et al., 2018). Thus, managerial interpersonal skills may be a key linchpin by which organizations can manage diversity and foster a more inclusive environment. The purpose of this chapter is twofold: To provide directions for future research on the role of MIPS in managing diversity and inclusion, and to provide organizations and managers with practical recommendations in terms of how to manage diversity and inclusion through MIPS.

In the sections that follow, theory and research on managerial interpersonal skills are reviewed; propositions are developed as to relationships between managerial interpersonal skills and diversity and inclusion management; and a framework for organizations and managers is offered to help them develop MIPS and hence optimize the value of their human resources.

MANAGERIAL INTERPERSONAL SKILLS (MIPS)

There is a relatively large literature on general social skills, otherwise known as interpersonal skills, which dates back at least to Thorndike's social intelligence research (Thorndike, 1920, 1936). He introduced the concept of social intelligence, i.e., the "ability to act wisely in social relations" (Thorndike, 1920). The literature has shown that social skills are related to psychosocial adjustment (Riggio, Watring, & Throckmorton, 1993), empathy (Riggio, Tucker, & Coffaro, 1989), leadership (Riggio & Reichard, 2008), and job performance (Ferris, Witt, & Hochwarter, 2001). Google recently found that social skills were more important to so-called Googler's performance than STEM skills (Glazer, 2018). This was surprising given the nature of Google's business and the skills needed to perform well at Google, namely technical skills such as computer programming. At the same time, most organizations rely on extensive social interaction to deliver their products and are increasingly reliant on service effectiveness (Klein, DeRouin, & Salas, 2006). The business and popular press are therefore increasingly interested in the role of soft skills, including interpersonal skills, in organizational effectiveness (e.g., Morgan, 2018).

Management and organization scholars have been interested in the importance of interpersonal skills to the managerial role and role performance for some time. Mintzberg (1980) proposed that managers occupy three key interrelated roles: informational, decisional, and interpersonal, each tied to three key skill sets namely, technical, conceptual, and interpersonal, respectively. Using O*Net data, research on the leadership strataplex model (Mumford, Campion, & Morgeson, 2007) revealed four broad skill sets important to managerial performance, that is, cognitive, interpersonal, business, and strategic. Although technical skills may be relatively important for entry-level managers, and conceptual skills for senior managers (Mumford, Campion, & Morgeson, 2007), interpersonal skills are important for managers in all organizational strata (Scullen, Mount, & Judge, 2003). Managers spend most of their time interacting with others (Hinds & Kiesler, 1995), thus it is not surprising that interpersonal skills are more strongly related to managerial performance than other skills (Abraham, Karns, Shaw, & Mena, 2001).

Despite the importance of interpersonal skills to managerial performance and organizational success, there is no widely-accepted definition or model of the managerial interpersonal skills construct (Beenen, Pichler, & Davoudpour, 2018). This being the case, a variety of constructs and, relatedly, measures of skills that might be considered interpersonal have flourished, such as communication (Rubin & Martin, 1994), conflict management (Van de Vliert, & Kabanoff, 1990), and political skills (Ferris et al., 2005). In fact, in a review of the interpersonal skills literature, Klein, DeRouin, and Salas (2006) identified 58 theoretical frameworks that included 400 skills that could be considered interpersonal. Thus, Pichler and colleagues (Beenen, Pichler, & Davoudpour, 2018; Pichler & Beenen, 2013; Pichler, Beenen et al., 2018) have attempted to develop a model— and validate a measure—of managerial interpersonal skills. Their goal was to identify a relatively parsimonious set of skills that represents the managerial interpersonal skills domain and are the most important for managerial success, which could be used for purposes of assessment, training, and development.

Pichler and colleagues' research program involved several phases- from an extensive literature review, to structured interviews with practicing managers about which interpersonal skills are most important to their success, to pilot testing of a preliminary set of items, and ultimately to a validation study with matched supervisor-subordinate data (Pichler & Beenen, 2013; Pichler, Beenen et al., 2018). Their literature review suggested that five different skills represented the construct domain of managerial interpersonal skills: self-management, communication, supporting, motivating, and managing conflict (Pichler & Beenen, 2013). These dimensions were consistent with the dimensions that MBA programs officers used when assessing applicant's interpersonal skills (Beenen, Pichler, & Davoudpour, 2018). One key finding from structured interviews was that practicing managers highlighted the importance of individuation, that is of tailoring their interpersonal behavior to each employee's unique backgrounds and needs (Pichler, Beenen et al., 2018). The authors developed items to map onto each of these five dimensions based on their literature review as well as interviews with managers. Preliminary factor analyses did not support a five-factor solution; instead, a three-factor model was the best fit to the data (see Pichler, Beenen et al., 2018). Results indicated that (1) self-management items did not seem part of the MIPS construct, and (2) communication items cross-loaded onto the other three factors (supporting, motivating, and managing conflict).

In hindsight, these results made sense: self-management is intrapersonal and a precursor to interpersonal skills. Based on interviews with practicing managers, self-management was comprised of initiative, emotional control, and self-awareness (see Pichler & Beenen, 2013). This is consistent with how MBA admissions officers conceptualize self-management, that is, to include determination, emotional intelligence, and self-awareness (Beenen, Pichler, & Davoudpour, 2018). As others have argued, self-management is critical to interpersonal skill development (e.g., Robbins & Hunsaker, 2011). If an individual is not aware of his or her own attitudes, values, and beliefs, and lacks self-control and emotion management, it will be difficult to communicate and interact with others effectively. It will be especially difficult for managers who are low on self-management to interact with others in an individualized way. Thus, we propose that self-management is a starting point for managerial interpersonal skill development.

Moreover, communication is essential to providing support, motivating others, and managing conflict. Thus, their revised model was one with a superordinate latent MIPS factor with three dimensions—supporting, motivating, and managing conflict—each of which had items about communication and individuation (Pichler, Beenen et al., 2018). Subsequent confirmatory factor analyses supported this model. They define managerial interpersonal skills as "skills that help managers support and motivate others, and effectively resolve conflicts in goal-directed organizational settings" (Pichler, Beenen et al., 2018). Results from their pilot and validation studies indicated MIPS is correlated with related constructs as expected, such as personality traits, and predicts incremental validity in outcome variables, such as job satisfaction and performance, above and beyond measures of related constructs, such as general social support, interpersonal justice, and conflict management styles (Pichler, Beenen et al., 2018). Figure 8.1 represents the MIPS model developed by Pichler and colleagues, which will be used as a guide for this chapter.

THEORETICAL BACKGROUND: CONNECTING MIPS TO DIVERSITY AND INCLUSION

Before explaining how managerial interpersonal skills could be related to the management of diversity and inclusion, it is important to provide an overview of relevant theories, namely social identity, leader-member exchange, and self-determination theories. Social identity theory proposes that individuals classify others into social categories based on identity-relevant information (e.g., demographics) and assign stereotypes to members

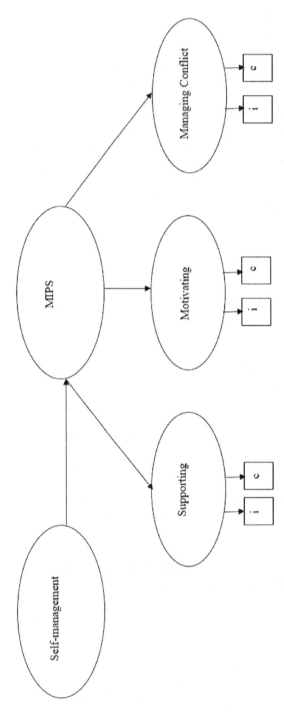

Notes: i = is meant to symbolize that each MIPS dimension features at least one item about individuation, c = is mean to symbolize that each MIPS dimension features at least one item about communication.

Figure 8.1. Model of Managerial Interpersonal Skills (MIPS).

of these categories (Turner, 1982). Research based on social identity theory has shown that individuals categorize others into in-groups and out-groups based on identity-relevant information, which helps individuals understand how to behave in social contexts (Hogg & Terry, 2000). Differentiation into in- and out-groups results in preferential or discriminatory treatment, respectively (e.g., Tajfel & Turner, 1979). In connection, the basic premise of leader-member exchange theory is that leaders form differentiated exchanges of relatively high- and low-quality with their subordinates— high-quality exchanges are characterized by higher levels of trust, support, and resources (Liden & Maslyn, 1998). Leader-member exchange theory posits that leaders will want to form high-quality exchanges with the most promising subordinates, for example, in terms of skill or motivation (Graen & Scandura, 1987). In addition to potential, similarity between supervisors and subordinates is a key predictor of exchange quality and favorability of treatment (Brouer, Duke, Treadway, & Ferris, 2009).

Self-determination, simply put, is the extent to which behavior is deter-mined by the individual. Human beings have an innate desire to feel that their actions and behaviors are self-determined. Self-determination theory proposes that when basic or organismic needs—namely for auton-omy, competence, and relatedness—are fulfilled, motivation will increase because an individual's sense of self-determination is enhanced (Deci & Ryan, 2011). In addition to job characteristics, supervisors are a key way by which employees' organismic needs are fulfilled (Gagné & Deci, 2005). When supervisors provide employees with discretion about how to do their, develop a sense of competence among employees through feedback, and help promote a sense of relatedness through support, employee motivation and performance should increase. An issue here is that if managers treat employees differently based on social categories, as well as in- and out-groups formed on the basis of demographic differences, this will impact how individuals from different backgrounds receive the nutriments they need for motivation.

Research has shown that social categorization is a natural tendency for human beings (Billig, 1985), as is forming in- and out-groups based on demographics. It takes effort and skill to mitigate this natural tendency to socially categorize others, or at least the outcomes of such categorization, such as preferential treatment. As will be explained in more detail in sec-tions to follow, development of managerial interpersonal skills—at least as conceptualized by Pichler and colleagues (e.g., Pichler, Beenen et al., 2018) —should mitigate the negative effects of social categorization. Man-agers who are more self-aware, who tailor their interpersonal interactions to individual differences in background and preferences, should be less likely to be perceived as biased or discriminatory. They should also be less likely to be perceived as forming in- and out-groups based on demographic differences. Indeed, high quality interpersonal exchanges can mitigate demography-based social categorization (Kim, Bhave, & Glomb, 2013), and highly interpersonally skilled managers should be more effective in forming high-quality relationships with employees of diverse backgrounds. This being the case, diverse employees working with interpersonal skilled managers should be more likely to have their organismic needs fulfilled, and thus should perform better.

THE ROLE OF MIPS IN DIVERSITY AND INCLUSION MANAGEMENT

Although leader-member exchange theory has generally not considered the role of manager's interpersonal skills in leader-member exchanges, these skills are essential to the development of high-quality exchanges. Thought leaders tend to agree that interpersonal skills are learnable and therefore trainable (see Beenen & Pichler, 2013). Research supports this proposition. For instance, Hunt and Baruch (2003) found that a managerial training program using pre- and post-training assessments revealed improvement across a variety of interpersonal skills. This is good news for managers and organizations: If managerial interpersonal skills are important in connection to diversity management, then interpersonal skills training may be a way to improve the management of diversity and inclusion in organizations. In the next section, each of the three skills in the MIPS model reviewed above (i.e., supporting, motivating, and managing conflict, Pichler & Beenen, 2013; Pichler, Beenen et al., 2018) will be considered as they relate to managing diversity and inclusion.

Supporting

There is a rich literature on the role of social support in individual psychological and physiological health (Caplan, Cobb, & French, 1975). Social support is related to happiness (Schnittker, 2008), the suppression of cortisol and hence to subjective responses to stress (Heinrichs, Baumgartner, Kirschbaum, & Ehlert, 2003), longevity (Brown, Nesse, Vinokur, & Smith, 2003), and mortality (Blazer, 1982). Social support is also related to success in relationships including friendships (Siebert, Mutran, & Reitzes, 1999), marriages (Bryant & Conger, 1985), coworker relationships (Varma, Budhwar, & Pichler, 2011), and supervisor-subordinate relationships (Pichler, 2012). There is a relatively extensive literature on the importance of social support to supervisor-subordinate relationships, which has shown that the supervisor support is related to employee job performance and work-family conflict (see Muse & Pichler, 2011). This literature has also shown that managers can be trained to be more supportive (e.g., Hammer Kossek, Anger, Bodner, & Zimmerman, 2011).

Social support comes in a variety of types. Early research differentiated social support across three types: emotional, informational, and instrumental (House, 1981), that is, concern for well-being, providing valuable information, and providing resources. More recent research specifically on supervisor support has suggested that specific forms of social support are more strongly related to outcomes of a similar bandwidth. For instance, supervisor work-family support is more strongly related to work-family conflict than general social support (Kossek, Pichler, Bodner, & Hammer, 2011). This line of research has identified two additional types of support, namely role modeling and creative work-family management (Hammer Kossek, Yragui, Bodner, & Hanson 2009)—that is, demonstrating how to balance work and nonwork demands and helping employees meet scheduling demands. The *supporting* dimension of managerial interpersonal skills identified by Pichler and colleagues is broader and includes features such as showing concern for employee well-being, treating others with dignity and respect, encouraging open conversations, demonstrating care for employee's lives outside of work, among others (Pichler, Beenen et al., 2018). In other words, *supporting* encompasses features of emotional, instrumental, and work-family support, among others, such as fair interpersonal treatment.

Social support, as a buffer of stress and a key resource for healthy psychological functioning, is increasingly important in a modern, global economy given increased job pressures and work intensification (Macky & Boxall, 2008). A key issue here is that supervisors are more likely to form high-quality relationships with, and thus provide more support to, employees who are more similar to them both demographically and in terms of more "deep-level" characteristics, such as personality, attitudes, and beliefs (e.g., Harrison, Price, & Bell, 1998). Supervisors create in-groups and out-groups based on similarity, and in-group employees receive more support (e.g., Ensher, Grant-Vallone, & Marelich, 2002). This could create a self-fulfilling prophecy (Rosenthal & Jacobson, 1968), such that employees who are demographically or otherwise similar to their supervisors receive more support, hence they perform better thus confirming supervisor expectations of higher performance among more similar subordinates.

Since managers tend to be majority-group members (e.g., White, male, heterosexual, able-bodied, etc.), it is likely that a key challenge that minorities face in organizations is a relative lack of perceived social support, especially from supervisors. This is consistent with research that has suggested minorities have fewer ties to similar others and thus less stable social networks in organizations compared to majority group members

(Ibarra, 1993). Managerial treatment is a key referent by which individuals judge the extent to which they are valued members of a workgroup (e.g., Tyler & Lind, 1992). Social support is important to employees, in part, because it signals the extent to which they are valued by their organization (Eisenberger, Stinglhamber, Vandenberghe, Sucharski, & Rhoades, 2002; Kossek, Pichler, Bodner, & Hammer, 2011). Moreover, interpersonal treatment experienced by a workgroup member, that is, another minority group member, can affect one's own perception of interpersonal treatment by a manager (Colquitt, Zapata-Phelan, & Roberson, 2005; Pichler et al., 2016). Research supports the colloquialism that employees leave managers, not organizations (Lipman, 2015). It is likely that minority employees leave organizations, even those that may have diversity management policies in place, due to unsupportive managers specifically because they feel unvalued. This should be especially true of high-potential or high-talent minority employees given their relative market power.

A central proposition of this chapter is that a key way for managers to manage diversity and create perceptions of an inclusive environment is to provide consistent levels of support to all of their employees regardless of their background. When employees feel supported, they are more likely to feel that their manager truly cares about their well-being, which leads them to feel that their organization values them and their contributions. Perceptions of being valued by one's organization are related to improved attitudes (e.g., mood), lower turnover intentions, higher levels of job performance and extra-role behavior (Rhoades & Eisenbeger, 2002). This proposition may seem intuitive or even obvious, but it goes against manager's natural behavioral tendencies to form differentiated exchanges based on interpersonal similarity (Billig, 1985; Tajfel & Turner, 1979). Getting managers to provide consistently high levels of support to employees from diverse backgrounds probably requires some sort of organizational intervention.

Motivating

Although motivating others is essential to effective management and leadership, motivating has not been a salient feature of models of leader interpersonal skills. For instance, in their leadership strataplex model (Mumford et al., 2007), interpersonal skills were represented by four items, and only one item, that is, persuasion, was closely tied to motivating others. The model of managerial competencies developed by Rubin and Dierdorff (2009) included "selling or influencing others" as an example of managing the task environment, but motivating others was not one of the competencies in their model. In a paper on managerial role requirements and work context (Dierdorff, Rubin, & Morgeson, 2009), managing human capital and interpersonal skills were included, but motivating others specifically was not a feature of their work. As above, research by Pichler and colleagues (Beenen, Pichler, & Davoudpour, 2018; Pichler & Beenen, 2013; Pichler, Beenen et al., 2018), including structured interviews from practicing managers, has indicated that *motivating* is a key dimension of managerial interpersonal skills.

The management and organization literature is replete with theories of motivation. One highly-cited theory that is closely tied to managerial interpersonal skills is self-determination theory (Deci & Ryan, 2011). The reason managerial interpersonal skills are relevant here is because self-determination theory specifically considers the role of the supervisor and supervisor behaviors as related to employee motivation (in addition to job characteristics, that is, Gagné & Deci, 2005). Unlike some of the classic theories of motivation (e.g., Maslow, 1954), self-determination theory includes propositions not only about motivators, but the regulatory processes that explain the direction of behavior (see Gagné & Deci, 2005), namely the fulfillment of basic or "organismic" needs, as described below. This makes self-determination theory particularly useful for connecting managerial interpersonal skills to work outcomes, including managing diversity and inclusion.

Self-determination, simply put, is the extent to which behavior is determined by the individual as opposed to an outside force. In self-determination theory, self-determination refers to initiation and regulation of behavior along an intrinsic-extrinsic spectrum (Ryan & Deci, 2000). Intrinsic motivation is characterized by actions that are self-determined, internalized, and integrated with one's self-concept. Extrinsic motivation is characterized by actions that are externally driven. Self-determination theory posits that individuals have an innate desire to choose actions themselves and to control their own behavior. Research has shown that self-determined motivation is related to outcomes such as self-esteem and general well-being (e.g., Deci & Ryan, 1985), as well as job attitudes and performance (e.g., Gagné & Deci, 2005).

There are three basic or "organismic" needs that lead to self-determined motivation and provide the "nutriments" for performance, that is, autonomy, competence, and relatedness (Ryan & Deci, 2000). In other words, individuals have a basic need to feel that their actions are self-determined; that they are effective in their behavior; and that they are socially connected to others. Since extrinsic motivators are pervasive in work organizations, it is important to note that social-contextual stimuli that support these basic needs, such as autonomy-supportive supervisor behavior, can increase the extent to which behavior is perceived as self-determined (Beenen, Pichler, & Levy, 2017; Deci & Ryan, 1985; Ryan & Deci, 2000). Supervisors in particular are an important source of esteem, feedback, autonomy, and social support that contribute to the fulfillment of these basic needs (Beenen, Pichler, & Levy, 2017; Pichler, 2012). Note the developmental nature of managerial interpersonal skills such that *supporting* is important to and a precursor of *motivating*; this will be discussed in more detail below in the discussion section.

As above, Pichler and colleagues (Beenen, Pichler, & Davoudpour, 2018; Pichler & Beenen, 2013; Pichler, Beenen et al., 2018) found that *motivating* is a key dimension of managerial interpersonal skills. In their model, motivating includes features such as providing rewards based on individual's unique values, providing learning opportunities based on employee's unique needs, encouraging employees with specific feedback, and communicating clear goals and expectations, among others. A key feature of the of MIPS as conceptualized by Pichler and colleagues is individuation, that is, tailoring one's behavior to the employee. This requires that managers get to know each member of their workgroup on an individual basis. Developing high-quality, supportive relationships with each of their employees should be helpful in this connection. In order to do so, they must spend time getting to understand what drives each of their workgroup members, what motivates them, what their needs are, and how each employee is different from the other in terms of how their organismic needs should be fulfilled. Managers with higher levels of managerial interpersonal skills should therefore provide higher levels of motivation to employees regardless of their background or similarity. In fact, they should be more likely to carefully tailor their motivators to each employee's background.

Managing Conflict

As mentioned in the introduction of this chapter, there are inconsistent findings across studies in the diversity literature as to the effects of diversity in workgroups (e.g., van Knippenberg & Schippers, 2007). Research has shown that higher levels of workgroup diversity are related to conflict in groups (see Christian, Porter, & Moffitt, 2006; King, Hebl, & Beal, 2009) including relational conflict (Jehn et al., 1999; Williams & O'Reilly, 1998). Relational conflict, also known as emotional conflict, is "characterized by disagreements or tensions with regard to personal taste or interpersonal style" (King et al., 2009, p. 265). Unlike task- and process-oriented conflict (Bradley, Klotz, Postlethwaite, & Brown, 2013), relational conflict is generally counterproductive (see De Dreu & Weingart, 2003; Pelled, Eisenhardt, & Xin, 1999). Thus, relational conflict can stymie group performance. In other words, relational conflict may be part of the explanation as to why there are mixed findings as to whether or not diversity in workgroups leads to positive outcomes.

Social identity theory helps to explain why relational conflict occurs in diverse workgroups. Similar individuals focus on each other's positive attributes and find each other more attractive than dissimilar individuals, which creates a more positive social identity (Tsui, Porter, & Egan, 2002). This positive social identity is related to individuals thinking of the self in more collective, that is, in-group, terms and internalizing the group's interests (van Knippenberg & Ellemers, 2003). Individuals will also treat similar others more favorably than dissimilar others (Tajfel & Turner, 1986). In other words, when group boundaries are salient, which tends to be the case for socially important categories such as race and gender, this can create social categories or an "us" and "them" mentality (see King, Hebl, & Beal, 2009). It is important, therefore, that managers are able to handle different forms of conflict in workgroups, perhaps especially relational conflict, and to address this "us" and "them" mentality.

Managing conflict was found to be one of three key interpersonal skills in the research by Pichler and colleagues (Beenen, Pichler, & Davoudpour, 2018; Pichler & Beenen, 2013; Pichler, Beenen et al., 2018). Conflict management is centrally important to the effectiveness of individuals, groups, and organizations (De Dreu et al., 2001). There is an extensive body of work, which has shown that individuals, including managers, have different conflict management styles or strategies (e.g., De Dreu et al., 2001). These styles are based, in part, on individual differences, such as differences in personality traits (Antonioni, 1998). Dual concern theory (Pruitt & Rubin, 1986) posits that there are five different conflict management styles, which are determined based on two dimensions: concern for self, and concern for others. Problem-solving, an ideal form of conflict management, is based on high levels of concern for the self and others. Conflict management strategies are related to levels of conflict (Weider-Hatfield, D., & Hatfield, 1995), group decision making (Kuhn & Poole, 2000), and team outcomes (Behfar, Peterson, Mannix, & Trochim, 2008). Research has shown that conflict management strategies (i.e., more active than passive) and leader behaviors (managing their own emotions) mitigate the negative relationship between relational conflict and performance in diverse teams (Ayoko & Konrad, 2012).

In addition to conflict management strategies, research by Pichler and colleagues (e.g., Pichler, Beenen et al., 2018) suggests that certain skills are important when it comes to managing conflict in workgroups. The *managing conflict* dimension of MIPS includes features such as remaining calm when handling disputes, managing one's emotions when managing conflict, effectively diffusing emotionally charged situations, understanding how unique personalities contribute to conflict, and communicating effectively to resolve interpersonal disputes (Pichler, Beenen et al., 2018). Previous research has shown that managing one's emotions is important when problem-solving and resolving conflict in workgroups (Jordan & Troth, 2004), especially diverse workgroups (Ayoko & Konrad, 2012). Effective communication also seems essential when managing conflict in diverse groups (Lam & Chin, 2005), particularly when it comes to managers helping resolve communication breakdowns (Ayoko Härtel, & Callan, 2002). Again, communication is an element of *supporting*, *motivating*, and *managing conflict*. A key proposition of this chapter is that more interpersonally skilled managers should be able to more effectively manage relational conflict in diverse workgroups, thereby enhancing workgroup performance.

What seems especially important in this connection is the feature of individuation in conflict management. Research by Pichler and colleagues (Pichler & Beenen, 2013; Pichler, Beenen et al., 2018) suggests, for instance, that being able to understand how individual differences and unique personalities contribute to a particular conflict is essential to conflict management. In other words, in order to effectively manage conflict, a supervisor or manager must understand the unique backgrounds and viewpoints of the parties involved in the conflict. When it comes to relational or emotional conflict, that is, conflict based on personal taste or style, understanding each party's individual "style" is paramount. Moreover, if social categories (e.g., race, gender) are related to relational conflict, understanding how individual differences contribute to this conflict should be helpful in addressing the root cause of the conflict and therefore finding a solution. If managers are to help individuals from diverse backgrounds work together and resolve interpersonal conflicts, not only must they manage their emotions and keep a level head, they must understand how workgroup diversity is related to conflict.

Self-Management as a Necessary Precondition for MIPS

Although Pichler and colleagues originally proposed that self-management (i.e., self-awareness and managing one's emotions) is an important element of managerial interpersonal skills based on their literature review (Pichler & Beenen, 2013), results from factor analyses in pilot studies indicated that self-management items caused poor model fit overall (Pichler, Beenen et al., 2018). Thus, the authors concluded that self-management is not a part of the MIPS construct, but is instead a precursor, or necessary precondition for the development of managerial interpersonal skills. Self-awareness is also important for managers to be able to understand how their personality, attitudes, beliefs, and so forth, differ from their subordinates. This sort of self-awareness is crucial for the individuation that is an essential element of supporting, motivating and managing conflict. This is perhaps why self-awareness is so important to leadership effectiveness (Bratton et al., 2001). Self-management in terms of managing one's emotions is also necessary for effective conflict management, that is, in terms of maintaining composure (Ayoko & Konrad, 2012). Thus, for managers to develop MIPS, they must first develop self-management skills.

DISCUSSION

Workplaces across the globe are becoming more diverse due to a variety of factors including technological advancements, globalization, labor force migration, and increased labor force participation of traditionally under-represented groups (Kossek & Pichler, 2007; Roberson, 2012). Although it seems intuitive that workforce diversity should be related to positive outcomes such as increased workgroup performance through factors such as increased creativity, the evidence is not as clear. Diversity in workgroups and organizations can indeed be fruitful, so long as organizations effectively manage the diversity of their workforce and create an inclusive environment within which to operate (Kossek & Pichler, 2007; Roberson & Park, 2007). The question that organizations must grapple with, given the variety of approaches to managing diversity and inclusion, is how best to do so.

The central thesis of this chapter is that one potentially useful approach is to focus on managerial interpersonal skills. Highly talented individuals tend to leave managers, not organizations. Managerial treatment signals to employees the extent to which their organization values them. Thus, it seems that since managerial interpersonal skills are closely related to how employees are treated, both as individuals and workgroup members, focusing on these skills, for example, when making selection, placement or training and development decisions, could be an important way for organizations to manage diversity and inclusion. In connection, the purpose of this chapter was two-fold: To direct future research on diversity and inclusion management as it relates to managerial interpersonal skills, and to provide practical recommendations for managers and organizations on how to manage diversity and inclusion through managerial interpersonal skills. Each of these will be considered in turn in the sections that follow.

Future Research Directions for Diversity and Inclusion Management

There is a growing literature on managerial interpersonal skills (e.g., Beenen et al., 2018; Mumford et al., 2007; Pichler, Beenen et al., 2018; Rubin & Dierdorff, 2009). This literature has shown that interpersonal skills are more important for managerial success than other skill sets, such as technical and conceptual skills (Scullen et al., 2003). This makes sense—managers spend most of their time interacting and communicating with others (Hinds & Kiesler, 1995). That said, to date there has been no attempt to link managerial interpersonal skills to diversity and inclusion management. This is surprising since managers are on the front lines, so to speak, when it comes to managing diversity and inclusion. Managerial interpersonal skills are, based on the logic developed in this chapter, important not only to managerial success, but to managing diversity and creating an inclusive environment.

One of the propositions developed above was that a key way for managers to create an inclusive environment is through *supporting*, that is, providing consistent levels of support to all of their employees. This is consistent with literature on procedural justice, which has shown that consistency of treatment across individuals within a workgroup is related to perceptions of fairness (e.g., Pichler et al., 2016). That said, research on procedural justice has focused on the consistency with which organizational policies and practices are implemented, not the consistency of support provided by managers. Future research could examine how consistency in support is related to diversity-related outcomes such as perceptions of interpersonal justice and diversity climate. It could be particularly interesting to measure perceptions of organizational support (POS), as a proxy for feelings of inclusion, as a mediator between managerial interpersonal skills and turnover among minorities (or among individuals who are demographically different from their managers). Consistent levels of support should be positively related to POS (i.e., feeling that the organization cares for them) and, hence, to lower turnover. This may be especially the case when support is not only consistent but individuated.

Another proposition developed in this chapter was that *motivating*, namely tailoring rewards, feedback, and so forth, to each employee based on their unique background is a key way for managers to support the diversity of their workgroup and foster and inclusive environment. In other words, individuated motivation should not only increase motivation, it should signal to employees that their manager truly cares about them. Thus, future research could examine the extent to which motivating is related to the fulfillment of basic psychological needs, namely for autonomy, competence, and relatedness and, hence, to feelings of inclusion. By providing individuated motivators, managers can potentially break-down feelings among their workgroup members that more similar employees are treated more favorably. Put differently, when managerial interpersonal skills are high, this could reduce differences in relative LMX (Henderson, Liden, Glibkowski, & Chaudhry, 2009) between employees of different backgrounds reporting to the same manager. If not that, minority employees working with majority group managers should be more likely to feel their basic needs are being fulfilled when motivators are tailored to their desires, needs, and background, thereby improving performance. Future research could how needs fulfillment is related to perceptions of inclusion and related outcomes, such as job performance.

Supporting and motivating, relatively speaking, tend to operate interpersonally between supervisors and subordinates. *Managing conflict*, on the other hand, is more closely related to perceptions and behavior at the workgroup level. A proposition developed in this chapter is that managerial interpersonal skills should be related to effective conflict management. In this connection, conflict management requires that managers understand the unique viewpoints and backgrounds of the parties involved. Future research could examine relationships between managerial interpersonal skills, relational conflict, and hence performance, among diverse workgroups. In other words, managerial interpersonal skills could be related to group performance by reducing relational conflict in diverse workgroups. It would also be interesting to examine how managerial interpersonal skills are related to conflict management styles or strategies. More interpersonally skilled managers may be more likely to use conflict management strategies that promote performance, such as problem solving. Since relational conflict is a key issue to be solved with diverse workgroups, managerial interpersonal skills may be essential to helping these groups resolve conflicts, solve problems, and perform to their full potential.

Implications for Managers and Organizations

Leader-member exchange research has shown that managers form in- and out-groups with their employees based, in part, on interpersonal similarity (Brouer et al., 2009). This is consistent with social identity theory, which proposes that individuals categorize others into groups based on socially-relevant information (Turner, 1982). This is problematic for a number of reasons. For instance, in-group members receive more favorable treatment, such as more support (Liden & Maslyn, 1998). This natural tendency for managers to form differentiated exchanges with their workgroup members could also create self-fulfilling prophecies such that in-group members perform better as a function of the support and resources they receive due to their in-group status. Thus many diversity initiatives, such as nondiscrimination policies, diversity training, and employee resource groups, highlight how persons are treated differently based on their membership in a class, and attempt to reduce unfair preferential treatment.

Assuming that managerial interpersonal skills are important for line managers when it comes to managing diversity and inclusion, this may be an alternative or additional area of focus to these more common or more traditional diversity initiatives. Managerial interpersonal skills training is generally uncommon, and rarely if ever conceptualized as a means by which to manage diversity and inclusion. There are several different ways by which organizations can try to ensure managers have the interpersonal skills needed to manage diversity and inclusion. A jumping off point, so to speak, might be job analysis. Job analysis is often call the bedrock of human resources management (Brannick, Levin, & Morgeson, 2007). This is because a key outcome of job analysis is a job description. Job descriptions become the basis by which other human resources decisions, such as selection, training and development, performance appraisal, among others, are made. It could be important, therefore, for organizations to consider the extent to which interpersonal skills are relevant to managerial roles. It could also be important for organizations to consider, more specifically, the extent to which interpersonal skills are important in connection to managing persons of diverse backgrounds and to managing conflict in diverse groups and teams.

Organizations may also want to consider interpersonal skills in selection and placement decisions, including promotion decisions. It's common knowledge that individuals are often selected to be managers based on their job performance in a professional role, such as their technical proficiency, but not necessarily their leadership potential or managerial skills. In order for organizations to make selection decisions based on interpersonal skills, there needs to be a validated measure of some kind of interpersonal skills relevant to the managerial role. There is scant research on interpersonal skills assessment for personnel selection, and few tools available. Again, one of the intended purposes of Pichler and colleagues' research program was to develop such a measure, that is, a questionnaire that could be used for self- and other-report purposes (Pichler, Beenen et al., 2018). That said, a variety of requirements must be met before a given tool can be used for purposes of personnel selection as outlined by the Uniform Guidelines on Selection Procedures (see https://www.eeoc.gov/laws/regulations/).

A central theme of this chapter is that managerial interpersonal skills training could be a key organizational intervention by which to manage diversity and inclusion. Interpersonal skills are learnable and therefore trainable (see Beenen & Pichler, 2013); MIPS training is a type of skills training (see Kulik & Roberson, 2008). In this sense, MIPS training could supplement or replace more traditional forms of diversity training. This could address the concerns and criticisms of diversity interventions mentioned above, such as an undue focus on group differences, results opposite those expected, lack of interest among participants, and even backlash (e.g., Kaplan, 2006; Sanchez & Medkik, 2004). Managers need social skills to be effective; thus, MIPS training may be more well-received by managers and other stakeholders than more traditional forms of diversity training. Thus, instead of focusing on group differences, for example, as a means by which to reduce stereotyping, which can be a source of frustration for trainees (Bregman, 2012), MIPS training encourages managers to tailor interpersonal exchanges to individual's unique backgrounds. In this way, diversity plays prominently in MIPS training without focusing on group differences per se. Put differently, MIPS training can not only increase employee motivation and performance—it can potentially help organizations manage diversity and inclusion with fewer unintended negative unintended consequences.

For MIPS training to be effective, a number of steps should be taken. Before training is considered, an organization should conduct a needs analysis to determine what diversity and inclusion issues might need to be resolved and accordingly what sort of training might be needed (Roberson, Kulik, & Pepper, 2003). If MIPS training is deemed a good match to the needs of an organization (e.g., after having assessed managers' average levels of interpersonal skills), it is important that organizations ensure trainees are ready for this sort of training and, if implemented, foster a supportive climate for training transfer (Roberson, Kulik, & Pepper, 2009). This seems especially important if MIPS training is used as a form of diversity training. It is also important that the organization provide managers with opportunities for these skills to be used in the managerial role (Baldwin & Ford, 1988), and to receive regular and ongoing feedback on their skill development (Kelloway, Barling, & Helleur, 2000).

If MIPS training is implemented, it should be done in a developmental way to be optimally effective (Pichler, Beenen et al., 2018), which is represented in Figure 8.2. The specific types of behaviors that managers could be trained to exhibit are presented in Table 8.1. Managerial interpersonal skills training programs should focus first on developing managers' self-management skills, that is, intrapersonal skills, before developing interpersonal skills. This is consistent with research that has shown self-awareness is important in connection to leadership development (Bratton, Dodd, & Brown, 2001). Being aware of one's own attitudes and biases, for instance, is essential to being aware of how individuals in one's workgroup differ from the manager, and from each other. Developing self-management skills is difficult for anyone. Some evidence-based ways by which managers can do so include better understanding the nature of emotions and how they relate to behavior (Locke, 2009), practicing predicting one's emotions (Salovey & Sluyter), collecting and evaluating multisource feedback (McCarthy & Garavan, 1999), and purposefully controlling one's thoughts through self-dialogue (London & Smither, 1999).

Figure 8.2. Model of Sequence for Managerial Interpersonal Skills (MIPS) Training.

Table 8.1.

Key Features and Example Behaviors of Managerial Interpersonal Skills (MIPS)

MIPS Precursor	Key Features of Dimension	Example Behaviors
Self-management	• Initiative • Emotional control • Self-awareness	• Take responsibility for actions • Prevent outbursts when angry • Demonstrate reflection of one's values
Communication	• Active listening • Effective outbound communication	• Reflecting what one has heard • Carefully choosing communication medium

MIPS Dimension	Key Features of Dimension	Example Behaviors
Supporting	• Seems approachable • Shows genuine concern • Demonstrates understanding • Fair interpersonal treatment • Helps employees with work-nonwork balance	• Maintain an open-door policy • Listen to employee concerns • Demonstrate empathy • Repeats-back to employees key ideas/phrases during conversation • Provide consistent treatment across employees • Coordinate schedules between employees
Motivating	• Understands how differences relate to motivation • Provides tailored rewards • Offers unique learning opportunities • Encourages employees • Communicates clear goals and expectations	• Ask employees about what drives them • Get to know employees on an individual basis • Assign tasks or projects based on employee's unique development needs • Provide feedback in a way that is motivating to each employee • Communicate goals based on conversations about employee motivators
Managing Conflict	• Manages one's emotions • Remains calm during conflict • Diffuses emotionally charged situations • Understands how different personalities relate to conflict • Communicates clearly to resolve disputes	• Think about and reflect on one's emotions • Take brief notes during a confrontation to help remain calm • Help employees take "breaks" when conflict gets heated • Reflect on each employee's personality and how this contributes to conflict • Discuss different possible solutions to a conflict with parties

The next sequence of a managerial interpersonal skills training program should be communication skills training. Research by Pichler and colleagues (Pichler & Beenen, 2013; Pichler, Beenen et al., 2018) suggests that communication skills are necessary for the effective use of supporting, motivating, and managing conflict. There is a robust literature on communication skills training in the clinical, that is, medical literature (e.g., Brown, Boles, Mullooly, & Levinson 1999), as well as the broader communications literature (e.g., Stokoe, 2014). One useful model of communication skills in organizations is that provided by Van der Molen and Gramsbergen-Hoogland (2005). Their model involves three modules: First, basic communication skills (e.g., listening skills), next, communication skills in applied dialogues, such as the employment interview, and finally communication in group situations, such as managing conflict. This model overlaps nicely with the model of managerial interpersonal skills developed by Pichler Pichler, Beenen et al. (2018) in that it includes basic skills (needed for supporting, motivating, and managing conflict), as well as the applied nature of the model. This literature suggests that managers' communication skills can be enhanced to the extent that they are trained to actively listen (Helms & Haynes, 1992) and communicate outbound messages effectively (Barrett, 2006).

Next, managers should be trained in skills related to supporting, motivating, and managing conflict in that order. Teckchandani and Pichler (2015) provide a framework by which managers can develop perceptions of support among employees in their workgroup. They suggest, for instance, that managers work to find common ground with their employees, seek to understand their employees on an individual basis, and create a virtuous cycle of reciprocity by helping employees with key work-related challenges. These behaviors are consistent with the *supporting* dimension of MIPS developed by Pichler and colleagues (Pichler & Beenen, 2013; Pichler, Beenen et al., 2018), as well as the behaviors listed in Table 8.1. These behaviors could be the basis for a training program designed to increase supervisor support, or to improve managerial interpersonal skills more generally. In addition to providing the emotional support described by Teckchandani and Pichler (2015), it is important that managers provide support for work-family balance (Kossek, Pichler, Bodner, & Hammer, 2011). Managers can role model effective behaviors and help employees with schedule conflicts (Hammer et al., 2009).

A key way for managers to support the diversity of their workgroup and foster a sense of inclusion is to develop skills around motivating as conceptualized by Pichler and colleagues (Pichler & Beenen, 2013; Pichler, Beenen et al., 2018). Tailoring motivators to employee's unique needs and backgrounds should fulfill organismic needs. For instance, providing learning opportunities should increase a sense of autonomy; specific feedback should increase competence; and communicating clearly with an employee should increase his or her sense of relatedness with the manager. Moreover, individuating motivators, such as rewards, based on employees' unique backgrounds and needs could increase perceptions of self-determination, thereby increasing motivation. Fulfilling organismic needs will increase motivation, but it should also increase the extent to which the employee feels like a valued group member because these behaviors signal to the employee that they are cared about (Tyler & Lind, 1992). Providing individuated motivators may mitigate a manager's tendency to form in- and out-groups based on similarity; if not that, it should give employees the sense that they are valued not only regardless of, but because of their unique background.

To manage conflict effectively, managers should learn to develop conflict management strategies that help address both concern for the self and for others, namely problem-solving (Pruitt & Rubin, 1986). To use this conflict management style effectively, managers must also learn to manage their emotions when handling conflict (Jordan & Troth, 2004). Social learning, or observing others manage conflict effectively is one way by which managers can learn to implement problem-solving as a conflict management style (see Berkes, 2009). Ultimately, managing conflict is perhaps one of the most complex challenges managers face, and it seems is the most sophisticated interpersonal skill for effective management of people (Pichler, Beenen et al., 2018). Thus, conflict management takes extensive practice. It could be useful for managers to engage in extensive role-playing with feedback from more experienced managers (Brown, 1994). This could be especially useful in helping managers deal with relational conflict, as well as developing skills in managing conflict between people from different backgrounds.

ACKNOWLEDGMENTS

This research was funded by a Management Education Research Institute (MERI) grant from the Graduate Management Admissions Council (GMAC). The author would like to thank those scholars who provided feedback on various aspects of this research program, namely Kim Cameron, Cary Cherniss, Shane Connelly, Sean Hannah, Paulo Lopes, Bob Rubin, Robert Tett, and Darren Treadway. The author would also like to thank the thought leaders who participated in a managerial interpersonal skills caucus at the 2010 Academy of Management meeting, namely Tim Baldwin, Gerard Beenen, Hillary Anger Elfenbein, Paulo Lopes, Tom Mayes, Lori Muse, Bob Rubin, and David Whetten. I would like to thank Quinette Roberson for her valuable and constructive comments on this chapter.

REFERENCES

Abraham, S. E., Karns, L. A., Shaw, K., & Mena, M. A. (2001). Managerial competencies and the managerial performance appraisal process. *Journal of Management Development, 20*(10), 842–852.

Antonioni, D. (1998). Relationship between the big five personality factors and conflict management styles. *International journal of conflict management, 9*(4), 336–355.

Ayoko, O. B., & Konrad, A. M. (2012). Leaders' transformational, conflict, and emotion management behaviors in culturally diverse workgroups. *Equality, Diversity and Inclusion: An International Journal, 31*(8), 694–724.

Ayoko, O. B., Härtel, C. E., & Callan, V. J. (2002). Resolving the puzzle of productive and destructive conflict in culturally heterogeneous workgroups: A communication accommodation theory approach. *International Journal of Conflict Management, 13*(2), 165–195.

Baldwin, T. T., & Ford, J. K. (1988). Transfer of training: A review and directions for future research. *Personnel psychology, 41*(1), 63–105.

Barney, J. B., & Wright, P. M. (1998). On becoming a strategic partner: The role of human resources in gaining competitive advantage. *Human Resource Management, 37*(1), 31–46.

Barrett, D.J. (2006). Leadership communication: A communication approach for senior-level managers. In *Handbook of business strategy* (pp 385–390). Houston, TX: Emerald Publishing Group, Rice University.

Beenen, G., & Pichler, S. (2016). A discussion forum on managerial interpersonal skills. *Journal of Management Development, 35*(5), 706–716.

Beenen, G., Pichler, S., & Davoudpour, S. (2018). Interpersonal skills in MBA admissions: How are they conceptualized and assessed. *Journal of Management Education, 42* (1), 34–54.

Beenen, G., & Pichler, S., & Levy, P. (2017). Self-determined feedback seeking: The role of perceived supervisor autonomy support. *Human Resource Management, 56* (4), 555–569.

Behfar, K. J., Peterson, R. S., Mannix, E. A., & Trochim, W. M. (2008). The critical role of conflict resolution in teams: a close look at the links between conflict type, conflict management strategies, and team outcomes. *Journal of Applied Psychology, 93*(1), 170.

Berger, L. J., Essers, C., & Himi, A. (2017). Muslim employees within 'white'organizations: The case of Moroccan workers in the Netherlands. *International Journal of Human Resource Management, 28*(8), 1119–1139.

Berkes, F. (2009). Evolution of co-management: Role of knowledge generation, bridging organizations and social learning. *Journal of environmental management, 90*(5), 1692–1702.

Billig, M. (1985). Prejudice, categorization and particularization: From a perceptual to a rhetorical approach. *European Journal of Social Psychology, 15*(1), 79–103.

Blazer, D. G. (1982). Social support and mortality in an elderly community population. *American Journal of Epidemiology, 115*(5), 684–694.

Bradley, B. H., Klotz, A. C., Postlethwaite, B. E., & Brown, K. G. (2013). Ready to rumble: How team personality composition and task conflict interact to improve performance. *Journal of Applied Psychology, 98*(2), 385.

Brannick, M. T., Levin E. L., & Morgeson, F. (2007). *Job and work analysis: Methods, research and applications for human resource management.* Thousand Oaks, CA: SAGE.

Bratton, V. K., Dodd, N. G., & Brown, F. W. (2011). The impact of emotional intelligence on accuracy of self-awareness and leadership performance. *Leadership & Organization Development Journal, 32*(2), 127–149.

Bregman, P. (2012). Diversity training doesn't work. *Forbes*, March, 12.

Brouer, R. L., Duke, A., Treadway, D. C., & Ferris, G. R. (2009). The moderating effect of political skill on the demographic dissimilarity - Leader-member exchange quality relationship. *Leadership Quarterly, 20*, 61–69.

Brown, J. B., Boles, M., Mullooly, J. P., & Levinson, W. (1999). Effect of clinician communication skills training on patient satisfaction: A randomized, controlled trial. *Annals of Internal Medicine, 131*(11), 822–829.

Brown, K. M. (1994). Using role play to integrate ethics into the business curriculum a financial management example. *Journal of Business Ethics, 13*(2), 105–110.

Brown, S. L., Nesse, R. M., Vinokur, A. D., & Smith, D. M. (2003). Providing social support may be more beneficial than receiving it: Results from a prospective study of mortality. *Psychological Science, 14*(4), 320–327.

Bryant, C. M., & Conger, R. D. (1999). Marital success and domains of social support in long-term relationships: Does the influence of network members ever end?. *Journal of Marriage and the Family*, 437–450.

Caplan, R. D., Cobb, S., & French, J. R. (1975). Relationships of cessation of smoking with job stress, personality, and social support. *Journal of Applied Psychology, 60*(2), 211.

Christian, J., Porter, L. W., & Moffitt, G. (2006). Workplace diversity and group relations: An overview. *Group Processes & Intergroup Relations, 9*(4), 459–466.

Colquitt, J. A., Zapata-Phelan, C. P., & Roberson, Q. M. (2005). Justice in teams: A review of fairness effects in collective contexts. *Research in personnel and human resources management* (pp. 53–94).

Deci, E. L., & Ryan, R. M. (1985). Conceptualizations of intrinsic motivation and self-determination. In *Intrinsic motivation and self-determination in human behavior* (pp. 11–40). Boston, MA: Springer.

Deci, E.L. & Ryan, R. M. (2011). Self-determination theory. *Handbook of theories of social psychology, 1,* 416–433.

De Dreu, C. K., Evers, A., Beersma, B., Kluwer, E. S., & Nauta, A. (2001). A theory-based measure of conflict management strategies in the workplace. *Journal of Organizational Behavior 22*(6), 645–668.

De Dreu, C. K., & Weingart, L. R. (2003). Task versus relationship conflict, team performance, and team member satisfaction: A meta-analysis. *Journal of Applied Psychology, 88*(4), 741.

Dierdorff, E. C., Rubin, R. S., & Morgeson, F. P. (2009). The milieu of managerial work: an integrative framework linking work context to role requirements. *Journal of Applied Psychology, 94*(4), 972.

Eisenberger, R., Stinglhamber, F., Vandenberghe, C., Sucharski, I. L., & Rhoades, L. (2002). Perceived supervisor support: Contributions to perceived organizational support and employee retention. *Journal of Applied psychology, 87*(3), 565.

Ensher, E. A., Grant-Vallone, E. J., & Marelich, W. D. (2002). Effects of perceived attitudinal and demographic similarity on protégés' support and satisfaction gained from their mentoring relationships. *Journal of Applied Social Psychology, 32*(7), 1407–1430.

Esen, E. (2005). *Workplace diversity practices survey report.* Alexandria, VA: Society for Human Resources Management.

Ferris, G. R., Witt, L. A., & Hochwarter, W. A. (2001). Interaction of social skill and general mental ability on job performance and salary. *Journal of Applied Psychology, 86*(6), 1075.

Ferris, G. R., Treadway, D. C., Kolodinsky, R. W., Hochwarter, W. A., Kacmar, C., Douglas & C., & Frink, D. (2005). Development and validation of the political skill inventory. *Journal of Management, 31,* 126–152.

Gagné, M., & Deci, E. L. (2005). Self-determination theory and work motivation. *Journal of Organizational behavior, 26*(4), 331–362.

Glazer, L. (2018). Google finds STEM skills aren't the most important skills. Blog Entry for Michigan Future Inc. Retrieved March 7 2018, from http://michiganfuture.org/01/2018/google-finds-stem-skills-arent-the-most-important-skills/

Graen, G. B., & Scandura, T. A. (1987). Toward a psychology of dyadic organizing. *Research in Organizational Behavior, 9,* 175–208.

Hammer, L. B., Kossek, E. E., Yragui, N. L., Bodner, T. E., & Hanson, G. C. (2009). Development and validation of a multidimensional measure of family supportive supervisor behaviors (FSSB). *Journal of Management, 35*(4), 837–856.

Hammer, L. B., Kossek, E. E., Anger, W. K., Bodner, T., & Zimmerman, K. L. (2011). Clarifying work–family intervention processes: The roles of work–family conflict and family-supportive supervisor behaviors. *Journal of Applied Psychology, 96*(1), 134.

Harrison, D. A., Price, K. H., & Bell, M. P. (1998). Beyond relational demography: Time and the effects of surface-and deep-level diversity on work group cohesion. *Academy of Management Journal, 41*(1), 96–107.

Heinrichs, M., Baumgartner, T., Kirschbaum, C., & Ehlert, U. (2003). Social support and oxytocin interact to suppress cortisol and subjective responses to psychosocial stress. *Biological Psychiatry, 54*(12), 1389–1398.

Helms, M. M., & Haynes, P. J. (1992). Are you really listening? The benefit of effective intra-organizational listening. *Journal of Managerial Psychology, 7*(6), 17–21.

Henderson, D. J., Liden, R. C., Glibkowski, B. C., & Chaudhry, A. (2009). LMX differentiation: A multilevel review and examination of its antecedents and outcomes. *Leadership Quarterly, 20,* 517–534.

Hinds, P., & Kiesler, S. (1995). Communication across boundaries: Work, structure, and use of communication technologies in a large organization. *Organization Science, 6*(4), 373-393.

Hogg, M. A., & Terry, D. I. (2000). Social identity and self-categorization processes in organizational contexts. *Academy of Management Review, 25*(1), 121–140.

House, J. S. (1981). The nature of social support. *Work Stress and Social Support,* 13-30.

Hunt, J. W., & Baruch, Y. (2003). Developing top managers: The impact of interpersonal skills training. *Journal of Management Development, 22*(8), 729–752.

Ibarra, H. (1993). Personal networks of women and minorities in management: A conceptual framework. *Academy of Management Review, 18*(1), 56–87.

Jehn, K. A., Northcraft, G. B., & Neale, M. A. (1999). Why differences make a difference: A field study of diversity, conflict and performance in workgroups. *Administrative Science Quarterly, 44*(4), 741–763.

Jordan, P. J., & Troth, A. C. (2004). Managing emotions during team problem solving: Emotional intelligence and conflict resolution. *Human Performance, 17*(2), 195–218.

Kaplan, D. M. (2006). Can diversity training discriminate? Backlash to lesbian, gay, and bisexual diversity initiatives. *Employee Responsibilities and Rights Journal, 18*(1), 61–72.

Kelloway, K., Barling, J., & Helleur, J. (2000). Enhancing transformational leadership: The roles of training and feedback. *Leadership & Organization Development Journal, 21*(3), 145–149.

Kidder, D. L., Lankau, M. J., Chrobot-Mason, D., Mollica, K. A., & Friedman, R. A. (2004). Backlash toward diversity initiatives: Examining the impact of diversity program justification, personal and group outcomes. *International Journal of Conflict Management, 15*(1), 77–102.

Kim, E., Bhave, D. P., & Glomb, T. M. (2013). Emotion regulation in workgroups: The roles of demographic diversity and relational work context. *Personnel Psychology, 66*(3), 613–644.

King, E. B., Dawson, J. F., Kravitz, D. A., & Gulick, L. M. (2012). A multilevel study of the relationships between diversity training, ethnic discrimination and satisfaction in organizations. *Journal of Organizational Behavior, 33*(1), 5–20.

King, E. B., Hebl, M. R., & Beal, D. J. (2009). Conflict and cooperation in diverse workgroups. *Journal of Social Issues, 65*(2), 261-285.

Klein, C., DeRouin, R. E., & Salas, E. (2006). Uncovering workplace interpersonal skills: A review, framework, and research agenda. *International review of Industrial and Organizational Psychology, 21,* 79.

Kochan, T., Bezrukova, K., Ely, R., Jackson, S., Joshi, A., Jehn, K., ... & Thomas, D. (2003). The effects of diversity on business performance: Report of the diversity research network. *Human Resource Management, 42*(1), 3–21.

Kossek, E. E., Ollier-Malaterre, A., Lee, M. D., Pichler, S., & Hall, D. T. (2016). Line Managers' rationales for professionals' reduced-load work in embracing and ambivalent organizations. *Human Resource Management, 55*(1), 143–171.

Kossek, E.E., & Pichler, S. (2007). EEO and the management of diversity. In P. Boxell, J. Purcell, & P. Wright (Eds). *Handbook of human resource management* (pp. 251–272). Oxford, England: Oxford University Press.

Kossek, E. E., Pichler, S., Bodner, T., & Hammer. L. (2011). Workplace social support and work-family conflict: A meta-analysis clarifying the influence of general and work-family specific supervisor and organizational support. *Personnel Psychology, 64*(2), 289–313.

Kuhn, T. I. M., & Poole, M. S. (2000). Do conflict management styles affect group decision making? Evidence from a longitudinal field study. *Human Communication Research, 26*(4), 558–590.

Kulik, C. T., & Roberson, L. (2008). 8 Diversity initiative effectiveness: What organizations can (and cannot) expect from diversity recruitment, diversity training, and formal mentoring programs. *Diversity at Work*, 265–317.

Lam, P. K., & Chin, K. S. (2005). Identifying and prioritizing critical success factors for conflict management in collaborative new product development. *Industrial Marketing Management, 34*(8), 761–772.

Liden, R. C., & Maslyn, J. M. (1998). Multidimensionality of leader-member exchange: An empirical assessment through scale development. *Journal of Management, 24*, 43–72.

Lipman, V. (2015, August 4th). People leave managers, not companies. *Forbes*.

Macky, K., & Boxall, P. (2008). High-involvement work processes, work intensification and employee well-being: A study of New Zealand worker experiences. *Asia Pacific Journal of Human Resources, 46*(1), 38–55.

Locke, E. A. (2009). Attain emotional control by understanding what emotions are. In *Handbook of principles of organizational behavior: Indispensable knowledge for evidence-based management*, 145–160.

London, M., & Smither, J. W. (1999). Empowered self-development and continuous learning. *Human Resource Management, 38*(1), 3–15.

Maslow, A.H. (1954). *Motivation and personality*. New York, NY: Harper.

McCarthy, A. M., & Garavan, T. N. (1999). Developing self-awareness in the managerial career development process: the value of 360-degree feedback and the MBTI. *Journal of European Industrial Training, 23*(9), 437–445.

Mintzberg, H. (1980). *The nature of managerial work*. Engelwood Cliffs, NJ: Prentice-Hall.

Morgan, B. (2018, January). Why every employee in your company should have communications training. *Forbes*.

Mumford, T. V., Campion, M. A., & Morgeson, F. P. (2007). The leadership skills strataplex: Leadership skill requirements across organizational levels. *The Leadership Quarterly, 18*(2), 154–166.

Muse, L., & Pichler, S. (2011). A comparison of types of support for lower-skill workers: Evidence for the importance of family-supportive supervisors. *Journal of Vocational Behavior, 79*(3), 653–666.

Ng, E. S. (2008). Why organizations choose to manage diversity? Toward a leadership-based theoretical framework. *Human Resource Development Review, 7*(1), 58–78.

Pelled, L. H., Eisenhardt, K. M., & Xin, K. R. (1999). Exploring the black box: An analysis of work group diversity, conflict and performance. *Administrative Science Quarterly, 44*(1), 1–28.

Pichler, S. (2012). The social context of performance appraisal and appraisal reactions: A meta-analysis. *Human Resource Management, 51*(5), 709–732.

Pichler, S. & Beenen, G. (2013). Toward a model and measure of managerial interpersonal skills. In R. Riggio & S. Tan (Eds.), *Leader interpersonal and influence skills: The soft skills of leadership*. Abington, England: Routledge.

Pichler, S., Beenen, G., Livingston, B., & Riggio, R. (2018). *The good manager: Development of a model and validation of a measure of managerial interpersonal skills (MIPS)*. Working Paper: California State University, Fullerton.

Pichler, S., Ruggs, E., & Trau, R. (2017). Worker outcomes of LGBT-supportive policies: A cross-level model. *Equality, Diversity and Inclusion: An International Journal, 36*(1), 17–32.

Pichler, S., Varma, A., Michel, J., Levy, P.E., Budhwar, P., & Sharma, A. (2016). Leader- member exchange, group- and individual-level procedural justice and reactions to performance appraisals. *Human Resource Management, 55*(5), 871–883.

Pichler, S., Varma, A., & Bruce, T. (2010). Heterosexism in employment decisions: The role of job misfit. *Journal of Applied Social Psychology, 40*(8).

Pruitt, D. G., & Rubin, J. Z. (1986). *Social conflict: Escalation, impasse, and resolution*. Reding, MA: Addision-Wesley.

Purkiss, S. L. S., Perrewé, P. L., Gillespie, T. L., Mayes, B. T., & Ferris, G. R. (2006). Implicit sources of bias in employment interview judgments and decisions. *Organizational Behavior and Human Decision Processes, 101*(2), 152–167.

Rhoades, L., & Eisenberger, R. (2002). Perceived organizational support: a review of the literature. *Journal of Applied Psychology, 87*(4), 698.

Riggio, R. E., & Reichard, R. J. (2008). The emotional and social intelligences of effective leadership: An emotional and social skill approach. *Journal of Managerial Psychology, 23*(2), 169–185.

Riggio, R. E., Tucker, J., & Coffaro, D. (1989). Social skills and empathy. *Personality and Individual Differences, 10*(1), 93–99.

Riggio, R. E., Watring, K. P., & Throckmorton, B. (1993). Social skills, social support, and psychosocial adjustment. *Personality and Individual Differences, 15*(3), 275–280.

Robbins, S. P., & Hunsaker, P. L. (2011). *Training in interpersonal skills: Tips for managing people at work*. United States: Pearson Higher Education.

Roberson, L., Kulik, C. T., & Pepper, M. B. (2003). Using needs assessment to resolve controversies in diversity training design. *Group & Organization Management, 28*(1), 148–174.

Roberson, L., Kulik, C. T., & Pepper, M. B. (2009). Individual and environmental factors influencing the use of transfer strategies after diversity training. *Group & Organization Management, 34*(1), 67–89.

Roberson, Q. M. (2012). Managing diversity. In *The Oxford handbook of organizational psychology, Volume 2*.

Roberson, Q. M., & Park, H. J. (2007). Examining the link between diversity and firm performance: The effects of diversity reputation and leader racial diversity. *Group & Organization Management, 32*(5), 548–568.

Rubin, R. S., & Dierdorff, E. C. (2009). How relevant is the MBA? Assessing the alignment of required curricula and required managerial competencies. *Academy of Management Learning & Education, 8*(2), 208–224.

Rosenthal, R., & Jacobson, L. (1968). *Pygmalion in the classroom: Teacher expectation and pupils' intellectual development*. New York, NY: Holt, Rinehart and Winston.

Rubin, R. B., & Martin, M. M. (1994). Development of a measure of interpersonalcommunication competence. *Communication Research Reports, 11*, 33–44.

Ryan, R. M., & Deci, E. L. (2000). Intrinsic and extrinsic motivations: Classic definitions and new directions. *Contemporary Educational Psychology, 25*(1), 54–67.

Salovey, P. E., & Sluyter, D. J. (1997). *Emotional development and emotional intelligence: Educational implications*. New York, NY: Basic Books.

Sanchez, J. I., & Medkik, N. (2004). The effects of diversity awareness training on differential treatment. *Group & Organization Management, 29*(4), 517–536.

Schnittker, J. (2008). Happiness and success: Genes, families, and the psychological effects of socioeconomic position and social support. *American Journal of Sociology, 114*(S1), S233–S259.

Scullen, S. E., Mount, M. K., & Judge, T. A. (2003). Evidence of the construct validity of developmental ratings of managerial performance. *Journal of Applied Psychology, 88*(1), 50.

Siebert, D. C., Mutran, E. J., & Reitzes, D. C. (1999). Friendship and social support: The importance of role identity to aging adults. *Social work, 44*(6), 522–533.

Stevens, F. G., Plaut, V. C., & Sanchez-Burks, J. (2008). Unlocking the benefits of diversity: All-inclusive multiculturalism and positive organizational change. *The Journal of Applied Behavioral Science, 44*(1), 116–133.

Stokoe, E. (2014). The Conversation Analytic Role-play Method (CARM): A method for training communication skills as an alternative to simulated role-play. *Research on Language and Social Interaction, 47*(3), 255–265.

Tajfel, H., & Turner, J. C. (1979). An integrative theory of intergroup conflict. In W. G. Austin & S. Worchel (Eds.), *The social psychology of intergroup relations* (pp. 33–47). Monterey, CA: Brooks-Cole.

Teckchandani, A., & Pichler, S. (2015). Quality results from performance appraisals. *Industrial Management, 57*(4).

Thomas, D. (2004). Diversity as strategy. *Harvard business review, 82*(9), 98–98.

Thorndike, E. L. (1920). Intelligence and its uses. *Harper's Magazine*. Retrieved from https://harpers.org/archive/1920/01/intelligence-and-its-uses/

Thorndike, R.L. (1936). Factor analysis of social and abstract intelligence. *Journal of Educational Psychology, 27*, 231–233.

Truxillo, D. M., Fraccaroli, F., Yaldiz, L. M., & Zaniboni, S. (2017). Age discrimination at work. *Palgrave Handbook of Age Diversity and Work* (pp. 447–472). London: England: Palgrave Macmillan.

Tsui, A. S., Porter, L. W., & Egan, T. D. (2002). When both similarities and dissimilarities matter: Extending the concept of relational demography. *Human Relations, 55*, 899–929.

Turner, J. C. (1982). *Towards a cognitive redefinition of the social group. In Social identity and intergroup relations*. Cambridge: Cambridge University Press.

Tyler, T. R., & Lind, E. A. (1992). A relational model of authority in groups. In *Advances in experimental social psychology* (Vol. 25, pp. 115–191). Cambridge, MA: Academic Press.

Van de Vliert, E., & Kabanoff, B. (1990). Toward theory based measures of conflictmanagement. *Academy of Management Journal, 33*(1), 199–209.

Van der Molen, H. T., & Gramsbergen-Hoogland, Y. (2005). *Communication in organizations: Basic skills and conversation models.* New York, NY and London, England: Psychology Press.

Van Knippenberg, D., & Ellemers, N. (2003). *Social identity and group performance. Social identity at work: Developing theory for organizational practice.* New York, NY and London, England: Psychology Press.

Van Knippenberg, D., & Schippers, M. C. (2007). Work group diversity. *Annual Review of Psychology, 58.*

Varma, A., Budhwar, P., & Pichler, S. (2011). Chinese country nationals' willingness to help expatriates: The role of social categorization. *Thunderbird International Business Review, 53*(3), 353–364.

Weider-Hatfield, D., & Hatfield, J. D. (1995). Relationships among conflict management styles, levels of conflict, and reactions to work. *The Journal of Social Psychology, 135*(6), 687–698.

Williams, K. Y., & O'Reilly, C. A., III. (1998). *Demography and Research in Organizational Behavior, 20,* 77–140.

ABOUT THE AUTHORS

THE EDITORS

Mikki Hebl is the Martha and Henry Malcolm Lovett Professor of Psychology and Professor of Management at Rice University, where she has been for the last 19 years. She graduated with her BA from Smith College and her PhD at Dartmouth College. She is an applied psychologist whose research focuses on workplace discrimination and remediation. Her particular area of expertise is in the area of gender discrimination. She has published over 125 articles, received 20 teaching awards, been awarded major NIH and NSF funded grants, and recently received both the lifetime award for Gender and Diversity in Organizations at the Academy of Management (2014) and the national Cherry Professor of the Year Award (2016).

Eden King is an Associate Professor of Industrial-Organizational Psychology at Rice University. She is pursuing a program of research that aims to make work better for everyone. This research—which has yielded over 100 scholarly products and has been featured in outlets such as the New York Times, Good Morning America, and Harvard Business Review—addresses three primary themes: (1) current manifestations of discrimination and barriers to work-life balance in organizations, (2) consequences of such challenges for its targets and their workplaces, and (3) individual and organizational strategies for reducing discrimination and increasing support for families. In addition to her scholarship, Dr. King has partnered with organizations to improve diversity climate, increase fairness in selection systems, and to design and implement diversity training programs. She is currently an Associate Editor for the *Journal of Management* and the *Journal of Business and Psychology* and is on the editorial board of the Journal of Applied Psychology.

Quinetta Roberson is the Fred J. Springer Endowed Chair in Business Leadership at Villanova University, prior to which she was an Associate Professor at Cornell University. She has been a visiting scholar at universities on six continents, and served an appointment as Director of the Science of Organizations Program at the National Science Foundation (NSF). Dr. Roberson has published over 30 scholarly journal articles and book chapters, edited a *Handbook of Diversity in the Workplace*, and served as an Associate Editor at the *Journal of Applied Psychology*. She also has over 20 years of global experience in teaching courses, facilitating workshops, and advising organizations on how to drive performance through diversity, inclusive cultures, and leadership. Her work is informed by her experiences as a financial analyst and small business consultant prior to obtaining her doctorate. She earned her PhD in Organizational Behavior from the University of Maryland, and holds undergraduate and graduate degrees in Finance.

THE AUTHORS

Derek R. Avery, PhD, is the David C. Darnell Presidential Chair in Principled Leadership in the Wake Forest School of Business. He is an active member of the Academy of Management and a fellow of the Society for Industrial/Organizational Psychology and Association for Psychological Science. His publications total more than 80 articles and chapters and this research, which has earned commendation from the Academy of Management, has appeared in various outlets such as the *Journal of Applied Psychology*, *Personnel Psychology*, *Organization Science*, *Organizational Behavior and Human Decision Processes*, the *Journal of Management* and the *Journal of Organizational Behavior*.

Mindy Bergman is a Professor in the Department of Psychological and Brain Sciences, Affiliated Faculty in Women's and Gender Studies, and Faculty Fellow in the Mary Kay O'Connor Process Safety Center at Texas A&M University. She is a Fellow of the Society for Industrial and Organizational Psychology and the American Psychological Association. Her work focuses on mistreatment and marginalization of minoritized persons in organizations, occupational health, workplace safety, and organizational commitment. She teaches Psychological Aspects of Human Sexuality at the undergraduate level.

Briana G. Capuchino is a graduate student studying Industrial/Organizational Psychology at Texas A&M University. She is broadly interested in research on the impact of gender and race on various workplace experiences with particular interest in parenthood and pregnancy.

Jaee Cho is an Assistant Professor in the Department of Management at the Hong Kong University of Science and Technology. She studies how people make sense of cultural differences and how their cultural beliefs influence their decision making, judgment, and performance. She received her PhD from Columbia University and her BA from Korea University.

Rifat Kamasak is Professor of Management and Strategy at Bahcesehir University, Istanbul, Turkey. He also holds board membership positions in several companies. He worked in the food, textile, and consulting industries for nearly 15 years. His primary interest areas are business strategy, diversity management, and knowledge and innovation.

Alison M. Konrad, PhD, joined the Richard Ivey School of Business, U. of Western Ontario in 2003 as a Professor of Organizational Behavior and holder of the Corus Entertainment Chair in Women in Management. Professor Konrad has been Chair of the Academy of Management's Gender and Diversity in Organizations Division, President of the Eastern Academy of Management, and President of the International Society for the Study of Work and Organizational Values. She is past Editor of *Group and Organization Management*, and has served on the Editorial Boards of *AMR*, *AMLE*, *Administrative Science Quarterly*, the *British Journal of Management*, *Equality, Diversity and Inclusion: An International Journal*, *Group & Organization Management*, and *Human Resource Management*. She has published over 100 refereed articles and chapters, and her current research focuses on diversity in social networks, and the effectiveness of diversity and inclusiveness initiatives.

Andrew Lam is a master's student in the Department of Sociology and Social Anthropology at Dalhousie University. His research focuses on the impact political satire on social media networks affects young people's civic engagement. His research interests extend towards areas of migration, diversity management and inclusion. He is the Program Coordinator for the Family Wellness and Community Enhancement Program at Catholic Social Services Immigration and Settlement Service which helps integrate immigrant and refugee families into Canadian life.

Sin-Ning Cindy Liu is a graduate student studying Industrial/Organizational Psychology at Texas A&M University. She is broadly interested in research on diversity and inclusion in the workplace. Specifically, her research examines challenges related to understudied aspects of social identity, including religion, sexual orientation, parenting status, and immigrant status.

Brent Lyons is the York Research Chair in Stigmatization and Social Identity and an Assistant Professor of Organization Studies at the Schulich School of Business. His research involves the study of stigma in organizations and how individuals with stigmatized social identities, such as disability, navigate their work and interpersonal relationships to reduce consequences of stigmatization. Brent has published his work in journals such as *Academy of Management Review, Journal of Applied Psychology, Journal of Management*, and *Organizational Behavior and Human Decision Processes*.

Eddy Ng is the James and Elizabeth Freeman Professor of Management at Bucknell University. Previously, he held the F.C. Manning Chair in Economics and Business at Dalhousie University. His research focuses on managing diversity for organizational competitiveness, the changing nature of work and organizations, and managing across generations. His work has been funded by the Social Sciences and Humanities Research Council of Canada grants. He has published more than 80 peer-reviewed journal articles and book chapters. His latest book (with S. Lyons and L. Schweitzer) is on *Generational Career Shifts: How Veterans, Boomers, Xers, and Millennials View Work* (2018). He is the Editor of *Equality, Diversity and Inclusion*, and he serves on the editorial board of multiple management journals.

Mustafa F. Özbilgin is Professor of Organisational Behaviour at Brunel University London. He also holds two international positions: Co-Chaire Management et Diversité at Université Paris Dauphine and Visiting Professor of Management at Koç University in Istanbul. His research focuses on equality, diversity and inclusion at work from comparative and relational perspectives.

Susan E. Perkins is an Associate Professor of Strategic Management at the University of Illinois –Chicago and previously held faculty appointments at the Kellogg School of Management, Northwestern University and MIT Sloan School of Management. Her research focuses on global strategy, leadership in organizations and how the leadership's strategic decisions shape organizations and societal-level outcomes. Her research has been published in academic and practitioner journals including the *Harvard*

Business Review,Administrative Science Quarterly, Global Strategy Journal, and the *Journal of International Affairs.* She received her MBA and PhD from the Stern School of Business, NYU and her BBA from Howard University.

Katherine W. Phillips is the Reuben Mark Professor of Organizational Character and Director of the Sanford C. Bernstein Center for Leadership & Ethics at Columbia Business School in New York City. Her research focuses on the value of diversity, information sharing in groups, and building relationships across boundaries in organizations. Professor Phillips received her undergraduate degree from University of Illinois, Urbana-Champaign, and her PhD in organizational behavior from Stanford University. She has published her research in leading academic journals, and her work has been featured in numerous media outlets. She shares her work on diversity and leadership with executives and organizations around the world.

Dr. Shaun Pichler (PhD, Michigan State University) is a professor and chairperson of the department of management at the Mihaylo College of Business & Economics at California State University, Fullerton. Shaun has published in journals such as *Human Resource Management, Journal of Vocational Behavior,* and *Personnel Psychology,* among others. He is an associate editor for the *Journal of Occupational & Organizational Psychology* and a current or former editorial board member for journals such as *Equality, Diversity, & Inclusion, Group & Organization Management, Journal of Vocational Behavior,* among others.

Rose L. Siuta is a doctoral student in the Industrial/Organizational Psychology Program at Texas A&M University. She has previously earned a Master of Arts degree in Industrial/Organizational Psychology from Fairleigh Dickinson University. Her research focuses largely on discrimination and diversity-related issues, with specific interests in body-related stigmatization, sexual harassment, and women and gender studies.

Negin R. Toosi is an experimental social psychologist with a special focus on diversity and intergroup relations. She is currently an assistant professor of psychology at the California State University, East Bay. Prior to that, she completed her undergraduate degree at Stanford University and her PhD at Tufts University, before spending some time at Columbia Business School and the Technion–Israel Institute of Technology.

Raymond Trau is a Senior Lecturer in the Department of Management at Macquarie University in Sydney, Australia. His research focuses on the impact of psychological and contextual influences on the workplace experiences of women, minorities and stigmatized groups, and the extent to which these experiences shape their wellbeing, work attitudes, career development and job performance. Raymond's research has been published in international scholarly journals such as *Journal of Applied Psychology*, *Human Resource Management* and *British Journal of Management*.

Sabrina D. Volpone is an assistant professor at the University of Colorado Boulder's Leeds School of Business. Dr. Volpone's research focuses on diversity management and identity management in organizations. Specifically, she uses both qualitative and quantitative methods to understand how organizations manage their diverse workforces and how diverse individuals flfourish through the management of their identities at work. This work focuses on examining the workplace experiences of traditionally underrepresented employees, as she has work on the topics of diversity and identity management published in the context of race, gender, race, disability, sexual orientation, and immigrant status. Her research has been published in peer-reviewed journals such as the Academy of Management Journal, Journal of Applied Psychology, *Organizational Behavior & Human Decision Processes, and Personnel Psychology,* among others.

Meltem Yavuz is a postdoctoral researcher at Istanbul University and lecturer at Bahcesehir University Istanbul, Turkey. She also works as an independent consultant. Her primary interest areas are organizational behavior, human resource management and business strategy in terms of both individual and organizational contexts.

Made in the USA
Monee, IL
19 October 2021